Discovering FURNITURE

COLLECTING
FOR PLEASURE

Discovering FURNITURE

BRACKEN BOOKS

Editor Dorothea Hall
Art Editor Gordon Robertson
Production Inger Faulkner

Concept, design and production by
Marshall Cavendish Books
119 Wardour Street
London W1V 3TD

This edition published 1992 by Bracken Books
an imprint of Studio Editions Limited,
Princess House, 50 Eastcastle Street
London W1N 7AP England

Typeset by Litho Link Ltd.
Printed and bound in Hong Kong

ISBN 1 85170 911 8

Some of this material was previously published in the Marshall Cavendish partwork *Times Past*

CONTENTS

INTRODUCTION

Who can resist the glowing patina of antique furniture? For the new collector, however, the choice can be pretty daunting. Most people who set out to buy may know a little about the subject, and in general terms, have a good idea of what they would like; perhaps a chaise longue, a set of chairs, a grandfather clock or a desk. They rarely set out to become experts or collectors of more than a few pieces – but many often do.

Collecting furniture often begins when people become householders for the first time, or have a little extra money to invest in something that is not only practical and can give immense visual pleasure, but will appreciate in value over the years.

This beautifully illustrated book serves two main purposes – firstly, to give the reader a sound knowledge of antique furniture styles, and secondly, to point out their current value. By focusing on the wide variety of everyday furniture that is available, and concentrating on those periods from which the reader is most likely to find examples, the book sets out to identify the different periods, styles and designs of furniture. Here each piece is carefully examined and tells the would-be-collector exactly what to look for, how to recognize the work of different craftsmen, how to determine the various qualities of workmanship, avoid fakes and reproductions, and how to check for damage and repairs. Each major item of furniture discussed is set out in chronological order so that period changes and stylistic development can be seen in proper progression, and at a glance.

The second most important feature of the book is the price guide. This is given at the end of each entry and consists of a panel containing several contrasting pieces of furniture of the type and period under discussion, each one captioned and price coded. (See the Price Guide below for the key to the

price codes.) On the whole, the items of furniture throughout the volume represent the middle section of the market with the addition of one or two rarer pieces, included to further contrast design and price.

While the current value of everyday collectable furniture can vary enormously from one area to another, and where fashion obviously plays a part in determining which pieces become 'much sought after', as well as its condition and availability, collecting can be exciting and most rewarding particularly when you can recognize the real bargains and buy them without paying vastly inflated prices.

Whatever your interests are in antique furniture, I hope through this volume you will be encouraged to collect – and remember that the most important consideration when buying is your own taste. So always buy the things that you like, after all, you are going to live with them. Enjoy the search.

Tony Curtis

PRICE GUIDE

KEY	
❶ £15-£30	❺ £200-£400
❷ £30-£60	❻ £400-£750
❸ £60-£100	❼ £750-£1500
❹ £100-£200	❽ £1500-£6000
	❾ £6,000 plus

The 18th Century Dining Chair

The dining chair was essentially an early 18th-century introduction,
and its evolution encapsulates a history of
18th-century furniture styles

A fine set of dining chairs, consisting of two carvers, or elbow chairs, and at least six side chairs, were an important part of the well-furnished Georgian house. Such chairs comfortably seated the refined company at dining tables laden with a vast array of dishes. These chairs also handsomely lined the walls of the dining room when it was not in use.

Like elegant dining itself, however, the dining chair was virtually unknown until the beginning of the 18th century. Throughout the 16th century and for much of the 17th, meals were taken at long trestle tables. The head of the household ensconced himself on a solid-backed oak armchair; lesser members perched on stools or benches.

Cane-seated chairs suitable for use at table were in existence from the 1660s, but it was not until the turn of the century that true dining chairs came into existence.

QUEEN ANNE CHAIRS
The history of the dining chair effectively begins during the reign of Queen Anne (1702-14). The characteristic features of the Queen Anne dining chair were a broad seat, a high back consisting of a cresting rail and vase-shaped splat between two uprights, and cabriole legs ending in paw, hoof or, most often, ball and claw feet. The arms of carvers rose up a little way behind the front legs. The upholstered seat was either of the stuff-over or drop-in variety. This was to be the basic form of all later 18th-century dining chairs.

Queen Anne dining chairs were also made in more ornate versions. In these, cabriole legs were embellished with rich carvings at the knee, and carved scallops, masks and leaves decorated the splat. The best chairs were invariably made in walnut. Plainer versions, with less ornament and cabriole legs at the front only, were sometimes made in oak, fruitwood or beech.

By the 1720s, the fully-developed dining chair had become an established feature of the upper-class dining room. Supplies of well-matured walnut wood were, however, running low; heavy frosts in 1709 had put paid to stocks of growing walnut which would have been ready for use ten years later. Mahogany, imported from Jamaica and Florida, was chosen as the best alternative. It had several advantages; it was very close-grained and extraordinarily

strong, making it eminently suitable for piercing and carving, and it could be polished to a dark, silky finish.

Mahogany dining chairs in the early Georgian period were modelled fairly closely on their walnut predecessors. From the 1740s, however, the dining chair underwent rapid stylistic changes. Extravagant, playful ornament, inspired by French rococo, was the order of the day. The craze for rococo gave rise to chinoiserie on the one hand, and the Gothic style on the other, each exercising the ingenuity of the best furniture-makers of the mid-18th century.

CHIPPENDALE CHAIRS
The most famous furniture-maker and designer of the time was Thomas Chippendale. His catalogue of furniture designs, *The Gentleman and Cabinet-Maker's*

◀ *One of a set of five, this walnut chair from the Queen Anne period shows a typical, flat vase-shaped splat. The early cabriole leg does not have the pronounced knee of later versions, but is well-carved.*

▶ *Dining chairs, as such, did not exist in the 17th century. Cane-seated chairs such as this were suited, if not intended, for dining. The special status of such chairs is attested to by the vigorous extravagance of the carving and turning on this example.*

◄ This print gently satirizes the unabstemious life of a typical Georgian parson. The rich, meat-filled diet of the middle classes produced substantial people who required strong, sturdy chairs on which to sit.

▶ The elegant proportions of Georgian and Regency chairs that led to their being so heavily reproduced allow them to sit harmoniously in most modern interiors.

ral variations. The characteristic feature of the 'ribband-back' chair, for example, was a splat beautifully carved in the shape of a ribbon tied in a rippling bow.

THE CHINESE TASTE

Chippendale, along with other mid 18th-century designers, also produced dining chairs in the Chinese taste. This style, indirectly copied from Chinese furniture, reached the zenith of its popularity in the 1750s. Dining chairs in the Chinese taste took a variety of forms. Some had a geometrical lattice-work back, which might either be plain or embellished with carved oriental motifs. The oriental flavour of the design was sometimes reinforced by a 'pagoda-roof' cresting rail. Chinoiserie dining chairs generally stood on square legs, which were either unadorned or covered in blind-fret carving in the Chinese style.

By comparison with the playful exuber-ance of rococo, the Gothic style was sober, if not, on occasion, downright lugubrious. The backs of typically Gothic chairs consisted of a tracery of pointed arches, quatrefoils or other motifs derived from medieval church architecture. Most chairs of this type stood on square legs with brackets. The Gothic style, championed by Horace Walpole, exerted considerable influence in the following century.

By 1760, however, each of these styles was beginning to pall. Disciplined neo-classicism, based on Ancient Greek and Roman designs, began to govern the look of everything from dining chairs to the rooms and even the buildings in which they stood. The neo-classical style's clean, orderly lines soon replaced the then outmoded fussiness of rococo, chinoiserie and Gothic.

▼ A plate from Chippendale's Director, showing three typically delicate chairbacks.

Director, was first published in 1754; later editions appeared in 1755 and 1762. With its detailed drawings, this comprehensive book disseminated to patron and maker alike a range of fashionable furniture styles. Not all were original to Chippendale.

What is now thought of as the typical Chippendale chair had a carved, bow-shaped cresting rail and, most notably, a delicately carved and pierced splat. Splat and rail were treated as one, the carving from one 'flowing' into that of the other. Seats were still either stuff-over or drop-in. The cabriole legs that had been fashionable in Queen Anne's day were retained, although Chippendale often favoured the lighter scroll-shaped foot. Square legs with stretchers between were a hallmark of cheaper Chippendale chairs.

The Chippendale dining chair had seve-

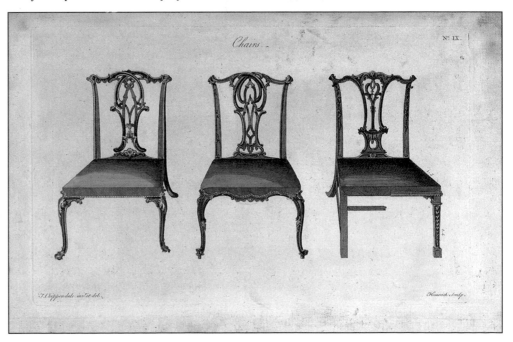

Chippendale Carver

THIS MAHOGANY CARVER, OR ELBOW CHAIR, WAS MADE AROUND 1770 AND SHOWS SEVERAL FEATURES TYPICAL OF THE CHIPPENDALE PERIOD. THE TOP RAIL HAS A CHARACTERISTIC BOW SHAPE, AND THE SPLAT IS PIERCED AND HIGHLY CARVED, WITH THE DESIGN FLOWING INTO THE TOP RAIL AND DOWN THE BACK SUPPORTS. THERE IS SIMILAR CARVING ON THE SUPPORTS OF THE DOWNWARD-SCROLLING ARMS. THE STUFF-OVER SEAT IS TEMPORARILY COVERED WITH CALICO. THE FRONT LEGS ARE OF CABRIOLE FORM, WITH ACANTHUS LEAVES ON THE KNEES, AND END IN BALL-AND-CLAW FEET. THE BACK LEGS, CONTINUING THE BACK SUPPORTS, ARE MUCH PLAINER.

① BOW-SHAPED TOP RAIL

② CARVED AND PIERCED SPLAT

③ DOWNWARD-SCROLLING ARMS

④ STUFF-OVER SEAT

⑤ ACANTHUS CARVING ON KNEE

⑥ BALL-AND-CLAW FOOT

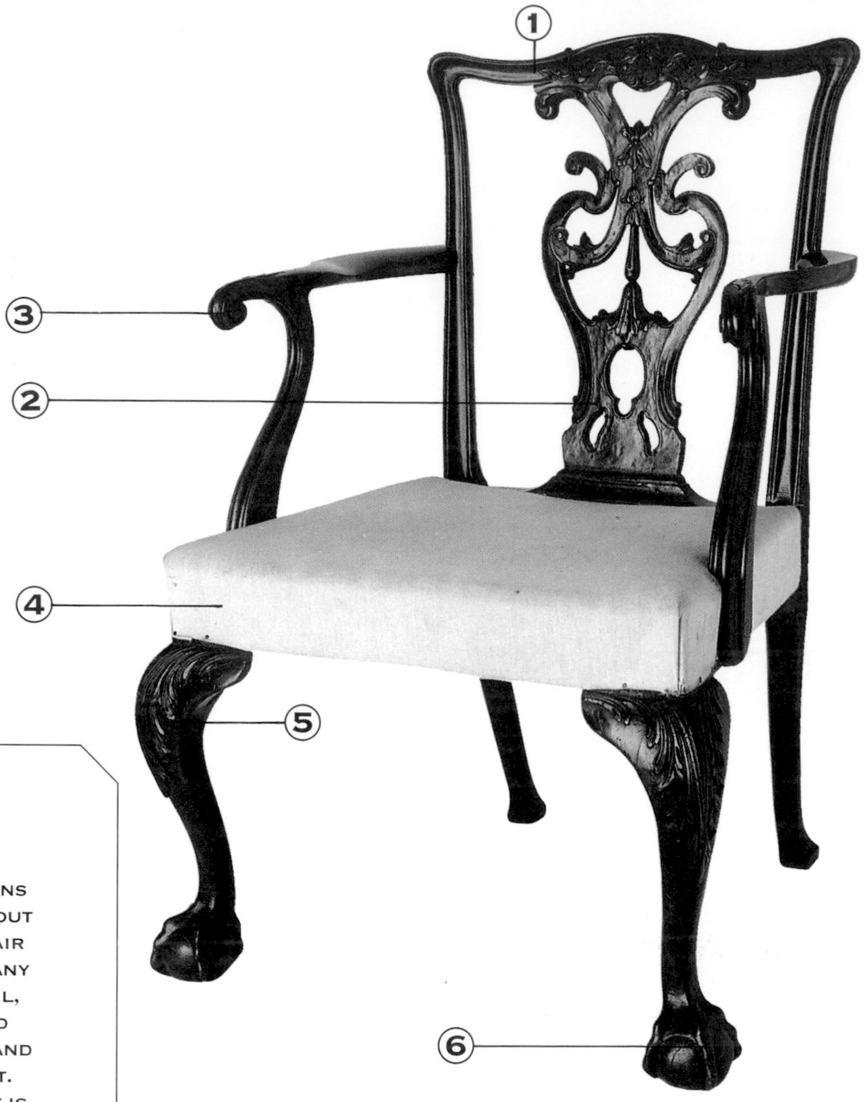

Victorian Chippendale

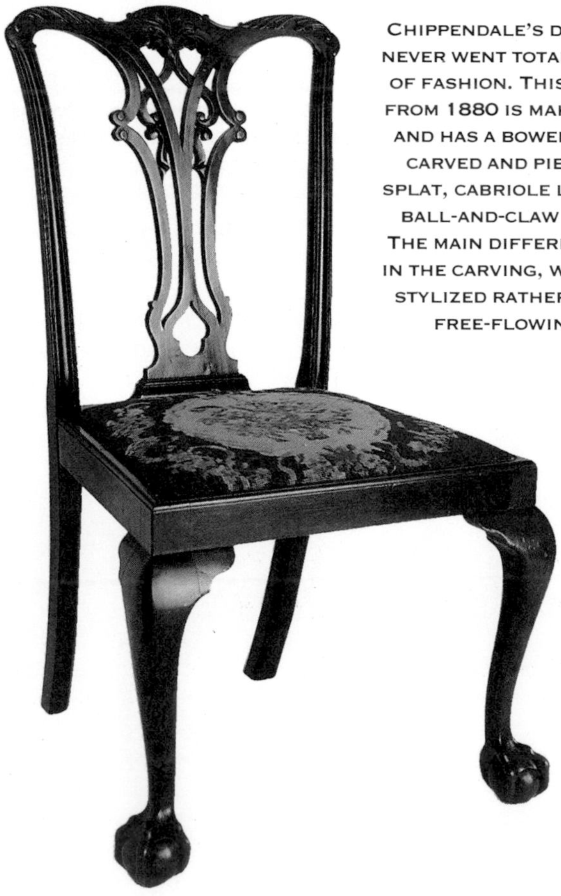

CHIPPENDALE'S DESIGNS NEVER WENT TOTALLY OUT OF FASHION. THIS CHAIR FROM 1880 IS MAHOGANY AND HAS A BOWED RAIL, CARVED AND PIERCED SPLAT, CABRIOLE LEG AND BALL-AND-CLAW FOOT. THE MAIN DIFFERENCE IS IN THE CARVING, WHICH IS STYLIZED RATHER THAN FREE-FLOWING.

It was Robert Adam who introduced the neo-classical style to English design. In his dining chairs he incorporated neo-classical motifs in a new and decorative way.

An important and typically 'Adam' type of dining chair was the 'lyre-back'. The lyre was a popular and recognizably neo-classical motif which appeared in many of Adam's designs. In the dining chair, it formed an attractive splat within the rounded outline of the chair-back. The whole framework of the chair was often decorated with other motifs such as husks, wheat ears, foliage and paterae carved in low relief or inlaid in contrasting woods.

Quite apart from the novel lyre-shape of the back, the outline of the neo-classical chair also changed. In typical examples, the front of the over-stuffed seat was either curved or serpentine. Legs were square, tapering to spade feet, or round, tapering to small peg feet. The arms of carvers were no longer set back on the seat rail but formed a continuous line with the front legs.

HEPPLEWHITE

As the neo-classical style developed, dining chairs were made around 1780 with oval, heart-shaped or shield-shaped backs. These shapes are particularly associated with the name

·PRICE GUIDE·   *Dining Chairs*

▶ A MAHOGANY CARVER OF THE SHERATON PERIOD WITH SQUARE BACK, HIGH ARMS AND TURNED TAPERED LEGS.

PRICE GUIDE **7**

▼ A LIGHT AND SIMPLE OVER-STUFFED DINING CHAIR OF THE HEPPELWHITE PERIOD WITH SQUARE, TAPERED LEGS.

PRICE GUIDE **7**

◀ THE TRAFALGAR BACK, WITH TURNED 'ROPE' CROSS-PIECE, WAS A POPULAR REGENCY STYLE.

PRICE GUIDE **7**

▼ THIS CHAIR FROM 1785, PART OF A SET OF TEN, HAS AN OVER-STUFFED SADDLE SEAT COVERED WITH SILK.

PRICE GUIDE **8**

▶ THE WIDE, SHAPED AND CARVED TOP RAIL AND THE REEDED SABRE LEGS DATE THIS MAHOGANY CHAIR WITH DROP-IN SEAT TO 1810.

PRICE GUIDE **6**

◀ A LESS ORNATE CHIPPENDALE CHAIR WITH SQUARE LEGS, STRETCHERS, AND A SPLAYED BACK SPLAT.

PRICE GUIDE **7**

---

of contemporary designer George Hepplewhite, although he invented none of them.

The back of such a chair was attached to the framework by short continuations of the back legs. The fact that it stood clear of the seat allowed the seat to be over-stuffed at the back as well as at the front and the sides.

The shield-shape itself enclosed delicate carvings that, emphasizing the vertical axis, took a variety of forms. The Prince of Wales' feathers was one, the wheatsheaf another. Urns and neo-classical swags were other devices which were frequently used. Oval backs often incorporated a radiating pattern of leaves.

Although Hepplewhite was a prolific designer, he may never have made any furniture himself. Dining chairs made to his designs have a delicate appearance, but nevertheless they are remarkably strong, well-crafted and of extremely handsome proportions.

SHERATON

The next stage in the development of the neo-classical dining chair is associated with Thomas Sheraton. Like Hepplewhite, Sheraton was a designer rather than a maker. His early designs for shield-back chairs virtually duplicated Hepplewhite's.

The dining chair most strongly associated with Sher-

aton was of a quite different design, however. In contrast to the heart, shield and oval shapes so characteristic of the Hepplewhite style, Sheraton's practical and elegant chairs have a rectilinear rather than a rounded outline.

The chair-back itself took the form of a neat rectangle, often filled with a tracery of finely carved motifs such as urn shapes within an arch or slender, stylized vase shapes between tapering rails. Further neo-classical ornament sometimes decorated the seat rail and the legs. In Sheraton-style carvers, the arms were set high on the back uprights. Legs were characteristically fluted or reeded.

POINTS TO WATCH

■ Most 'Chippendale' chairs refer to the style only and not the maker. Finding a similarity in a chair-back to one in *The Director* does add value, however.

■ Chairs made in sets were numbered by the maker. They should have a Roman numeral grooved in the framework beneath the seat.

■ Signs of wear will appear first in the back legs. Check the blocks joining the side rails; they may have had to be replaced or restored.

■ The webbing of stuff-over seats should be nailed to rails made of beech, which survives nailing without splitting. Elm or sycamore is also acceptable.

Regency Sideboards

The sideboard was still a relatively new piece of furniture in the
Regency period, but had already evolved a rich variety of styles,
ranging from the Ancient Greek to the Chinese

The sideboard as we know it today —
a fairly large piece of furniture
comprising a number of drawers and
cupboards for storing cutlery, table linen
and other eating and drinking accessories —
first appeared around 1770, and several
examples were illustrated and described in
detail in the pattern books of George
Hepplewhite and Thomas Sheraton. Its
name was derived from the medieval *sytte
board,* a board (or tiered arrangement of
several boards) which stood near the high
table in the medieval hall. This was used
principally for the display of precious plate
but, at times, also temporarily housed
platters, condiments, drinking vessels and so
forth while a meal was in progress.

AN AGE OF MANNERS

Meal-times in the 18th century were gov-
erned by strict social etiquette. Before 1700
both food and drink were served by footmen
from a number of side tables standing
against the walls. During the 18th century it
became customary for the main roast of the
meal to be placed before the host for him to
carve and for a number of dishes to be laid
on the table to allow guests to serve themselves. Supplementary dishes were positioned
on the side tables from which the footmen
could serve guests as required.

Wine was brought in to the room before
the meal and cooled in a special ice-filled
cooler on the floor. When not in use, the
cooler was stored beneath a side table.
Food was carried in hot at the beginning of
a meal — but was often cold before all the
guests were seated.

SIDE TABLES

Until the late 1760s the majority of items
required for the serving and consumption of
the meal were stored in the service area of
the house, although some 17th-century side
tables had a small storage drawer in their
frieze. Early side tables were made of
carved oak and were usually covered with a
cloth while in use, but during the Restoration period (about 1660-1700) they were
fashionably made in walnut and had turned
legs joined by stretchers.

After 1700, stretchers disappeared and
in very grand examples the legs were elaborately carved and the tops made of marble
or scagliola, a composition of cement and
stone chips resembling marble. Although

similar in appearance to pier tables, they
were a little lower in height and sometimes
had a drawer in their deep, moulded frieze.
Simpler pieces were made all in walnut (and
after about 1730 in mahogany) and had
cabriole legs. Towards the middle of the
century more decorative carving was introduced, at first of classical design, then
rococo and, sometimes, chinoiserie.

THE FIRST SIDEBOARDS

Some of the earliest examples of the
provision of storage space within the dining
room itself were designed by the famous
neo-classical architect Robert Adam in the
early 1770s. Several designs for side table
ensembles comprising a large table, a
cooler, and a pair of pedestals supporting a
pair of urns, appeared in his *Works of
Architecture,* 1773.

The pedestals and vases had a number of
functions. Generally one pedestal was lined
with tin and contained a plate-warmer,
while the other held either a chamber pot
(for the gentlemen's use after dinner) or a
cellaret for wine. One vase was sometimes

▲ *An illustration of 1826 showing the
arrangement of board, urns and wine cooler.*

▼ *The generous proportions of pedestal
sideboards are best suited to spacious rooms.*

now with drawers etc. in a genteel style to hold bottles', implying that they were a fairly recent invention.

Between about 1780 and 1810 these sideboard tables were made in very large numbers. The standard form had a shallow central drawer flanked on either side by a pair of deeper drawers or a cupboard, or one of each. The cupboard doors were sometimes faced with dummy drawer fronts. The central recess was usually rounded at the top corners with small arched brackets.

The largest number were bow- or serpentine-fronted, but semi-circular and straight-fronted examples were also made. The most expensive were evidently those with an 'eliptic' (hollow) middle. The majority had six legs, four at the front and two at the back, but some had eight.

Legs were commonly square in section, ending in spade feet, but could also be round. Both styles were sometimes reeded or fluted. The most popular wood was mahogany, which was often inlaid in lighter woods with simple stringing lines and small fan shapes. Cock-beading on drawers and cupboard edges was fairly common up to about 1800.

Sheraton designs for sideboards included a decorative back rail or 'brass rod to support large dishes'. Some had adjustable brass candelabra attached to 'give a very brilliant effect to the silver ware'. Brass rails were particularly popular after 1800 and were sometimes hung with a curtain which prevented the walls from being splashed with food or drink.

used as a knife case and the other was fitted with a tap and contained either iced drinking water or warm water for washing wine glasses.

CELLARET SIDEBOARDS

These sideboard tables, as they were called, were popular for large dining rooms until about 1800, but for smaller rooms cellaret sideboards, in which the various features were combined in a single piece of furniture, were evidently preferred. The records of Gillows of Lancaster for 1779 referred to a 'new sort of sideboard table

◀ An early serving table in the Queen Anne style. Made of oak, it has three drawers cross-banded in walnut and retains its original brass drop handles.

▲ A mid 18th-century side table in the French style, with marble top and gilt decoration based on a mask of Hercules. Food was served from tables like this in the Regency.

Cellaret Sideboard

1. **SHALLOW CENTRAL DRAWER**
2. **TAPERING, SQUARE-SECTIONED LEGS**
3. **RESTRAINED MARQUETRY DECORATION**
4. **FALSE-FRONTED CELLARET DRAWERS**
5. **BLIND KEYHOLES**

MADE IN THE FIRST 20 YEARS OF THE 19TH CENTURY, THIS MAHOGANY CELLARET SIDEBOARD SHOWS SEVERAL TYPICAL REGENCY FEATURES. THE OVERALL LIGHTNESS OF THE DESIGN IS EMPHASIZED IN THE SIX TAPERING, SQUARE SECTIONED LEGS AND THE RESTRAINED, BUT TELLING USE OF INLAID ORNAMENT.

THE CENTRAL DRAWER HAS TWO PLAIN BRASS DROP HANDLES AND AN ALMOND-SHAPED PANEL OF INLAY BENEATH THE KEYHOLE, WHICH IS ALSO INLAID. THE DEEP CELLARET DRAWERS ON EITHER SIDE BOTH HAVE A FITTING FOR SIX BOTTLES. EACH CELLARET IS ELABORATELY DISGUISED AS TWO SHALLOWER DRAWERS, COMPLETE WITH HANDLES AND BLIND KEYHOLES.

Side Cabinet

THIS SMALL DOOR IN THE SIDE OF THE PIECE LETS ON TO A CABINET BEHIND THE CELLARET DRAWER.

False Drawer

THE SIDES OF THE CELLARET DRAWERS REVEAL THICK HAND-CUT VENEERS AND TYPICAL DOVETAIL CONSTRUCTION.

Regency Side Table

A SIDE TABLE WAS AN ALTERNATIVE TO A SIDEBOARD. THIS SPADE-FOOTED MAHOGANY TABLE HAS THREE SHALLOW DRAWERS WITHOUT HANDLES.

During the Regency period, the sideboard almost completely replaced the side table ensemble and became a more impressive piece of furniture. It was frequently used for the permanent display of ornamental plate and ceramics and often dominated the dining room.

PEDESTAL SIDEBOARDS

Although the earlier sideboards of Sheraton and Hepplewhite type were still made, after about 1810 further design developments took place. The shallow central drawer was retained, but the side sections were extended downwards to form pedestals and the legs were replaced by feet.

The next step was to project the pedestals upwards and provide a decorative wooden splash-back to join them together. Wooden boards with boldly carved ornamentation gradually replaced brass rails hung with curtains. These rather grand pedestal sideboards were often made with a matching wine cooler which stood underneath their central recess.

·PRICE GUIDE·

Sideboards

▼ THIS MAHOGANY PEDESTAL SIDEBOARD INLAID WITH EBONY AND BRASS HAS A BOW-FRONTED CENTRAL DRAWER. IT WAS PROBABLY MADE IN IRELAND.
PRICE GUIDE 8

▲ A NORTH COUNTRY SIDEBOARD FROM THE END OF THE REGENCY PERIOD ALREADY SHOWING VICTORIAN CHARACTERISTICS, WITH A CUPBOARD FILLING THE CENTRAL SPACE.
PRICE GUIDE 8

▲ THIS REGENCY-STYLE SIDEBOARD WITH A SLIGHT BOW FRONT IS AN EDWARDIAN REPRODUCTION WHICH LACKS A LITTLE OF THE DEFINITION OF THE ORIGINAL.
PRICE GUIDE 8

▼ SATINWOOD IS USED EXTENSIVELY AS AN INLAY IN THIS BOW-FRONTED MAHOGANY PIECE FROM THE END OF THE 18TH CENTURY.
PRICE GUIDE 8

▼ ANOTHER EDWARDIAN VERSION OF A REGENCY PIECE WITH A SERPENTINE FRONT. ITS DATE IS REVEALED BY THE RATHER THIN LEGS AND FIGURELESS VENEERS.
PRICE GUIDE 7

▲ MADE AROUND 1800, THIS SIDEBOARD IS SIGNED BY W. WILLIAMSON OF GUILDFORD. THE LEGS ARE FLUTED AND THE DRAWER FRONTS INLAID WITH CROSS-BANDING.
PRICE GUIDE 9

Mahogany was still used a great deal, but rosewood became a particularly fashionable finish in the Regency period. Many pieces were still inlaid with thin stringing lines and other refined decoration in lighter woods, but brass inlay was more fashionable, and found on the best quality pieces.

Regency pedestal sideboards were made largely in the prevailing Grecian, or classical, taste advocated by the scholar and architect Thomas Hope. Popular designs were published by the cabinet maker George Smith in 1808 and included coolers in the form of sarcophagi and feet of paw form.

GOTHIC AND GREEK

Smith also included Gothic designs in his book and his later *Cabinet Maker and Upholsterer's Guide* of 1826 added Louis Quatorze and other fashionable styles to his repertoire, foreshadowing early Victorian taste.

Grecian designs for sideboards and for separate splashbacks using classical motifs such as anthemia, paterae and swags were similarly widely copied from Peter Nicholson's *Practical Cabinet Maker*, also published in 1826. He also included Gothic designs, using carved Gothic architectural ornament applied to otherwise very simple, almost austere, forms.

By 1825 massive side tables with a separate cooler below had once again replaced the sideboard proper in large homes as chiffoniers (or side cabinets) became popular for storage purposes. From the 1830s onward, chiffoniers began to replace the sideboard altogether in smaller Victorian homes.

POINTS TO WATCH

■ Watch out for cutting down; look for suspicious joints on the back and sides.

■ The survival of interior fittings adds to a piece's value, particularly a compartmentalized, lead-lined cellaret drawer.

■ Brass rails went out of fashion and may have been removed; look for filled holes on the top and back.

■ Drawer handles are often replacements. Check inside for signs of previous handle fixings.

■ Decorative inlay and carved legs add value.

The Occasional Table

Movable tables in all shapes and sizes were a feature of any Victorian parlour, and were used for entertaining and for ornaments

Victorian householders were an enthusiastic buying public, enamoured with 'new styles' appropriate for a 'new age', and much of their income went towards the comforts of the home. Integral to comfort was the need for everyday furniture on which to take refreshment, to read, rest books or to sew. After all, where was the family to put its knick-knacks, so necessary to the well-appointed Victorian parlour, or display its family photographs? The answer lay in one of the most diverse and multitudinous examples of Victorian home furnishings – the occasional table.

ORIGINS OF THE TABLE
In the 17th and 18th centuries, rooms were generally rather sparsely furnished and pieces were placed against the wall to leave the floor clear to show off splendid dresses.

By the Regency period, however, things began to change. One of the first *in situ* tables made its appearance: the sofa table. It was in demand from the early years of the 19th century and was regarded as a proper part of the furniture of the parlour, drawing room or library. Of a convenient size and shape, it stood immediately before a sofa, intended primarily for the use of ladies, who had moved out of their private rooms to enjoy publicly such pursuits as reading or writing. Its small rectangular end-flaps could be raised to extend the table. The popularity of this design – usually in mahogany or rosewood – continued until the mid-Victorian period.

The sofa table is a direct descendant of the delicate Pembroke table, which dates from the 1750s. This table was also retained by the Victorians and used for serving refreshments. Instead of folding end-

▲ *A passion for things oriental or eastern manifested itself in Moorish-style tables, inlaid with mother-of-pearl, ivory or shell.*

flaps, the Pembroke table has side-flaps, which lift up to give a square or oval surface.

By the later part of the Regency period, the placing of small tables around the room had become general practice in the houses of the well-to-do. In addition to the 19th century sofa and Pembroke tables, there was the multi-purpose tripod table (see following pages). These became very popular with the Victorians who found them invaluable additions to the parlour, especially when entertaining, as they were easily moved about. The quartetto or trio nest tables, originally designed by Thomas Sheraton in the 18th century, also found their way into the Regency home.

By the 1850s and 1860s, the fever for ingenious creations had reached a new height – and a much wider market. Mechanical sawing and turning became widespread and styles were extremely varied.

DIVERSITY OF STYLES

Classical fashions, popular in the Georgian period, mingled freely with bastardized Gothic, Chinese or Ancient Egyptian pieces, although they tended to be of sturdier proportions. Work tables with attached baskets or boxes underneath, containing sewing equipment, or teapoys with the caddy attached to the pedestal and with a lifting top, were very popular. The Sutherland table – a gateleg with two wide flaps, named after Queen Victoria's mistress of the robes – came into its own for serving tea. When the flaps were lowered, the table became very narrow and could be pushed against a wall or behind a sofa.

A plentiful choice of raw materials echoed the diversity of styles. Mahogany, oak, rosewood and walnut were favourite woods, and papier mâché enjoyed a major vogue from 1830 onwards. However, little in the mid to late 19th-century parlour was left unadorned and more often than not shawls, cloths and brocades covered every surface.

Towards the end of the 19th century, tables with three or four legs replaced the tripod table in popularity. They had the advantage of greater stability, and the growing use of castors made movement easier. Undershelves and side shelves on these multi-legged tables were in great demand to accommodate the excess trinkets demanded by Victorian taste, as well as the growing opulence of Victorian teas!

LATER DESIGNS

Reproduction pieces based on European designs of the last four centuries became the vogue from the 1890s through the Edwardian period to the 1920s. Neo-classical French styles were popular for drawing rooms. Queen Anne, Chippendale, Hepplewhite, Sheraton and Regency variations were mass-produced.

The modern day lifestyle calls for the occasional table even more than did that of our great-grandparents. Nest tables for TV suppers, tripod tables for ornaments, and, perhaps, a reproduction Pembroke table in the hall are not uncommon features in today's homes.

▼ *A small octagonal table fits neatly into any corner, and an undershelf gives more space for ornaments.*

▲ *Small loo tables – used for the popular 19th century card game 'loo' – made useful side tables. This decorative tilt-top is inlaid with blue silk and embellished with silver and silver-gilt. The raised rim kept play in order and prevented objects from sliding off the rounded edge.*

▼ *The Victorian love of ornament led to the popularity of flamboyant designs. The tilt-top table was the ideal vehicle for this type of decoration. This one, for example, with a painted top and papier mâché base, is as much an attractive object of display as a functional piece of furniture.*

The Tripod Table

THE VICTORIAN VERSION OF THE TRIPOD TABLE IS OF AN ALTOGETHER STURDIER DESIGN THAN ITS 18TH CENTURY PREDECESSOR, WITH A MORE STABLE BASE.

SCROLL-ENDED AND PILLAR-AND-CLAW FEET ARE BOTH COMMON FEATURES OF 19TH CENTURY TRIPODS, COMPLEMENTING THE HEAVIER TABLE DESIGNS.

TABLE TOPS MAY BE ROUND, SQUARE OR OCTAGONAL, AND ARE SOMETIMES INLAID WITH WOOD OR ARE CARVED.

ORNAMENTAL STEMS REPLACE THE PLAINER, EARLIER COLUMN AND BALUSTER. THE SHOULDERS OF THE LEGS ARE THICKER AND THE SHAPE IS SOMETIMES FLATTER.

① CARVED GROOVE TO CATCH SPILLS, TOGETHER WITH A DECORATIVELY CARVED BORDER.

② STURDY STEM OR COLUMN, TURNED AT THE TOP AND CARVED ALONG ITS LENGTH.

③ BALUSTER AT BASE OF STEM IS ORNATELY CARVED AND PROMINENT TO COUNTER-BALANCE THE TOP.

④ THICK, CABRIOLE-STYLE LEGS WITH ACANTHUS LEAF CARVING ON THE KNEES.

⑤ SCROLL CARVING STARTS AT THE TOP OF THE UNDERSIDE OF THE LEGS AND ENDS AT THE FEET.

Table Bases

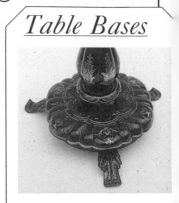

A CIRCULAR PLATFORM AND SPLAYED LEGS REPLACE THE CLASSIC TRIPOD BASE.

THIS FLOOR-LEVEL PLINTH ALMOST ELIMINATES THE FEET ALTOGETHER.

The Piecrust

A GEORGIAN TRIPOD TABLE WITH PIECRUST RIM. FEATURES ARE FINER THAN LATER EXAMPLES.

The elegant tripod, or pillar-and-claw table, has remained in fashion and manufacture from early Georgian times. Originally the table developed from the candle-stand, whose three feet were considered more stable than a single pedestal candlestick. It was this stability and their convenient size that made tripod tables ideal for entertaining.

Mahogany was the principal wood adopted for tripod tables from the middle of the 18th century through to the Victorian period – although often elaborately embellished with other materials. Many of these tables were veneered – topped with a thin strip of good-quality wood to give a grained surface. Originally, this was an expensive decorative effect. Later, it was used to top cheaper wood for an expensive finish.

The top of the table could reach a considerable size and generally had a rim to catch spills and prevent objects from sliding off. A variation on this was a table with eight dished circles around the edge. This was known as a supper table, as the dishes could be placed in the carved circles. It was a pattern revived in the Victorian era.

The tilt-top feature was already in use in 1740. This

·PRICE GUIDE·

Occasional Tables

▲ 'QUARTETTO' OR NEST OF FOUR TABLES, NEATLY FUNCTIONAL IN PLAIN, LACQUERED WOOD.

PRICE GUIDE **8**

▲ PAPIER MÂCHÉ TRIPOD TABLE WITH MOTHER-OF-PEARL INLAY AND RIDGED TABLE EDGE. TABLE TOP SURFACE IS DAMAGED.

PRICE GUIDE **4**

▲ LATE VICTORIAN HEXAGONAL TABLE SHOWING ARABIC INFLUENCE IN BOTH SHAPE AND INLAY PATTERN.

PRICE GUIDE **7**

▲ OCTAGONAL TRIPOD TABLE, WITH TURNED STEM AND TOP INLAID WITH WOOD. NEEDING EXTENSIVE REPAIR TO INLAY AND VENEER.

PRICE GUIDE **4**

▲ RECTANGULAR SUTHERLAND TABLE WITH THUMB-NAIL EDGE MOULDING AND GATELEGS ON CASTORS.

PRICE GUIDE **6**

▲ ARTS AND CRAFTS TABLE WITH MINTON CHINA TRAY TOP AND EBONISED WOODEN BASE.

PRICE GUIDE **8**

allowed the table to be truly 'occasional', since it could be stored upright in a corner. The tilt-top became popular with the early Victorians but as the designs became heavier and more elaborate so they became unsuited to this fragile means of support. Square, rectangular and octagonal-topped pedestal tables became more common. From 1840 onwards, japanned and papier mâché examples

were à la mode, encouraged by the flamboyant designs for the Great Exhibition of 1851.

The Regency period introduced a design which suited the Victorians for practical purposes. The turned pillar was mounted directly on a floor-level pedestal. This made the tables more stable and able to withstand the knocks of bulky Victorian dresses.

By the turn of the century the

heavier treatment of the Victorian style had been rejected in favour of 18th century simplicity. The workmanship in these revival pieces is not as delicate and often the tops are larger in proportion to their supports. Many of the tripod tables surviving today are from this revival, and while they may lack authentic origins, they can blend into the style of almost any modern room.

Real or Fake?

■ CHECK FOR 'MARRIAGE' — NEWER OR DIFFERENT PIECES ADDED ON.
■ AN UNNATURALLY THIN TOP COULD INDICATE ALTERATION.
■ THE TOP SHOULD FIT PERFECTLY ON ITS BASE. IF UNSTABLE, IT MAY BE A LATER ADDITION.
■ CHECK FOR GLUED BORDERS.

The Longcase Clock

The languorous ticking and sonorous chimes of long-case clocks
provided a soothing backdrop to everyday life in the Georgian and
Regency periods

From around 1290, when the earliest known mechanical clock was produced (driven by weights, having neither face nor hands, but simply intoning the hours by means of a bell), scientists and clockmakers worked towards improving the accuracy of timepieces. The major breakthrough came in 1657, with the introduction of pendulum-driven clocks.

There is continuing debate about who should take the credit for this. Most authorities agree that it was the Dutch physicist and mathematician Christiaan Huygens van Zulichen. In the following year, his innovation was introduced into England by his friend Ahasuerus Fromanteel, who began to manufacture and sell pendulum clocks in London. Shortly afterwards Fromanteel encased them as 'longcase' clocks.

Because they were tall and needed a stable base, longcase clocks were usually positioned in the hall, where the sound of their striking could be heard by everyone in the house. Some clocks had fretted panels backed with silk, to allow freer transmission of the sound.

Movements usually consisted of two 'trains' or sets of interconnecting wheels. The 'going' train controlled the movement of the single hour hand and the 'striking' train the tolling of the hours and quarters. The precise swing of the pendulum, a weighted rod, regulated the co-ordinated movements of both trains, ensuring more accurate time-keeping than hitherto possible.

Unfortunately, early iron rod pendulums contracted and expanded with the fluctuating temperature of their surroundings, affecting their precision. This problem was only resolved in 1726 when clockmaker George Graham produced a compensating, mercury controlled pendulum.

EARLY CASINGS

Encasing the pendulum clock was a logical, practical step. It kept dust out of the movement, concealed unattractive workings and, most important, protected the pendulum from accidental knocks that could disrupt its swing. Incidentally, it also allowed for decoration of the case and plinth and in so doing helped to transform the

clock into an elegant, useful piece of furniture.

The dial, protected by a hood casing, was viewed through an inset glazed panel. Initially, the hood had to be raised to wind up the clock or adjust the single hand. Early dials were only about 9 inches (23cm)

across and the short swing of the pendulum required only a narrow case, so the overall design was streamlined and simple. Some 17th-century clocks had bun feet rather than a plinth. Later Stuart clocks usually had bracket feet or a low plinth.

▶ *This engraving of the Grand Staircase at
Carlton House, London residence of the Prince
Regent, shows a longcase clock covered with
fanciful rococo gilding in the French taste.*

all kinds of embellishment – particularly popular images being Father Time, a waning moon, or a rising sun. The faces got ever more complicated, with as many as four hands, separate, enclosed second-hand dials, engraving and painting inside the chapter ring as well as in the spandrels, and bevelled winding-holes. Around 1750 the task of reading the time was eased by the introduction of a 'white' dial of silvered brass. This was widely adopted. Less grand versions had enamelled dials.

By the middle of the 18th century – after a long succession of changes and adaptations – every feature of the longcase clock, from plinth to pediment, had reached its perfected form.

◄ A less grand stairwell in Hinton Ampner, Hampshire, houses a more typically British clock, made around 1730, with a burr walnut case.

▶ The clock on the right dates from around 1710. It was made by Joseph Windmills of London. The carcase is of oak covered with delicate and intricate seaweed marquetry. The hood has a 'caddy' top, so named for its resemblance to a tea caddy, and has been converted to slide forward rather than lift off as originally. That on the far right is by Thomas Tompion, made of walnut-veneered oak around 1685. It also has a converted hood, with twist columns supporting a carved, crested cornice.

From about 1670, when taller cases were made to accommodate longer pendulums, rising hoods became impractical and the glazed panel was replaced by a hinged, glazed door.

In the early 1690s minute hands, 8-day movements and calendar circles were introduced. Master clockmaker Thomas Tompion made for William III a three-month movement clock with a perpetual calendar – which automatically adjusted for months in which there were less than 31 days, and even for leap years.

LONDON CLOCKS

Until 1750, London was the centre for clockmakers and cabinet-makers. Their combined skills produced clocks that were not only the most accurate timepieces then available, but also handsome pieces of furniture. Among the great clockmakers of that golden age of horology were Thomas Tompion, Daniel Quare, William Clement and William Kent.

Their guild, the powerful Clock Makers' Company, compelled its members to record their name on the dial of every clock they produced. Many surviving clocks can therefore be dated with reasonable accuracy, though less scrupulous dealers have been known to add inscriptions to anonymous clocks. Unfortunately, the cabinet-makers

left no such records on the magnificent decorated cases.

London-made clocks were cased in a variety of imported woods as well as English ones, but there tended to be fashions in what was used, and how. In the first half of the 18th century, a number of trends followed in quick succession; first ebony and walnut, then exotic veneers, marquetry designs featuring birds and flowers, japanning and lacquerwork, and finally mahogany. Clocks cannot be dated positively by this yardstick alone however, because periods overlapped, some makers favouring a particular finish long after its heyday, while provincial makers usually lagged behind the London fashions. Outside London, oak and walnut were long popular, possibly because they were often local woods.

When japanning and lacquer were in fashion, the case door and the front panel of the plinth were despatched to China to be black japanned with gilded scenes of Chinese life. The case was assembled and the other panels lacquered in England. This tended to be more skilfully executed in London than in the provinces. Later, red, blue and green lacquers were also used.

THE ARCHED DIAL

An arch over the square clock-face was introduced in about 1715, giving space for

Regency Longcase Clock

Several makers called Grove produced clocks in London in the early Regency period. One of them signed this mahogany clock, which dates from the last few years of the 18th century.

The hood has a pagoda top. Silk-lined fretwork in the top and the sides of the hood let the sound of the strike out. A pair of brass ball and spire finials establish a theme carried through the case, with brass hinges and key escutcheon on the hood door and brass stringing in the reeded columns of the hood and on the chamfered, reeded edges of the trunk.

The door panel of the trunk has a flame mahogany veneer, and a similar well-figured veneer is used for the base, which has a double plinth and bracket feet.

① PAGODA TOP WITH BRASS FINIALS

② FRETWORK SOUND HOLES

③ REEDED COLUMNS WITH BRASS STRINGING

④ FLAME VENEER DOOR PANEL

⑤ CHAMFERED, REEDED EDGES

⑥ DOUBLE PLINTH

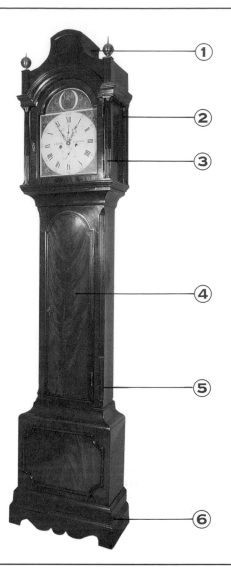

Pendulum Wall Clock

Not all pendulum clocks had standing cases. This clock from 19th-century Vienna is half the height of a contemporary longcase.

Painted Dial

In the arch is a figure of Justice in a cartouche. Flowers fill the spandrels. A seconds dial and a calendar dial fill the centre, while the chapter ring has Roman hours and Arabic minute numerals.

Towards the end of the 18th century, with the rise of new monied classes at the beginning of the Industrial Revolution, the demand for clocks increased dramatically. Many of these new customers could not afford top quality materials and simply wanted a reliable timepiece, so overall standards inevitably dropped, though of course top quality pieces were still being made in small numbers.

Clockmakers from other parts of the country who had previously bought their casings in London now had them made locally, increasing the use of local woods and creating regional styles. Lancashire, for instance, became a centre of some excellence, making superb mahogany cases from wood landed at Liverpool.

Jeremiah Standring of Bolton was one of many first-rate provincial makers. Another was Will Kent of Saffron Walden, who incorporated bird, butterfly and foliage designs into the centre of his chapter rings.

REGENCY CLOCKS

In the Regency period, some very fine clocks in a classical revival style were made in satinwood, with delicate marquetry, but overall standards of workmanship and design continued to fall as mass production techniques were brought in to meet the ever-escalating demand.

Yorkshire clocks deteriorated markedly, with a fashion for larger and larger cases that tended to be clumsy, rather than imposing as was probably intended. One explanation offered for this is that architects of the period took to designing the cases along with other items of furniture commissioned by wealthy clients who wanted everything to be 'in proportion and style'. And as the houses of the nouveau riche became grander and ceilings higher, so did the clocks, often to the detriment of their proportions.

While the body of the case became somewhat shorter, and the doors almost square, the height of the plinth increased substantially and hoods became huge, often topped by clumsy

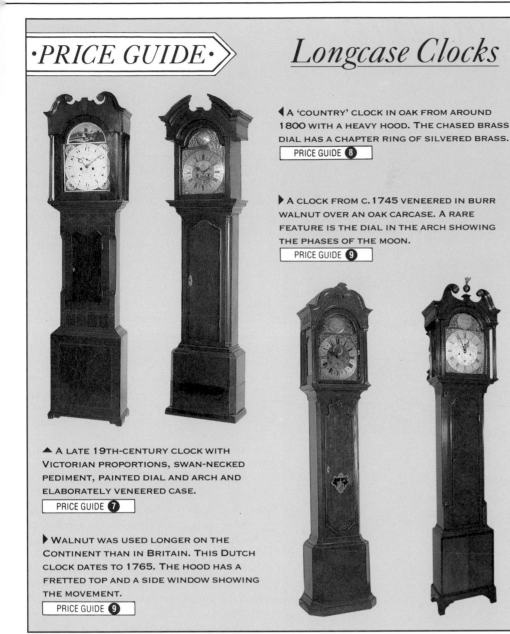

Longcase Clocks

◄ A 'COUNTRY' CLOCK IN OAK FROM AROUND 1800 WITH A HEAVY HOOD. THE CHASED BRASS DIAL HAS A CHAPTER RING OF SILVERED BRASS.

> PRICE GUIDE **8**

► A CLOCK FROM C.1745 VENEERED IN BURR WALNUT OVER AN OAK CARCASE. A RARE FEATURE IS THE DIAL IN THE ARCH SHOWING THE PHASES OF THE MOON.

> PRICE GUIDE **9**

▲ A LATE 19TH-CENTURY CLOCK WITH VICTORIAN PROPORTIONS, SWAN-NECKED PEDIMENT, PAINTED DIAL AND ARCH AND ELABORATELY VENEERED CASE.

> PRICE GUIDE **7**

► WALNUT WAS USED LONGER ON THE CONTINENT THAN IN BRITAIN. THIS DUTCH CLOCK DATES TO 1765. THE HOOD HAS A FRETTED TOP AND A SIDE WINDOW SHOWING THE MOVEMENT.

> PRICE GUIDE **9**

►▲ A REGENCY CLOCK BY WILLIAM VALE OF LONDON. IT HAS AN ENGRAVED SILVERED BRASS DIAL AND A RICH MAHOGANY CASE FINISHED IN BRASS.

> PRICE GUIDE **9**

◄ JAS. HOWDEN OF EDINBURGH MADE THIS CLOCK LATE IN THE 19TH CENTURY. IT HAS A SLENDER FLAME-VENEERED CASE AND A HOOD WITH REEDED COLUMNS.

> PRICE GUIDE **9**

pediments. Dials, too, were correspondingly larger, measuring 14 inches (35cm) across. This gave scope for unrestrained painted decorations.

These sometimes commemorated major events such as the Battles of Trafalgar and Waterloo – celebrated in paintings of flags, ships and muskets. Another popular subject was scenes of local interest, which may help to identify the area from which a particular clock originally came.

As if this vogue for painted decoration was not enough, the arched section above the dial often housed automata of Old Father Time and other such popular characters.

The numerals around the chapter ring were usually large, too, perhaps in an attempt to make them clearly readable among the distractions. The Arabic minute numerals were often as large as the Roman hour numerals.

Makers' names still appeared on dials, but by this time many makers purchased the various components from workshops in centres such as Coventry and Bristol and simply assembled them for sale. However, where a single maker was involved, his name or initials are often found on the engraved back plate of the movement.

Oak, pine and mahogany were now the woods most popularly used, with the latter reserved for 'better' clocks. In fact, better often simply meant larger; cumbersome, heavy pieces that would overwhelm an average-sized room.

After 1850, there was a huge influx of cheap mantle and bracket clocks from America and the Continent and these helped to hurry the fall from favour of the longcase clock.

Ironically, this was the very time when the longcase clock was affectionately re-christened the 'grandfather clock', apparently inspired by a contemporary popular song about 'my grandfather's clock' that 'stopped short, never to go again, when the old man died'.

Many clocks offered for sale today are 'marriages' of parts from two or more originals. The following signs should alert a buyer to this possibility.

POINTS TO WATCH

■ A square dial in an arched hood, filled in with wood.

■ A square hood containing a dial with signs of sawn-off lunar movements or other arch decorations.

■ A minute hand on a dial with no minute markings.

■ A small dial set within a bezel; this may have been added to disguise the fact that the dial is too small for the case.

■ Blind winding holes serving no practical purpose.

■ No signs of shrinkage or cracking on the case door; this may indicate that the door has been relatively recently replaced.

The Sideboard

The sideboard was an essential part of the Victorian dining room,
where its foremost function was the display
of the family's fine tableware

The sideboard was often the most expensive piece of furniture in a Victorian middle-class home, and it was therefore only right that it should be heavy, richly polished and impressive. When loaded with sparkling plate and glass, it became a status symbol, exhibiting family wealth, taste and adherence to convention.

Alternatively, on a more functional level, it might be used for serving dishes and for carving the meat.

At the beginning of the 18th century, the sideboard was little more than a large side

▲ The pedestal sideboard – effectively a table top supported on two cupboards – was the original design produced by Robert Adam.

table within the dining room, on which the crockery was stacked and the food was served. It was not until Robert Adam, the famous architect, was commissioned to design a dining-room side table that the sideboard became recognizable as the long cupboard we know today. Adam designed his table in an 'architectural' manner, mounting the flat top on two 'pedestals' which contained cupboards. This style of

table was copied by cabinetmakers throughout the country, often with the cupboards designed for a specific use. One cupboard, for instance, may have been lined with lead or zinc and used as a wine cooler.

TYPES AND STYLES

The Victorians furnished their dining rooms in conventional style. Sideboards in a variety of revival styles, including Sheraton, Elizabethan, French Empire, 'antique oak', Italian, Early English, Queen Anne and Chippendale, were all available. Later in the 19th century they could be created more cheaply because of the improvements in machine finishing.

The craze for 'Tudor Revival' furniture led to the construction of pieces cannibalized from original Tudor furniture. Many curiously styled, buffet-type sideboards or sideboard tables were made from old chests, bedposts, Tudor floorboards, wall panelling and doors.

The Great Exhibition of 1851 had a lasting effect on furniture styles, as many of the impressive exhibition pieces, made especially to win acclaim, were copied by the large furniture factories for commercial sale. The sideboards produced were considerably reduced in scale, and much of the fine ornamentation was lost, as machines were used to execute the carving.

Around the time of the Exhibition, mirrors were incorporated into furniture for the first time and these proved especially popular for the sideboard. Mass production of sheet glass began in the 1840s, enabling large mirrors to be produced for the first time. Large mirrors enhanced the effect of carving and looked well in combination with the rich colour of that all-popular wood, mahogany.

Throughout the second half of the 19th

century, the word 'sideboard' was used without precise definition. Many manufacturers chose the term 'buffet', presumably because of antique associations, while some trade catalogues used 'sideboard' for almost identical pieces. The word 'dresser' was also used in many instances to describe what would now be thought of as a basic sideboard. While the progressive were making use of the new mirrors to create Italianate pieces, others were still making sideboards in the 18th century style, with carved backboards and matching wine coolers. In one example, made by the famous furniture makers, Gillow, the delicate front legs of the 18th century have been replaced by large carved eagles, while the backboard is continued to ground level.

POPULAR TASTE

During the 1860s and 70s sideboards grew steadily larger and more ornate, with vast areas of machine decoration, a lavish use of mirrors, and a generous use of heavy woods, purely to give the weighty solidity so liked by the middle classes. This style of sideboard suited the masculine appearance of the Victorian dining room very well.

The Cabinetmaker's Assistant, published in 1853, gave specific advice to the fashion-conscious middle classes. It decreed that dining room furniture should have three qualities – convenience, solidity and absence of gaudiness – as richness of effect rather than mere show should always be the aim. Cabinetmakers in possession of this volume were able to offer clients a wide assortment of sideboards, from classical to romantic.

Many people obviously found the Italianate or Exhibition-style pieces too oppressive, and to satisfy popular demand many simpler types were made. Some were mere slab tops with a central drawer, standing on

◄ *A Victorian card showing children playing Oranges and Lemons in front of a carved buffet sideboard laden with a boar's head on a platter.*

▶ *An elaborately carved Victorian oak buffet with twin cupboards and drawers for storage with two shelves for displaying plate and glass.*

▲ *A pedestal sideboard with plate-glass top looks good in today's dining room and is ideal for displaying fruit and antique silver.*

▼ *A detail from the door panel of the oak buffet, left. It shows a wild boar and a gamebird: scenes from the hunt were popular.*

rectangular pedestals – a development of the Regency form. Another variation was a slab of marble, slate or wood, resting on four front legs and a continuous back, often standing on a platform base that could be used for a wine cooler. Mahogany and rosewood remained the most popular woods throughout the century, the brass fittings adding richness to the effect.

DESIGNER FURNITURE

Alongside the mainstream commercial furniture, there was also a strong art movement, inspired by designers such as William Morris and Charles Eastlake and Bruce J. Talbert. Designers of the Arts and Crafts and Art Nouveau schools deplored all factory-made work and attempted to educate the public in the new taste. As their furniture was individually designed and expensive, the influence was mainly limited to a small circle, though again there were some cheaper imitations. Long hinges, ring handles and inlaid pewter and brass were typical decorative features on 'art' furniture.

Eastlake, however, understood that to be viable furniture needed to be capable of commercial production. He favoured plain pieces made without glue, varnish, stains or polish and somewhat rustic in style. These were ideal for the large 'cottage' homes that were becoming more popular with the middle classes. The clutter of silver and glass that had brightened many a dull mid-Victorian pedestal sideboard was banished from many dining rooms, to be replaced with a single, finely potted bowl or a slender, coloured glass flagon.

Despite these advances in design, it must be said that the majority of Victorians favoured traditional styles and selected these from a wide range of factory-made pieces.

DESIGN IN FOCUS
The Chiffonier

THE DISTINCTION BETWEEN CHIFFONIER AND SIDEBOARD IS SOMEWHAT BLURRED AND A PIECE MAY BE REFERRED TO AS A CHIFFONIER-SIDEBOARD.

THE CHIFFONIER, HOWEVER, HAS TWO CENTRAL CUPBOARDS (OCCASIONALLY ONE) WITH SHELVES, RATHER THAN THE SEPARATE PEDESTAL CUPBOARDS IN THE ADAM-STYLE SIDEBOARD.

DOOR FRONTS MAY BE OF WOOD, GLASS OR PLEATED SILK. BRASS GRILLES IN A LATTICE PATTERN WERE ADDED TO PLEATED SILK DOORS FROM THE 1840s ONWARDS.

IN ADDITION TO SHELVES WITHIN THE CUPBOARDS, THERE COULD BE SHELVES ABOVE AND/OR SHELVES TO THE SIDE. SHELVES WERE SUPPORTED ON FLUTED PILLARS OR CARVED BRACKETS, AND WERE INTENDED ORIGINALLY FOR BOOKS.

CHIFFONIERS WERE MADE IN ROSEWOOD OR MAHOGANY, THOUGH FRENCH EXAMPLES FROM THE EARLY 19TH CENTURY USED VENEER ON AN OAK CARCASE.

BRASS STRINGING AND DECORATIVE INLAYS — PERHAPS IN EBONY OR IVORY — WERE COMMON FROM THE EARLY 1800s.

① **BOOKSHELVES SUPPORTED ON SHALLOW-TURNED SPINDLES.**

② **CURVED BACK WITH SCROLLED MACHINE-CARVING.**

③ **THE BACKBOARD OFTEN INCLUDED A MIRROR.**

④ **STYLIZED ACANTHUS-LEAF CARVING GIVES A CLASSICAL LOOK.**

⑤ **THE FLATTENED ARCH ON DOOR PANELS WAS IN VOGUE FROM THE 1840s.**

⑥ **PLAIN PLINTH BASE COVERS THE SMALL FEET.**

Shelf Supports

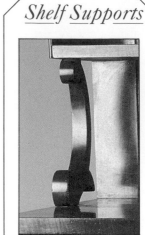

SIMPLE CURVING LINES OF THE EARLY 19TH CENTURY.

TYPICAL VICTORIAN TURNED SPINDLE WITH CARVING.

Queen Anne Style

A QUEEN ANNE-STYLE SERVING TABLE OF OAK WITH DRAWERS CROSS-BANDED IN WALNUT. IT WOULD BE USED FOR CARVING.

The **Victorian chiffonier** was a lowish cupboard with an enclosed front, often with drawers above and topped by open shelving. In the smaller Victorian dining room, this more compact piece of furniture frequently replaced the traditional sideboard, since it was of a rather more practical size.

The English chiffonier was, in fact, French in origin and was simply a commode with doors to conceal its drawers. In France it reached its height of popularity during Napoleon's reign when severe, classical styles were fashionable. Curved bombé fronts were therefore replaced by flat lines, embellished with ormolu and gilt-bronze mounts. Regency designers in England adapted this style to the English taste, and the Regency chiffonier was still popular in Victorian times. In style, this piece was low and slim with usually a marble top. Early examples were often made in solid rosewood, inlaid or with fine inlaid brass designs. The cabinets

·PRICE GUIDE· Sideboards

A FUNCTIONAL SIDEBOARD WITH MINIMAL CARVING; ITS CABRIOLE LEGS HAVE BALL AND CLAW FEET.

PRICE GUIDE **6**

TALBERT SIDEBOARD OF THE 1870S, WITH LONG HINGES, RING HANDLES AND BOXWOOD PANELS.

PRICE GUIDE **9**

A LATE REGENCY CHIFFONIER WITH A CONVEX DRAWER AND BRASS LATTICE DOORS BACKED WITH SILK.

PRICE GUIDE **7**

AN IMPOSING, LATE VICTORIAN CHIFFONIER OF EBONIZED WOOD, WITH TOP MIRRORS AND AMPLE SHELVING WITH TURNED AND FLUTED SUPPORTS.

PRICE GUIDE **7**

A VICTORIAN WALNUT CHIFFONIER OF SERPENTINE DESIGN WITH ELABORATE CARVED WOOD BRACKETS.

PRICE GUIDE **8**

often had open-pleated silk door-panels and were flanked on either side by bookshelves. Brass grilles were added to the door-panels from the middle of the century onwards. The Regency chiffonier was more suited to halls, passages and libraries, rather than the dining room, yet this low chiffonier, sometimes called a 'side cabinet' continued to be made throughout the 19th century. It is generally a more elegant piece of furniture than the dining room sideboard – and this is exempli-fied in its increasing popularity in salerooms today. It is note-worthy that many elaborate pieces have been dismembered and reassembled to reappear later as 'Regency' chiffoniers.

Chiffoniers intended for the drawing room, and slightly dif-ferent again in design, were produced in large numbers dur-ing the second half of the 19th century. A manufacturer's cata-logue of 1876 shows that these were invariably bow-fronted, lighter, and with large mirror backs rather than shelves.

Dining room chiffoniers were commonly made in rosewood or mahogany although late in the century thin veneer on a deal frame, or even stained deal, was used on very cheap pieces. Obviously, designs differed widely. Some have plinth bases, while others are on decoratively carved feet. As the century progressed, so did the decora-tion on dining room chiffoniers. Leaf and scroll carving was almost universal on late Victo-rian examples and generally designs are heavy and fussy.

Real or Fake?

■ PLINTH IS ALWAYS PLAIN, NEVER DECORATED.
■ GENUINE SILK-PANELLED DOORS HAVE NARROW FRAMES.
■ OAK CHIFFONIERS FROM REGENCY PERIOD ARE FRENCH IN ORIGIN.
■ HAND-FINISHED PILLAR SUPPORTS ARE NOT ABSOLUTELY IDENTICAL.
■ VENEERED DOOR PANELS ARE OFTEN REPLACED WITH BRASS LATTICE AND SILK TO SIMULATE REGENCY-STYLE CHIFFONIERS.

The Victorian Dining Chair

The dining chair was as much an essential in the breakfast room as the
dining room. Features changed dramatically over the centuries and
the Victorians developed many new designs

I t is hard to imagine life without chairs,
but just 500 years ago chairs were the
reserve of the nobility and ecclesiastics.
The bench and stool were the forerunners of
the armless side chairs and bobbin-turned
chairs of the 16th century. The Reforma-
tion frowned upon carving and other ornament on furniture, so it was not until the
Restoration that the chair became a medium
of creative expression.

William and Mary brought with them
refinements from the continent, so that the
aristocracy were able to indulge a new-
found delight in veneer, marquetry and
lacquerwork. The sturdy cabriole leg was
introduced, dispensing with the need for
stretchers and at this time some chairs lost
their arms, becoming single chairs – com-
panions to elbow chairs or 'carvers' – thus
forming the first sets. By the 18th century,
the dining chair had finally evolved.

THE RISE OF MAHOGANY
A landmark in furniture-making is the year
1720, when an embargo was placed on the
export of native walnut from France.
English craftsmen turned to American walnut, and mahogany from the Caribbean and
Honduras. The years 1720 to 1730 saw
the elaborate fashions of walnut transmuted
into those of mahogany. The abolition of tax
on imported mahogany in 1733 was the
final blow to the widespread use of walnut.

18TH CENTURY DESIGNERS
By the time Thomas Chippendale published
*The Gentleman and Cabinet-maker's
Director* in 1754, the chair – or set of chairs
– was an accepted proof of the furniture-
maker's art. The character of Chippendale
chairs was largely determined by the design
of the back. Ribbon patterns, Chinese frets
and trelliswork were his distinctive hallmarks, along with carved straight legs
rather than cabrioles.

Within the second half of the 18th
century, three other notable makers contributed their distinctive styles. Robert Adam
produced gilded classical chairs, which
incorporated lyre and oval backs and
serpentine seats. Hepplewhite, who can
claim no pieces as his own, left the

▲ *In grander Victorian homes even breakfast
was a formal and often lengthy affair that
necessitated comfortable seating. The Victorians
made sturdy dining chairs in a variety of styles,
often in sets of ten or more.*

inspiration for the shield-back chair and
saddleback seat as his legacy. Sheraton
synthesized all these current influences and
refined them, allowing the beauty of inlaid
woods, such as ebony, to show up in
banding and detail work. In his designs can
be seen the forerunners of the 19th century
dining chair. The hint of a concave curve in
the legs prefigured the sabre leg of the
Regency period.

REGENCY STYLE
True Regency style in its prime, from 1810
to 1830, is unmistakable. The top back-rest
was the central focus, and the sabre legs
ended bluntly at the foot. Brass and/or
ebony inlay and stringing decorated the
back panels and the arms of carvers.

In the earlier expressions of Regency
taste, the arms of carvers rested on exten-

sions of the front legs, which were either a series of small Greek balusters, lion's or ram's heads, or scimitar-shaped curves. The inspiration of these classically derived chairs was Greek, Roman or Egyptian.

VICTORIAN CHAIRS

After 1830, however, the heavier, early Victorian designs moved away from the overtly classical tradition. The chairs developed greater curves to the uprights. Simulation of exotic woods, like rosewood and coromandel — a type of ebony — was used as an alternative to painted motifs on the back panel.

The cresting and carving of the top rail became heavier until, finally, in about 1840, a reaction set in. The line of the back gradually became more of a curve, punctuated by a dip in the centre and a nipped-in waist. This change was partly due to the vogue for the French Rococo style, which required lighter chairs. The fashion for crinolines also demanded wider, rounder seats and curved backs.

Faithful reproductions of Queen Anne, Chippendale, Hepplewhite and Sheraton were produced in the 1870s. These are easily distinguished from the originals in most cases. The carving is less crisp and thin, machine-cut veneers are used on the chair back and seat frames. The chairs are made of brasher Victorian mahogany, even where the original pieces would have used walnut. Also noticeable is an imbalance of proportion, such as a bandy cabriole leg supporting a heavy seat frame. However, the best examples are difficult to distinguish from the original.

Also popular at this time were the sturdy oak chairs produced in Gothic and mock-medieval styles after designs introduced by Victorian reformer-designers such as Charles Eastlake. These, however, were often made with appearance rather than comfort in mind.

▲ *The lighter-weight balloon-back chairs produced by the Victorians were originally intended for the drawing room. Although these will not withstand rough usage, they can be used for occasional dining.*

▶ *A highly elaborate Chippendale chair with 'ribband' back and intricately carved cabriole legs after a design in* The Gentleman and Cabinet-maker's Directory.

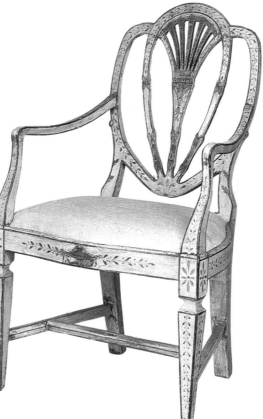

◀ *The late 18th century produced many simple but sophisticated designs such as this Hepplewhite chair with its shield-shaped back. The mahogany and beech frame is painted with stylized leaves and classical motifs.*

The Balloon-back Chair

THE MID-VICTORIAN BALLOON-BACK CHAIR COMBINED ELEGANCE WITH COMFORT AND STRENGTH. THE GRACEFULLY CURVED BACK WAS OFTEN NIPPED IN AT THE WAIST, WITH THE MORE ELABORATE EXAMPLES FEATURING CARVED CREST RAILS AND CROSS RAILS.

THE SOPHISTICATED TURNING AND JOINTING METHODS USED IN FACTORY PRODUCTION ENABLED THE SHAPED CREST RAIL TO BE JOINED TO THE BACK FRAME WITH AN ALMOST INVISIBLE SEAM.

STRONG FRONT LEGS MADE HEAVIER EXAMPLES MORE DURABLE AND SUITABLE FOR USE IN THE DINING ROOM. MACHINE TURNING PRODUCED A VARIETY OF SHAPES FOR HEAVY BALUSTER LEGS WHICH WERE SOMETIMES ALSO EMBELLISHED WITH VERTICAL GROOVES, KNOWN AS REEDING.

A COMFORTABLE SEAT WAS AN ESSENTIAL PREREQUISITE FOR A DINING CHAIR AND LATER DESIGNS NEARLY ALWAYS FEATURE A 'STUFFED-OVER' SEAT — A FIRM PAD OF COMPACTED HORSEHAIR HELD IN THE SEAT FRAME BY WEBBING FIXED TO THE UNDERSIDE AND BY AN UNDER-COVER OF CANVAS FIXED TO THE OUTER SEAT RAILS.

① SERPENTINE CREST RAIL.

② DEEPLY CARVED CROSS RAIL.

③ 'WAISTED' BALLOON BACK.

④ 'STUFFED-OVER' SEAT WITH UPHOLSTERY FIXED TO CHAIR FRAME.

⑤ STOCKY TURNED AND REEDED BALUSTER LEG.

The Sheraton Style

EARLY 19TH CENTURY SHERATON-STYLE CHAIRS FEATURE SQUARE BACKS: THE CREST RAIL IS FIXED BETWEEN THE BACK SUPPORTS.

Leg Styles

A STURDY TURNED AND REEDED BALUSTER LEG WITH ORIGINAL CASTOR (LEFT)

A CURVED CABRIOLE LEG CULMINATING IN A BALL AND CLAW FOOT (RIGHT)

The evolution of the balloon-back chair from Regency examples can most readily be seen in the front legs, which gradually became less like the concave sabre of the classical ideal, tending towards a heavier, more ornate baluster leg. Meanwhile, by the 1830s, the concave back legs began to sweep up into the curving back. The top rail became an extension of the verticals, culminating in a highly decorative crest of curls and swags.

By 1840, these chairs were beginning to be made in quantity, as sets for dining rooms, drawing rooms and parlours, and in pairs for use in the boudoir. They had by now lost all trace of the heavy, overriding top rail and were skilfully shaped to fit the sitter's back.

By 1850 the rounded balloon-back was to be found in every well-dressed house. Variations continued to be made for every room, and it is only from the sturdiness and ornament of an example that it is possible to tell its use. Drawing room and bedroom chairs are usually light and decorative.

Dining room chairs, in contrast, were tough; made for the

·PRICE GUIDE· ⟫ *Dining Chairs*

▲ MAHOGANY DINING CHAIR WITH UPHOLSTERED SEAT AND BACK AND TURNED BALUSTER LEGS. ONE OF A SET OF FOUR.

PRICE GUIDE ❻

▲ ONE OF FOUR FRENCH WALNUT CHAIRS WITH INTRICATE INLAY, PIERCED SPLAT, CABRIOLE LEGS.

PRICE GUIDE ❽

▲ STURDY DINING CHAIR WITH STUFFED-OVER SEAT AND BUTTONED BACK. ONE OF A SET OF FOUR CHAIRS.

PRICE GUIDE ❼

▲ MAHOGANY BALLOON-BACK CHAIR WITH SERPENTINE CREST RAIL AND BULBOUS TURNED AND REEDED LEGS.

PRICE GUIDE ❺

▲ AN ANGULAR VERSION OF THE BALLOON-BACK CHAIR WITH CARVED CROSS RAIL AND RE-COVERED STUFFED-OVER SEAT.

PRICE GUIDE ❹

▲ VICTORIAN 'CHIPPENDALE' CARVER WITH CABRIOLE LEGS, BALL-AND-CLAW FEET AND GOTHIC STYLE PIERCED SPLAT.

PRICE GUIDE ❻

long hours spent at the Victorian table. They almost always had the strong-reeded and/or turned baluster leg, and plainer, less fussy backs to accommodate a well-fed diner.

A variety of woods were called into use. Made for the homes of the wealthy, some of the finest chairs were in solid rosewood, with elegant cartouches carved on the cross rail and sometimes on the crest.

Other solid woods included mahogany and sometimes American walnut.

The seat frames could be made of beech or birch, veneered to match the solid wood legs and back. Less expensive versions were made entirely of the lighter wood, which could be stained, sometimes quite convincingly, to imitate rosewood or walnut.

The seat itself is a clue to the age and quality of a piece.

Earlier examples often had drop-in seats, while later designs almost always had a 'stuffed-over' seat, where the upholstery was attached to the chair frame, then trimmed with decorative brass studs or braid.

The universal stuffing was horsehair – white in the better pieces – and the upholstery itself ranged from durable woven horsehair, which can look as good as new today, to damask,

silk plush and Berlin woolwork.

Most well-known London furniture dealers produced their version of the balloon-back. As the demand increased and the fashion passed down to the less privileged, mass production took over in earnest and the quality of the design declined. By the 1870s and 80s, the chair had become an uninspired hoop-back with a plain back rail and straight or simply turned legs.

The Dresser

Evolved as a piece of working furniture for the kitchen or dining room, dressers came to be an essential item in the provincial parlours of the late 19th century

For the Edwardian working man and his family, whether they lived in the town or the country, accommodation was often very cramped. The majority of artisan cottages and terraced town houses contained only a handful of rooms, the most important of which was the parlour at the front of the house. This room was not for carrying out normal domestic activities, but for entertaining visiting friends and neighbours. It was also in the parlour that the family's most prized possessions were kept, many of them proudly displayed on the shelves of their best piece of furniture, the dresser. Where space was limited a dresser was ideal. The cupboards and drawers in its lower section provided plenty of storage room for table linen, cutlery and other items, while the upper shelves were used to display the family's precious collection of crockery and glassware.

MEDIEVAL ORIGINS

The term dresser (or dressoir) appeared frequently in medieval inventories and seems to have referred to some form of side-table on which food was 'dressed' before serving. The dresser as we know it today, with an arrangement of cupboards and

▶ This simple pine dresser, with its sturdy, home-made look and miscellany of well-used china, is totally at home in a late-Victorian farmhouse kitchen. Pine dressers were often painted in this period.

◀ Although originally built as working furniture for a kitchen, the pleasing lines and rich patination of an old dresser make it perfectly at home in a present-day dining room, where it acts as a showcase for family treasures.

drawers below a set of shelves surmounted by a cornice, began to evolve during the 17th century. It combined the medieval form of dresser, with the simple cupboards used for storage of drinking vessels, plate, crockery, cutlery and condiments, with the tiered arrangement of shelves which were draped with costly textiles and used in wealthy households for the display of valuable gold and silver items.

Until the last part of the 17th century dressers were mostly made without a superstructure and the majority were in the form of a long table with a single frieze of three or more drawers and a decorative apron below. The supporting straight legs were usually turned and joined by stretchers or, occasionally, a 'pot board' or platform on which large vessels could be stored. Sometimes the space below the drawers was completely filled with panelled cupboards and further drawers.

During the 18th century the 'rack' (or superstructure of shelves) became an essential feature of all dressers although, until the middle of the century, it was usually

small spice drawers running along the base of the rack is a particularly attractive, though unusual feature. Quality pieces often have a guard rail running along each shelf rather than a simple groove to prevent crockery from slipping off. On rare occasions clocks are fitted in the centre of the superstructure.

The most common wood for all dressers was oak, although pine, elm and various fruitwoods were also used. Occasionally oak pieces are found with mahogany crossbanding on the drawers and cupboards. It has to be remembered that oak continued to be used for country furniture long after walnut and mahogany became fashionable for smarter homes.

REGIONAL CHARACTERISTICS

As with all country furniture there were numerous variations, although many features were widely copied and so cannot be relied on as a positive method of identification. As a very general rule, Southern dressers tended to have open bases with open shelves above, in contrast to those in the North which usually had backboards on the rack and both cupboards and drawers below. Cabriole legs and integral clocks are also thought to be Northern features.

During this century the term 'Welsh dresser' has loosely been used to describe dressers of the more open Southern type, although the same North and South differences applied in Wales also. True Welsh dressers often have more elaborately scrolled uprights on the rack and more decorative, carved, or even pierced, aprons on both their bases and cornices than their English counterparts.

unattached and either simply sat on the top of the base or was fixed permanently to the wall above.

DRESSERS AND STATUS

The importance, and consequently the appearance, of the dresser depended to a large extent on the wealth of the household for which it was acquired. In wealthy houses the dining room contained no storage furniture at all, as everything required for a meal was being kept in the service areas of the house and only brought in for the occasion. The dresser therefore was situated in the kitchen and was quite utilitarian in appearance. Further down the social scale, the dresser had a higher profile – in the less grand houses of merchants, yeoman farmers and the gentry for instance, the dresser was a prominent feature of the dining room; in humbler cottages, where the dining room, parlour and sometimes the kitchen too, were combined within a single space, the dresser was often actually the most prestigious piece of furniture in the room, usually sporting a number of decorative features. Because

dressers were made for houses at all levels of society and in all parts of the country, there is considerable variation in their design and it is rare to find two identical examples.

By the 18th century, the characteristic shape of the well-known dresser was firmly established. There was now a general tendency for dressers to become larger and for the cupboards and drawers below to increase in number, although some very fine single-frieze dressers supported on cabriole legs were made early in the century. The rack, too, showed great variety. The side uprights could be either straight or decoratively shaped or have additional turned columns. The projecting cornice could have several rows of moulding and sometimes a shaped apron below.

Some pieces incorporated a cupboard into the rack, either a single one in the centre or a matching pair on either side. A row of

▶ *This impressive panelled and decorated George III dresser has small lockable cupboards at the base of the rack intended for tea and spices, then precious commodities.*

The Open-base Dresser

REGIONAL VARIATIONS IN DRESSER DESIGN ARE RARELY CLEAR-CUT. THIS EDWARDIAN EXAMPLE COMBINES SHELVES FIXED WITH A BACKBOARD (A FEATURE OF NORTHERN DRESSERS) AND AN OPEN BASE (TYPICAL OF THE SOUTH). THE UNFUSSY NATURE OF THE DESIGN AND THE PLATFORM BASE, RATHER THAN STRETCHERS, SUGGEST THAT IT WAS ORIGINALLY MADE FOR A WORKING KITCHEN.

THE IMAGE OF SOLID PRACTICALITY IS ENHANCED BY THE DEEP DRAWERS WITH THEIR BRASS HANDLES AND THE SIMPLIFIED BALUSTER LEGS. THE DECORATIVE FRIEZE — ANOTHER HALLMARK OF SOUTHERN STYLE — IS THE ONLY CONCESSION TO ORNAMENT.

① OPEN BASE WITH PLATFORM

② DECORATIVE FRIEZE

③ BALUSTER LEGS

④ DEEP, BRASS-HANDLED DRAWERS

George III Style

THIS 18TH-CENTURY DRESSER HAS AN OPEN, STEPPED RACK AND BASE CUPBOARDS WITH PANELLED SLIDING DOORS.

During the 19th century dressers became far more common. J. C. Loudon described the typical furnishings of the time in his book the *Encyclopedia of Cottage, Farm and Villa Architecture,* published in 1833, and referred to dressers as 'fixtures essential to every kitchen, but more especially to that of the cottager, to whom they serve both as dresser and sideboards'. Loudon illustrated a dresser suitable for cottages which had three panelled cupboards below three drawers, and three gradu-ated shelves in the rack above with backboards and a simple moulded cornice. The turned wooden knob handles and turned feet were typical of the period and were soon to become a standard feature of much Victorian furniture.

BUILT-IN DRESSERS

In the kitchens of large Victorian houses dressers were very often built-in to the walls and were often of massive size. Towards the end of the century the upper shelves were frequently enclosed by large glazed doors to protect the contents from dust and grease. Pine replaced oak as the most common wood for all dressers and was mostly stained, although on fixed examples it was sometimes painted. Because pine dressers have been so fashionable in recent years, many built-in examples have been removed from houses and fitted with backboards at both levels. On dressers of all dates, however, backboards are often found to be later additions and very often the entire superstructure can be a replacement.

·PRICE GUIDE·

Dressers

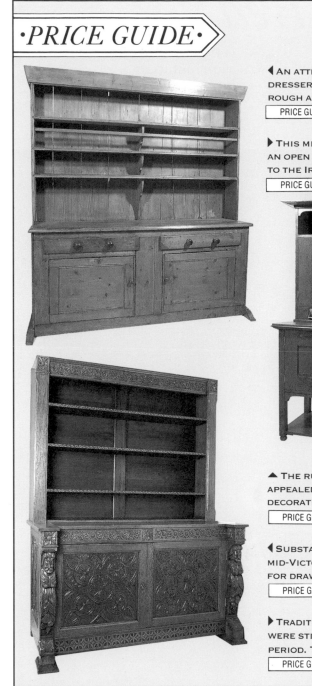

◀ AN ATTRACTIVE EARLY 19TH-CENTURY PINE DRESSER FROM IRELAND, SHOWING TYPICALLY ROUGH AND READY LOCAL CRAFTSMANSHIP.
PRICE GUIDE **8**

▶ THIS MID-VICTORIAN WELSH DRESSER WITH AN OPEN RACK HAS A BASE ALMOST IDENTICAL TO THE IRISH EXAMPLE OPPOSITE.
PRICE GUIDE **8**

▲ THE RUSTIC PRACTICALITY OF THE DRESSER APPEALED TO ARTS AND CRAFTS IDEALS. THIS DECORATIVE PIECE IS MADE OF FRUITWOOD.
PRICE GUIDE **8**

◀ SUBSTANTIAL OAK DRESSERS SUCH AS THIS MID-VICTORIAN EXTRAVAGANZA WERE INTENDED FOR DRAWING-ROOM DISPLAY, NOT KITCHEN USE.
PRICE GUIDE **7**

▶ TRADITIONALLY-STYLED WELSH DRESSERS WERE STILL BEING MADE IN THE EDWARDIAN PERIOD. THIS ONE SHOWS PLEASING WEAR.
PRICE GUIDE **8**

Dresser design varied considerably in the Victorian period, just as it had done in the previous century. Kitchen dressers were usually very plain and simple while the parlour type tended to be more decorative.

VICTORIAN STYLES

Throughout Victoria's reign it was fashionable for different rooms to be furnished in different styles, mostly pastiches of historical designs. For the dining room Renaissance and 'Jacobethan' furniture – the latter a combination of 16th- and 17th-century styles was popular. Many Jacobethan dressers were made, particularly towards the end of the century. The majority were cheaply produced and had poor quality, machine-carved panelling, and decorative mouldings. Spiral and bobbin turning on legs and side uprights was particularly popular. Handles were mostly of cheap stamped metal and their style was frequently incongruous with the rest of the piece. Art Nouveau handles, for example, were not uncommon on later Jacobethan pieces.

Most dressers of this type were made in oak and coated with brown stain. Their design was often rather fussy and their bases were frequently characterized by asymmetrical arrangements of drawers and cupboards. While not to everyone's taste, their appeal to the aspiring middle class was very great and they provided a suitable compromise between the more formal sideboards and china cabinets found in grander houses and the commonplace dressers found in the kitchens of more humble homes.

POINTS TO WATCH

■ Original drawers should show mortise-and-tenon joints on the outer surface of the uprights.
■ Decorative friezes and aprons may be later additions applied to add value. Saw marks on the underside and a softer feel to the wood may be give-away signs. Patination of original features should match that of adjoining wood.
■ Dresser tops added to bases at a later date do not necessarily detract from value if they are well matched.

The Brass Bed

Brass and iron superseded wood as the practical construction materials
for beds. Cast in elegant designs, they were sometimes embellished
with porcelain and mother-of-pearl

Brass beds became fashionable in the 19th century because they satisfied the Victorian's predilection for innovation and hygiene. The Victorians loved new inventions and, if they could afford them, they crammed their homes with the latest products of 19th century ingenuity.

At the beginning of the century, new developments in the metallurgy industries saw the production of cheap and durable metal products. Whereas, previously, the only metal beds were of wrought iron, now elegant brass and iron beds were manufactured in sections that could be easily joined together. These hollow, interlocking tubes were lightweight and simple to transport; the top and end sections and the connecting side rails were made separately, yet they could be slotted together in minutes.

DESIRE FOR HYGIENE

Initially, metal sections were used only to connect wooden frames. However, it was soon realized that wooden beds, especially those draped with heavy curtains, were a cosy and welcoming habitat for bedbugs. As the 19th century progressed, people became increasingly aware of the connection between cleanlinesss and good health. Soon wooden bedsteads with metal sections were replaced with frames made entirely of brass, iron or steel or a combination of metals.

METAL REPLACES WOOD

During the second and third decades of the 19th century, manufacturers competed with each other to develop and patent metal bedsteads. Samuel Pratt was granted a patent in 1825 to produce and sell metal rods designed to hold bed hangings. A year later, his rival, William Day, took out a patent for furniture made from interlocking and extending tubes, based on the same principle as the telescope.

By the 1840s, the metal bedstead was gradually ousting traditional hardwood frames of rosewood and mahogany. Some of the most important firms, R. W. Winfield, Hoskins and Sewell and Peyton and Harlow, were based in Birmingham.

From the beginning, the warm, golden shine of brass was preferred to the dark,

▶ *Turn-of-the-century children's beds were often made of iron, embellished with brass.*

◀ The brass bed is enjoying a revival in the modern bedroom. Early examples can be purchased from antique dealers, but there are also many modern reproductions. These beds often copied original designs. Generally, the plainer the line and decoration of the bedstead, the later the design. Original iron bedsteads are often painted white.

dull colour of iron. Cast iron, however, was rarely left naked; it was usually painted. One exception was an attractively burnished, cast-iron bedstead with elegant, curving rods and cast-brass finials, made by Winfield. This firm's catalogue illustrated several ornately decorated metal beds, some adorned with birds, acanthus leaves and classical figures. Such embellishment appealed to the lavish tastes of the Victorians. Four-poster beds were also made, but not everyone approved of these; some considered curtained beds unhygienic.

Some beds were made entirely of brass, but most brass beds had an inner core of iron. As cast iron was cheaper than brass, brass was usually reserved for covering the iron frame. The finials that topped the four corner-posts and other decorations were often made of cast brass.

THE HEYDAY OF BRASS

Brass-bed manufacturers, such as Winfield, proudly displayed their latest designs at the Great Exhibition of 1851. The public admired the quality of the metalwork and the detail of the decoration. From that point on, the brass bed was firmly established.

The second half of the 19th century saw the height of popularity for the brass bed. The number of styles available in furniture stores in London's Tottenham Court Road and in manufacturers' catalogues seemed infinite. Birmingham was still the centre of the industry and in the 1870s about 300,000 metal bedsteads were produced there each year. Many of these were exported to Europe and America. Throughout the 19th century, Britain was

the largest manufacturer of metal bedsteads. America did not begin to make metal beds until the turn of the century.

CHANGING STYLES

Brass-bed styles changed over the years. In the early Victorian period, the top and end rails were often highly decorated with brass scrolls, animals and flowers in urns. Such ornate embellishment continued into the 1880s, after which decoration became simpler. During the 1890s other materials, such as mother-of-pearl and porcelain, were also used to decorate the beds.

At the turn of the century, metal beds were influenced by Art Nouveau designs from Europe. The curved top rails that resulted were a graceful contrast to the straight, vertical lines of earlier examples. After the First World War, brass beds had little decoration and the metal sections were square-shaped, rather than tubular.

▼ This Victorian iron bed has bevelled glass plaques and brass rosettes on the spindles, with brass finials on the corner-posts.

The Edwardian Brass Bed

THE DESIGN OF THE EDWARDIAN BRASS BED WAS MUCH SIMPLER THAN ITS VICTORIAN PREDECESSOR. LESS ORNATE, THE DESIGNS CONCENTRATED ON FLOWING, CURVING LINES AND SIMPLE DECORATIVE EMBELLISHMENTS. THESE WERE USUALLY CAST AND TURNED ON THE LATHE. FROM THE 1890S, FITTINGS WERE OFTEN MADE OF PORCELAIN, MOTHER-OF-PEARL OR BEVELLED AND ENGRAVED MIRROR GLASS.

① SQUARED END SUPPORTS AND TOP RAIL SUGGEST A LATER DESIGN

② SQUARED BED KNOBS TO COMPLEMENT THE SQUARE TUBING

③ SPINDLES EMBELLISHED WITH SIMPLE BRASS FITTINGS

④ IRON MATTRESS BASE, COMMON ON BRASS BEDS

Decorative Fittings

ROSETTES IN DIFFERENT METALS WERE POPULAR ON SPINDLES.

DECORATED PORCELAIN WAS AN ALTERNATIVE FITTING.

The Iron Bed

AN EARLY VICTORIAN IRON BED, EMBELLISHED WITH ONE OF THE FIRST EXAMPLES OF CAST-IRON PLAQUES.

By the Edwardian period, the metal bedstead was commonplace; for several decades it had been more popular than the traditional wooden bed. Those made entirely of brass or of brass-covered iron were both more fashionable and more expensive than those made primarily of iron.

Charles Eastlake, the author of *Hints on Household Taste,* wrote: 'Some of the ordinary brass bedsteads are . . . stronger and better designed than those of iron. In selecting them, however, it will be well to choose those which are composed of simple bars and rods.'

Certainly, compared to its ornate Victorian ancestors, the Edwardian brass bed was of a fairly simple design. Yet, unless it was an inferior example for a servant or a poor family, it had some form of decoration.

The finials that topped the posts at the four corners of the bed were the most common form of decoration. At their simplest and cheapest they were merely

·PRICE GUIDE·

Victorian and Edwardian Brass Beds

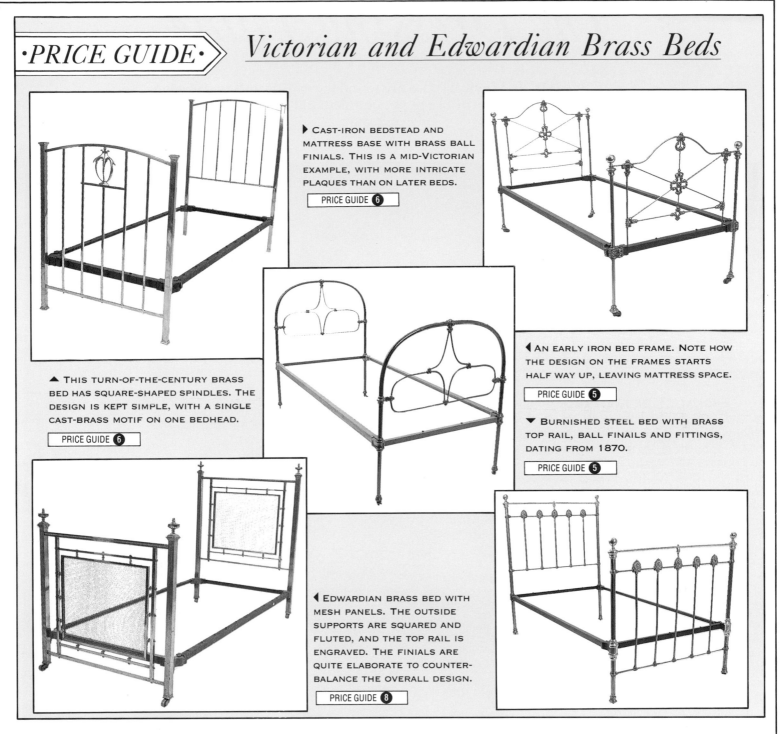

▶ CAST-IRON BEDSTEAD AND MATTRESS BASE WITH BRASS BALL FINIALS. THIS IS A MID-VICTORIAN EXAMPLE, WITH MORE INTRICATE PLAQUES THAN ON LATER BEDS.

PRICE GUIDE **6**

▲ THIS TURN-OF-THE-CENTURY BRASS BED HAS SQUARE-SHAPED SPINDLES. THE DESIGN IS KEPT SIMPLE, WITH A SINGLE CAST-BRASS MOTIF ON ONE BEDHEAD.

PRICE GUIDE **6**

◀ AN EARLY IRON BED FRAME. NOTE HOW THE DESIGN ON THE FRAMES STARTS HALF WAY UP, LEAVING MATTRESS SPACE.

PRICE GUIDE **5**

▼ BURNISHED STEEL BED WITH BRASS TOP RAIL, BALL FINIALS AND FITTINGS, DATING FROM 1870.

PRICE GUIDE **5**

◀ EDWARDIAN BRASS BED WITH MESH PANELS. THE OUTSIDE SUPPORTS ARE SQUARED AND FLUTED, AND THE TOP RAIL IS ENGRAVED. THE FINIALS ARE QUITE ELABORATE TO COUNTER-BALANCE THE OVERALL DESIGN.

PRICE GUIDE **8**

brass balls. More expensive beds had cast-brass finials, turned on a lathe and often in the shape of urns. Moulded brass fittings were sometimes added to other parts of the frame; these could be a row of brass shells on top of the end rail. Sometimes the rails were engraved with a leaf pattern.

A circular brass decoration was a common addition to the top and end rails as it broke up the stark, perpendicular lines of most brass beds. This circle was often in the form of a wheel or rosette, made entirely of brass, although it was also made of other materials, such as mother-of-pearl, engraved mirror glass or porcelain.

Round porcelain plaques were fitted to many brass beds between 1890 and 1910. They were transfer-printed or hand-painted with flowers, birds or historical scenes that helped to satisfy the Edwardian love of nostalgia. Porcelain and mother-of-pearl were also used to decorate spindles on the rails.

This was also the era of Art Nouveau, and brass was ideal for swirling floral designs. Many beds made in the period had gracefully curving top rails ending in scrolls.

Although brass was preferred, many beds were made of iron, sometimes with brass-covered top rails and finials. Iron beds were generally painted black, but sometimes blue or dark green, especially on Art Nouveau designs. Children's beds were often painted white. Iron beds were also electro-gilded to look like brass.

POINTS TO WATCH

■ Check a bed fits together before buying, and avoid purchasing unassembled bits.

■ Look for the manufacturer's name stamped on the frame.

■ Ask how much restoration has been done; too much can spoil the original appearance.

■ Make sure that the brass casing has not cracked.

■ Check that the iron rails are not damaged: they are expensive to replace.

■ Check that the joints have been tightened.

The Dressing Table

Both modern and revival styles are found in the Edwardian dressing table – an item of furniture in popular demand with the suburban lady-of-leisure

Elaborate make-up and hair styles have been a feature of almost all civilizations, both ancient and modern, and a variety of helpful beauty accessories have been developed over the years. In England the use of cosmetics, hair dyes, wigs and perfumes, for both men and women, became widespread during the reign of Elizabeth I, and were the height of fashion after Charles II was restored to the throne in 1660. The need for a suitable place to store all these beauty accessories led to the introduction of the dressing table and established it as an essential piece of bedroom furniture.

EVOLUTION OF THE TABLE

In the fashionable houses of the 17th century, the bedchamber was the most important room of the house. It was here that visitors were received, business transacted and letters written, often at the same time as the master or mistress were being attended to by their servants. The 'dressing' or beautifying procedures were enacted in front of a simple table, which was usually situated near the window for maximum light. Covered with a fine cloth or 'toilet', this was a convenient place on which to spread out the dressing accessories.

Around 1700 these draped tables were replaced by kneehole tables made of walnut. On top of the table stood a small 'toilet glass' – a swivel mirror on a stand. Kneehole desks were also introduced, which served as both writing and dressing tables. In some cases the top of the desk was hinged and it lifted to reveal a mirror and a number of compartments.

DIVERSE DESIGNS

The first half of the 18th century saw these tables and desks become generally larger and more complex. Mahogany replaced walnut after about 1730. Thomas Chippendale, in the 1762 edition of *The Director*, showed a number of 'buroe dressing tables', some 'dressing chests' – a chest of drawers with a fitted top drawer beneath a writing slide – some 'toylet tables' and a lady's dressing table. The latter was a rather elaborate kneehole table with the central recess hung with fringed draperies and had a long fitted drawer containing a 'miror to rise', as well as a novel feature, a central mirror on the top fixed between two narrow

▲ *The elaborate preparations for a grand social occasion were carried out in front of the Edwardian dressing table.*

cupboards. This was to be the prototype for most 19th- and 20th-century dressing tables.

After about 1775, furniture generally became lighter, more delicate and decorative, using materials such as satinwood in place of mahogany, or inlay, or marquetry finished with painted decoration. The elegant Neo-Classical designs of Robert Adam were adapted for the middle-class market by designers such as Thomas Shearer, George Hepplewhite and Thomas Sheraton, whose pattern books all show numerous ingenious variations on earlier styles. A new type of dressing table appeared, in the form of a dressing case on a simple stand, hinged at the sides and opening outwards to reveal the interior fittings.

During the early Victorian period, dressing tables were basically of two types: either the kneehole pedestal or a table supported on four legs with various arrange-

ments of small drawers and cupboards. A matching dressing glass stood on top. After about 1850 the glass was actually fixed to the base and was flanked by small cupboards or nests of drawers. This provided the basic formula for dressing tables until the end of the century and beyond. The only new type to appear before 1900 was the 'duchess', in which a full-length mirror was flanked by two pedestals of drawers.

THE EDWARDIAN SUITE

Edwardian tastes in furnishing were by and large those already prevailing around 1890. There were the historic styles that had been successively revived since 1840, which included 'Jacobethan', Gothic, Renaissance, Queen Anne, Chippendale, Neo-Classical and Louis Quinze, and there were also the modern Arts and Crafts and Art Nouveau styles (see overleaf). Since the 1880s it had become customary to buy bedroom furniture in suites. These usually consisted of one or more beds, a wardrobe, a dressing table, washstand, towel horse, chairs, cheval glass, pot cupboard and a separate chest of drawers.

The majority of bedroom suites in the so-called revival styles bore little relation to any original prototype, but simply had appropriate applied ornament and period-style handles. Perhaps the most successful revival was the Adam style, where delicate Neo-Classical swags, ribbons, bell-flowers and medallions were painted on, or moulded and applied to the surface of the wood. A desire for light, airy bedrooms resulted in a vogue for white-painted furniture for which the Adam style was suitable.

The most common woods for bedroom furniture of all styles were oak and mahogany, although a lot of cheap furniture was made in deal, and stained.

▲ *This 1890s Liberty & Co bedroom suite, including dressing table, shows an attractive simplicity of style.*

▲ *This wonderfully ornate pâpier maché dressing table, now in Temple Newsam, Leeds, dates from early Victorian times. As the century progressed, styles became simpler and more functional.*

◄ *This elegant dressing table in Neo-classical style is inlaid with satinwood and decorated with classical motifs and figures. Note the decorative brass stretcher below and the delicate embellishments on the mirror.*

Art Nouveau Dressing Chest

ART NOUVEAU FURNITURE, LARGELY PRODUCED BETWEEN 1890 AND 1910, WAS A REACTION TO THE MACHINE-MADE VICTORIAN FURNITURE WHICH COPIED EARLIER ELABORATE STYLES.

ART NOUVEAU DRESSING CHESTS WERE RESTRAINED YET DECORATIVE AND WERE OFTEN MADE IN PINE OR OAK.

DECORATION WAS FREQUENTLY CONFINED TO THE CRESTING RAIL ABOVE THE MIRROR AND TO THE CARVED MIRROR SUPPORTS.

ELABORATE METAL HANDLES, OFTEN IN FLORAL PATTERNS, WERE A FEATURE.

① ARTS AND CRAFTS-TYPE GALLERY UPRIGHTS, SET IN AT RIGHT ANGLES, SUPPORT THE CENTRAL AND SIDE MIRRORS

② ADJUSTABLE TRIPLE MIRROR, ALLOWING VIEWS FROM SEVERAL ANGLES

③ TWO CENTRAL JEWEL DRAWERS IN THE UPPER SECTION BENEATH THE MIRROR

④ MOULDED EDGE TO CHEST TOP AND SHELF

⑤ PRESSED METAL HANDLES

⑥ TURNED LEGS ON CASTORS, SUPPORTING THE CHEST

Mirror Supports

MINIMALIST DECORATION: A CARVED DETAIL FROM AN ART NOUVEAU MIRROR SUPPORT.

Dressing Chest

AN UNUSUAL VICTORIAN DRESSING TABLE, MADE AROUND 1850. NOTE THE ELABORATE CARVING AND THE OVAL ON THE CUPBOARD WHICH REFLECTS THE MIRROR SHAPE.

The most fashionable Edwardian bedroom furniture was made either in the Arts and Crafts or Art Nouveau styles. English Art Nouveau owed many of its features to the Arts and Crafts furniture designs.

ARTS AND CRAFTS STYLE
This movement, based on the ideals of William Morris, shunned mechanization and reverted to craftsmanship. The emphasis on functional design without unnecessary ornament was responsible for a large amount of plain, rather severe furniture with a preponderance of flat surfaces and a minimum of decoration. Most was made in oak, the traditional wood for English country furniture. On many pieces the only decorative elements present were large hinges, locks and handles, executed in beaten copper or pewter. Liberty's, the department store, sold a very distinctive range of this 'quaint' oak furniture, including many bedroom suites. Their pieces are characterized by heavy projecting cornices, and desk, table and washstand tops extending further than normal beyond the top of the carcase. This feature is emphasized by table legs and other uprights sloping inwards towards the top.

ART NOUVEAU
Unfortunately, this style was not ideally suited to the feminine interior of a lady's bedroom, although it helped if the room was decorated with plain, light-coloured walls beneath a deep frieze painted with stylized flowers and trees.

In contrast to this plain style was

·PRICE GUIDE·

Dressing Tables

▲ A BAMBOO AND RATTAN DRESSING CHEST, WITH A SINGLE SMALL JEWELLERY DRAWER.

PRICE GUIDE 6

▶ AN UNUSUAL BURNISHED BAMBOO CHEST WITH ORIENTAL DESIGNS IN RED AND BLACK LACQUER.

PRICE GUIDE 7

▶ A MORE TRADITIONAL DRESSING TABLE IN DARK WOOD, WITH A KNEEHOLE AND INLAID DRAWER EDGES.

PRICE GUIDE 6

◀ THE STRAIGHT LINES OF ARTS AND CRAFTS STYLE ARE RELIEVED BY DECORATIVE WOOD TURNING BY THE MIRROR.

PRICE GUIDE 3

▲ A CHUNKY ART NOUVEAU OAK CHEST WITH PEWTER DRAWER HANDLES. ALL ITS DRAWERS ARE LOCKABLE.

PRICE GUIDE 4

▲ THE OVAL MIRROR AND SURROUND, AND THE HERRINGBONE-PATTERNED WOOD SOFTEN THE SQUARE-NESS OF THIS DESIGN.

PRICE GUIDE 6

the continental Art Nouveau (known in France as *Le Style Moderne* and as *Jugendstil* in Germany). This was a popular alternative to Arts and Crafts furniture among the commercial furniture makers from 1895 to 1910. The basic elements of the style were forms copied from nature. However, the rather exaggerated swirling lines of French and Belgian Art Nouveau furniture were too flamboyant for British taste, and the style was strongly criticised by leading architect-designers. Nevertheless, many makers used stylized floral motifs for decorative purposes on the more straightforward Arts and Crafts furniture. In many cases these took the form of small panels of inlay, or occasionally beaten metal, on the front of cupboard doors.

Sometimes a table had this decoration on the front of its drawers and along a deep cornice over the mirror. Some firms, such as J. S. Henry, who made furniture for Heal's, designed pieces elaborately inlaid all over with floral Art Nouveau designs in contrasting woods, usually oak and pine.

The dressing chest was produced in both the modern styles and is a variation on the table. Much used by the Edwardians, it was quite impossible to sit comfortably at it, but as the majority of the middle-class sub-urban ladies had a maid to dress them, they did not feel the need to sit close to the mirror.

In smaller bedrooms, mostly in town houses where economy of storage space was crucial, these utilitarian chests doubled up as dressing table and chest of drawers.

Real or Fake?

■ PEDESTAL DRESSING TABLES WERE OFTEN CONVERTED TO DESKS BY REMOVING TRINKET DRAWERS AND MIRROR. CHECK THAT TOP FITTINGS MATCH THE BASE.
■ DRESSING CHESTS WERE OFTEN CONVERTED TO SIMPLE CHESTS OF DRAWERS. CHECK THAT TOP FITTINGS MATCH THE BASE.
■ THE MIRROR MAY BE A LATER REPLACEMENT.

The Chest of Drawers

Elegant, light and charming in the 18th century and solid, dark and imposing in the 19th, the style of a practical piece of furniture like the chest of drawers reflects that of its century

A chest of drawers was an essential piece of furniture for the Victorian bedroom. Apart from its purely practical purpose of providing storage for clothes, linen and personal possessions, its solid construction and often highly figured veneered finish helped set the tone of solid respectability that was the prime aim of most middle-class households.

17TH-CENTURY OAK CHESTS

The chest of drawers evolved from the plain box chest in the 17th century. During this period, chests and coffers with a drawer in the base, variously known as dowry chests, counter chests or mule chests, began to be made, and by mid-century complete chests of drawers first made an appearance.

These early chests of drawers were tall, with four flights of drawers, the top one generally shallower than the others. The drawers were not made as deep as the chest, leaving a space of two or three inches (5-7.5cm) at the back to permit the circulation of air.

The chests were made by filling a frame construction with oak panels. The drawer fronts of the best examples carried carved decoration and applied moulding and had brass drop handles. Every drawer had a lock, for chests of drawers were not merely units of storage, but also places to keep valuables secure.

In this basic, four-square, solid form, though perhaps with round wooden knobs instead of brass handles, the oak chest of drawers continued to be made as a piece of 'country' furniture into the 19th century.

THE AGE OF WALNUT

For most of the 18th century, chests of drawers remained essentially rich men's furniture. It was not that they were in themselves expensive, simply that only the rich had sufficient possessions to make the purchase of one worthwhile.

The first 30 years of the 18th century were the heyday of marquetry and inlaid work. Although some fine examples were made of solid walnut, most chests of this period were richly veneered in walnut and inlaid with marquetry in a variety of naturally-coloured or dyed woods.

At the beginning of the century there was a fashion for chests to be placed on stands fitted with two or three drawers. Stands were often made of solid walnut, dowelled into the bottom of the chest frame, and many have fallen victim to walnut's well-known susceptibility to woodworm.

Oak is rarely suitable as a base for veneering, and chest carcases were generally of Baltic pine, though the drawer linings continued to be made of oak. When walnut became scarce in the 1730s, mahogany was substituted without significantly altering the

basic structure or design of the chests.

The drawers were made using lapped dovetails, so that the veneer did not have to be laid against the end grain. Cock-beading was typically placed all around the front edges of the drawers. The handles, either drop-handles or cast brass knobs, were secured using hand-cut screws. Bun feet or a plinth replaced the block feet used in the previous century.

SERPENTINE CHESTS

Serpentine-fronted chests, introduced around 1730, were altogether showier pieces of furniture, and their popularity coincided with a period when chests of drawers became, for a while, drawing-room furniture, displaying to callers the status and taste of their owners.

The wavy front with canted corners that gives these chests their name was cut from a single piece of wood, often mahogany. The

▲ *Although they enjoyed a brief vogue as drawing-room furniture in the 18th century, chests of drawers were firmly established as a standard item of bedroom furniture by the middle of the 19th century.*

◀ *The practicality and the classic status of the bow-fronted chest of drawers make it an elegant and – at least in its Victorian version – affordable addition to most modern bedrooms.*

single graduated drawers, with the top one perhaps fitted out as a writing drawer, until around 1800. After this date, two drawers in the top flight were more likely, and after 1830 the most common arrangement was for five flights.

Although the bow remained popular, flat-fronted chests also came back into fashion in the Regency period under the influence of Hepplewhite. These were generally finished in mahogany, with the best examples veneered in highly figured San Domingo or Cuban mahogany on a plainer mahogany carcase.

From around 1820, methods of curving wood by steaming it, then clamping it into shape, provided a much cheaper alternative than shaping bows and serpentines with band-saws, chisels and planes. This helped the bow front to continue to hold its popularity into the Victorian era, though increasingly in the form of pine carcases covered with thin veneers.

curvilinear theme was carried through in ogee bracket feet and in decoratively carved aprons. There were three or four graduated, cock-beaded drawers; the top one was often fitted out for toilet accessories. A particularly desirable feature was the brushing slide, a pull-out surface between the top and the top drawer that was used for writing or for valeting clothes.

BOW-FRONTS

The bow-front, introduced around 1760, became the classic English shape for a chest of drawers. Early ones had brushing slides and curving bracket feet, but the latter were soon displaced, under the influence of Sheraton's designs, by splayed feet. All 18th-century bow-fronted chests were finished in dark mahogany, and were mainly a gentleman's piece, intended for the dressing room or bedroom.

The typical bow-fronted chest had four

▲ *This plain-fronted chest in well figured walnut dates from the 1720s. Set on a simply cut plinth, it shows a typical arrangement of drawers edged with cross-banding and cock-beading.*

◄ *A serpentine chest in the manner of Chippendale. Built of mahogany and set on bracket feet, this piece shows the desirable, well-carved canted corners so often lacking in later reproduction pieces.*

Victorian Bow-fronted Chest

BOW-FRONTED CHESTS WERE MADE IN GREAT NUMBERS FROM THEIR INTRODUCTION AROUND 1760 THROUGH INTO THE VICTORIAN ERA. THIS EXAMPLE FROM 1860 IS TYPICAL OF THE STYLE AND THE PERIOD. IT IS COVERED WITH A MAHOGANY VENEER THAT HAS VERY LITTLE FIGURING BUT FEATURES THE SOFT, GLOSSY SHEEN THEN FASHIONABLE.

THE DRAWERS CARRY MOST OF THE DECORATION ON WHAT IS OTHERWISE A VERY PLAIN PIECE OF FURNITURE. THEY ARE EDGED WITH NARROW COCK-BEADING AND INLAID WITH THIN STRINGING IN A LIGHTER WOOD, PERHAPS WALNUT, BUT MORE LIKELY BLEACHED YEW. THE HANDLES ARE STAMPED BRASS.

THE BOW IS NOT PARTICULARLY PRONOUNCED, AND HAS BEEN PRODUCED BY STEAMING. ITS SHAPE IS ECHOED IN THE MACHINE-CUT CURVE OF THE APRON. THE DRAWER LININGS ARE ALSO MACHINE CUT, AND THIS PIECE DEMONSTRATES THAT MACHINE TECHNIQUES DID NOT INEVITABLY LEAD TO LUMPISH, INELEGANT FURNITURE.

① NARROW COCK-BEADING AROUND THE EDGE OF THE DRAWERS.

② STRINGING IN CONTRASTING WOOD.

③ PLAIN TOP AND SIDES.

④ STAMPED BRASS HANDLES.

⑤ MACHINE-CUT CURVED APRON.

Miniature Wellington

THIS TABLE-TOP WELLINGTON CHEST, JUST 2 FEET (60CM) HIGH, WAS PROBABLY USED FOR JEWELLERY OR PAPERS.

The average mid-Victorian middle-class family had more choice in furniture than ever before. Just about every style that had ever been manufactured was available, either from craft workshops or from furniture factories, where mechanization produced cheap, if sometimes unlovely, furniture that made up in serviceability what it lacked in individuality and charm.

Pine became the preferred timber for chest frames and for drawers in the 19th century. The cheapest versions were finished with painting and staining to resemble the grains of more desirable woods. For the middle-class, however, solid respectability required massive mahogany. Large chests of drawers with dark, usually well figured, mahogany veneer on a carcase of pine or Honduras mahogany were the norm in middle-class homes and hotel bedrooms.

Sizes increased, both to fit new, larger rooms and to express the social status of the owner of the furniture. And as five flights of drawers became more usual, chests were supported more often on plinths or short, bulbous legs.

MACHINE TECHNIQUES

Thin machine-cut veneers replaced the more generous hand-cut versions from the previous century, and continued to get thinner through the 19th century. Bold figuring became less important so long as French polishing could give the veneer the preferred deep, glossy shine.

Serpentine and bow shapes were achieved by steaming and clamping soft woods. Drawer

·PRICE GUIDE·

Chests of Drawers

▼ THE CONTRASTING VENEERS ON THE DRAWERS AND BODY OF THIS MID-VICTORIAN CHEST COMPENSATE FOR THE RATHER WEAK SERPENTINE SHAPE.

PRICE GUIDE 6

▲ A WELL-FIGURED MAHOGANY VENEER ADDS VALUE TO A MID-VICTORIAN SERPENTINE CHEST.

PRICE GUIDE 7

▼ THIS IMPOSING FIVE-FLIGHT MAHOGANY CHEST WAS MADE IN SCOTLAND AROUND 1860.

PRICE GUIDE 7

▲ A PLAIN, FOUR-SQUARE CHEST IN FIGURED WALNUT WITH WOODEN HANDLES AND A PLINTH ON SQUAT BUN FEET, MADE AROUND 1860.

PRICE GUIDE 6

▼ AN OAK CHEST ON STAND FROM THE 1880S WITH FOUR CABRIOLE LEGS, THIS HYBRID WAS PROBABLY SOLD AS QUEEN ANNE.

PRICE GUIDE 6

▲ SMALL THREE-FLIGHT CHESTS NEVER WENT OUT OF PRODUCTION. THIS ONE, C.1860, HAS CANTED CORNERS AND BLEACHED WOOD INLAY.

PRICE GUIDE 6

linings, complete with dovetails, were machine-sawn a dozen at a time. Turning, planing, sawing and moulding all became the province of machines.

REVIVAL STYLES

Every major style of chest was reproduced in the Victorian period. The Jacobean or Tudor revival produced copies of 17th-century oak chests, sometimes with applied twist-turned columns. Genuine old oak panels and timbers were taken from older pieces or discarded wall panelling and successfully fitted into newer, stained oak frames.

Chests on stands were not often made in Victorian England, but many were imported from Holland and Germany, especially during the mid-century Gothic vogue.

Thinly-veneered, flat-fronted chests with machine-cut aprons and stamped brass handles were made in their thousands, though many have since had their veneer removed owing to the fashion for stripped pine.

The serpentine shape was revived, though without great success; the bold curves of the original versions were often merely hinted at. Large French versions, veneered over oak, were imported in the middle of the century.

Bow-fronted chests were not reproductions in the strict sense, as they continued to be made without a break into the 1850s and 1860s. In later versions, the bow became more and more accentuated, and after 1850 turned wooden knobs came to replace the traditional brass handles. Many large Victorian bow-fronts were later cut down to imitate Sheraton styles.

POINTS TO WATCH

■ Reproduction oak furniture can be identified by looking at the drawers; 19th-century oak has a strong, dark grain.

■ Drawer handles set close to the edge of a chest suggest it has been cut down to fit a smaller 20th-century bedroom.

■ Three drawers in the top flight suggest the chest was originally the top half of a chest-on-chest or tallboy.

■ Examine the carcase of bow or serpentine drawers. If the grain is continuous the drawer has been steam-shaped.

The Hall Chair

First developed in the 18th century, the hall chair began its life as a humble servants' seat but soon it became, and remained, a major source of ornament in the hall

The furnishings in the Edwardian lobby, limited as they may have been, would usually have included a pair of solid wood hall chairs. Easily recognizable by their almost flat polished seats and carved, upright backs, hall chairs were never intended to be comfortable.

Though the hall chair had really outlived its original purpose even by Victoria's reign, it continued as a decorative anachronism in many an Edwardian hall. By this time, hall chairs were usually made in pairs. In a main entrance hall, they were among the first things that a visitor would see, and so were used to give an impression of both style and substance to an ordinary middle-class home.

DESIGN ORIGINS

The hall chair evolved into a distinct type during the first half of the 18th century but its story really begins with the furnishings of the great halls of medieval and Elizabethan times. The hall was originally the communal gathering place for both family and visitors where banquets were held and armour displayed. The English house actually grew up around this great, high-ceilinged room, as chambers were added around and above it.

By the early Georgian period, the hall was still an important feature of large houses and was usually a two-storey 'stately centre' off which would lie the saloon, the library, withdrawing rooms and stairs leading to the upper storeys. It became customary for chairs to be set around the walls to provide seating for visitors while they waited to be admitted and also for tradesmen, who in the 18th century, still called at the front door. In addition, the hall was where the 'reserve team' of servants waited to be summoned for duties such as fetching carriages, carrying sedan chairs, lighting lamps and running messages, and where the servants of visiting guests also waited.

COLD COMFORT

Comfort was not a priority in chairs that were provided for use mainly by servants or tradesmen. They could not be upholstered like other chairs as the dripping-wet cloaks of messengers and the mud-splattered uniforms of chair carriers and footmen were hardly good for shot silk or damask. A shallow, circular dishing seat which pre-

vented the occupant from sliding off the highly polished surface was the only concession. Nevertheless, some 18th-century chairs were given a small measure of padding in the form of a flat cushion which fitted neatly into this circular hollow in the wooden seat.

Even so, by the second half of the 19th century, the hall chair was still apparently dogged by its earlier associations with the servile classes – in 1876 R. and A. Garret remarked in their *Suggestions for House*

▼ *The Georgian era was the real heyday of the hall chair but even by the late Victorian and Edwardian periods it was still customary to furnish the hall with at least a single chair, if not a pair. Some hall chairs came as part of special hall sets.*

could appeal to the more refined tastes of the gentry.

By the Victorian era, halls had become substantially smaller and though hall chairs were made in decreasing numbers, their styles reflected a whole gamut of fashionable trends that, one after the other, affected all furniture throughout the Victorian period.

VICTORIAN ECLECTICISM

From the mid 19th century onwards, virtually all furniture design was in some way derivative of an earlier style and, apart from the influences of India and the Orient, every successive trend had its roots firmly in the past. Tastes shifted relentlessly between Graeco-Roman, neo-classical, Regency revival, on to neo-Gothic, Queen Anne or mock Tudor. Victorian hall chairs bore witness to this profusion of influences with each style being imitated to a greater or lesser degree by cabinet maker and furniture factory alike.

▲ *Hall furniture is as sparse as ever in today's interiors. Nevertheless, hall chairs are still popular and continue to be used as decorative features.*

Decoration that 'the hall seat may be taken as the protest of the well-to-do classes against undue luxury in those below them; for it is generally constructed in such a manner as to form a stool of repentance for the unfortunate servant or messenger who is destined to occupy it!'

THE CLASSIC STYLE

Although the hall chair had started as an essentially simple item of furniture, it soon began to show personality. As the real arms and armour that had customarily adorned the walls of large entrance halls gradually disappeared, the armorial theme survived to a large extent in the carved decoration of hall chair backs.

To impress visitors, backs often displayed a painted or a carved crest (the classic shield-back styles were a direct descendant of these). The legs were usually columns, with reeding or a restrained cabriole; solid mahogany was the favoured wood. By the 1760s, sets of 12, 18 or even 36 chairs were being made. In Chippendale's third edition (1762) of his great tome, *The Gentleman and Cabinet Maker's Director,* six different designs for hall chairs were included, reflecting both Rococo and Gothic taste.

The influence of the famous designer Robert Adam introduced oval, round, shield and vase-backed chairs to the 18th-century hall and these were confirmed in popularity by their inclusion in Hepplewhite's *The Cabinet Maker and Upholsterer's Guide* (1788), published by his wife two years after his death.

The later, more elaborate fashions coincided with the changing character of the hall. The servants were now more confined to their own wing and, as they could be summoned by bells wired to a system which ran throughout the house, by the 1780s and 90s there was no need to have anyone dawdling in the hall. Tradesmen too now made their way to their own door, located in the servants' wing and with the lower elements thus kept at bay, hall furniture

◀ *This George III mahogany hall chair, one of a pair, is of particularly graceful design. Its unusual pierced back contributes much to its light feel but notice that it still incorporates the characteristic shield motif.*

◀◀ *Rare and valuable George II painted hall chair dated c.1735. The baluster-shaped back bears the arms of Thomas Osborne (1713-1789) who became 4th Duke of Leeds in 1731. It is part of a set of four chairs all with distinctive architectural painting.*

By the late 19th century, and particularly the Edwardian period, there was a great interest in later 18th-century styles. Especially popular were the revivals of Chippendale, Adam, Hepplewhite and Sheraton, though factories churned out pieces which were more 'in the style of' than true reproductions. A certain quantity of faithful Victorian copies were made, however, but these were produced by craftsmen for those who could pay the price. Such chairs were made by using original methods and the pattern books of the great 18th-century designers.

The Revival Chair

VICTORIAN AND EDWARDIAN REVIVAL CHAIRS CAN BE DIVIDED INTO TWO MAIN CATEGORIES — THOSE WHICH ARE MERELY ADAPTATIONS OF EARLIER DESIGNS WHICH DO NOT NECESSARILY ADHERE TO THE PROPORTIONS, MATERIALS OR CONSTRUCTION METHODS OF THE ORIGINALS; THEN THERE ARE THE CHAIRS WHICH WERE MADE AS FAITHFUL COPIES WHICH, ALTHOUGH TERMED AS REPRODUCTIONS, ARE OFTEN OF SUCH HIGH QUALITY THAT THEY FETCH CONSIDERABLE PRICES TODAY.

THE RUN-OF-THE MILL REVIVALS ARE NOT LIKELY TO DECEIVE THE EXPERT AND WERE MADE IN FACTORIES IN SUCH GREAT NUMBERS THAT, ALTHOUGH OFTEN ATTRACTIVE IN THEMSELVES, THEY ARE NOT USUALLY PARTICULARLY VALUABLE. GOOD QUALITY COPIES ARE NOT SO EASY TO SPOT.

THE YEARS BETWEEN 1830 AND 1860 REPRESENTED THE PEAK IN QUALITY OF 'OUT OF PERIOD' FURNITURE AND SO THERE IS INEVITABLY CONSIDERABLE AGEING INVOLVED. LIKE THE ORIGINALS, PIECES WERE MADE FROM FINE MAHOGANY USING TRADITIONAL TECHNIQUES.

LATER THERE WERE ALSO THOSE EXAMPLES MADE BY CABINET-MAKERS WHO RESISTED THE VOGUE FOR MASS PRODUCTION BY SPECIALIZING IN HAND-PRODUCING TRADITIONAL DESIGNS FOR THE WEALTHY. THE CHAIR SHOWN HERE DATES FROM THE MID-VICTORIAN PERIOD AND IS OF THE FORMER TYPE — IT DISPLAYS A CONFUSED MIXTURE OF BORROWED STYLES.

(1) SCROLLED DECORATION DERIVED FROM MID-18TH CENTURY ROCOCO

(2) HEAVY CARVING IS TYPICALLY VICTORIAN; THE ORIGINAL WOULD HAVE BEEN MUCH LIGHTER

(3) TINY SHIELD MOTIF STILL PRESENT BUT ALMOST LOST IN DECORATION

(4) THE TAPERING OF THE TURNED LEGS SUGGESTS EARLIER REGENCY STYLE

Heraldic Motif

THE SHIELD SHAPE REMAINED ON HALL FURNITURE LONG AFTER HALL TROPHIES DISAPPEARED.

Gothic Style

ECCLESIASTICAL ARCHITECTURE INSPIRED GOTHIC STYLES IN THE 18TH AND 19TH CENTURIES.

In retrospect, the extensive 'borrowing' of styles that took place in the Victorian and Edwardian periods added an extra touch of irony to hall chairs which in themselves were rather anachronistic. In the 1850s and 60s, the two most common styles of hall chair were 'Greek' and 'Elizabethan' – despite the fact that the hall chair had not even existed as a particular type as far back as the 16th century. The term 'Elizabethan' is often substituted by 'Jacobethan', since although the chairs were in oak, and combined usual hall chair attri-butes, the heavy carving of foliage, masks and animals which covered them harked back to the more massive Jaco-bean taste.

FASHIONABLE GOTHIC
Another favourite range was the 'Gothic' chair which displayed church-window tracery in its back, with tall, angular back rails and straight legs. All these styles tended to retain the dished seat characteristic of earlier chairs, sometimes enlivened with a marquetry motif in the centre.

The use of new materials was all part of the general fascination with experiment. Papier-mâché, or imitation painted oak, both embellished with mother-of-pearl and painted designs, lent an oriental appeal to the 19th-century halls.

·PRICE GUIDE·

Hall Chairs

◀ 19TH-CENTURY HALL CHAIR MADE OF CARVED AUSTRALIAN OAK. THE CABRIOLE LEG AND KNURL FOOT IMITATE 18TH-CENTURY STYLES.

PRICE GUIDE 5

◀ VARNISHED OAK CHAIR WITH BROAD BACK INCORPORATING STYLIZED BIRDS AND SWIRLING FOLIAGE DESIGN.

PRICE GUIDE 5

▲ SQUARE-FRAMED WALNUT HALL CHAIR DATED C. 1900 AND ONE OF A PAIR. THE BROKEN ARCHITECTURAL PEDIMENT WITH FINIAL IS DERIVED FROM 18TH-CENTURY DESIGN.

PRICE GUIDE 5

◀ EXTREMELY FINE GEORGE II FRUITWOOD CHAIR WITH PAINTED EAGLE CREST AND RECESS FOR A CUSHION.

PRICE GUIDE 7

▶ EARLY VICTORIAN MAHOGANY HALL CHAIR IN THE REGENCY STYLE, WITH CRESTED BACK.

PRICE GUIDE 5

◀ COALBROOKDALE-STYLE, CAST-IRON HALL CHAIR WITH PLAIN OAK SEAT.

PRICE GUIDE 6

By the late 1860s and 70s, matching hall sets began to be designed which could comprise table, umbrella stand, mirror and hall bench and chairs. One of the great designers of the Arts and Crafts Movement, Christopher Dresser, best known for his work with silver and metals, designed an entire hall set in iron; the malleability of the wire resulted in delicate shapes imitating plant forms.

The hall chair itself, however, did not really lend itself to the innovative side of the Arts and Crafts Movement; it was rather the Queen Anne and Georgian styles which inspired respectable reproductions.

MORRIS REVIVALS

The Morris factory turned out a number of these pieces, as did the companies who worked with the great Gothic designers, William Burges, R. J. Talbert and Charles Eastlake.

The sinuous designs of Art Nouveau twined themselves around slim, armless chairs which could be used both in halls or drawing rooms but there was no real repertoire of hall chairs. That was the preserve of the revived classic styles, the ever-popular Hepplewhites and the Chippendales which continued to be made well into the 20th century, although, by this time, the hall chair was hardly more than an indulgence.

POINTS TO WATCH

■ Although reproductions may be of some value in themselves, beware of them being passed off as the genuine article.

■ Matching pairs or sets of hall chairs will always sell at a premium; for instance, expect to pay three times the single chair price for a pair and so on.

■ Mortise and tenon joints characteristic of earlier chairs give a sturdier structure than later factory-made joints.

The Library Table

Whether rectangular or drum shaped, the library table was the focal
point of the country study, where the gentleman spent many quiet
hours reading and smoking

The gentleman's study was one of the most notable features of the Victorian country house. At its centre was the rectangular or drum library table where the gentleman dealt with the running of the estate, and pursued his hobbies. After 1850, it became fashionable to have a room where the gentlemen could smoke tobacco. In larger houses the library was maintained as a family room and the study that lay off it assumed the new guise of a 'smoking room'.

In the more modest country house the study served both purposes, although it was generally accepted to be a male domain where the country gentleman would spend his leisure time and entertain male guests. In the morning it would be used as a reading room and in the evening as a retreat for tobacco, male gossip and jokes – in fact, anything that the 'gentle creatures' of the household were not expected to take part in. Ladies were admitted only in the afternoon, when the gentleman and male guests were absent, usually fishing.

THE GENTLEMAN'S CLOSET

The earliest incarnation of the private study was as a personal retreat or 'gentleman's closet', referred to in 16th and 17th-century writings. It lay directly next to the master's bedroom, and books were kept in closed compartments along the four walls. It was an austere chamber and there was not much call for comfortable or even utilitarian furnishings. But by the latter part of the 17th century, the room had grown in proportion. Stairs or ladders were needed to reach books and tables were required for taking notes and consulting large volumes.

But in the early years of the 18th century, the character of the literate rich man underwent a change. In the 1700s, he had to become a host interested in all manner of things and willing to share his interests with a multitude of guests. In the grander households, the library had to become yet again larger to accommodate family and guests. While the master of the house might keep his own smaller study as a bulwark against the world, family entertaining passed to what was in effect a literary sitting room.

In the centre of this room stood the pedestal table which, by 1740 had a drawer in the apron, with one on each of the

pedestals, as well as a large cupboard or further drawers. The kneehole allowed ample room for the legs and was sometimes embellished with corner pilasters. Typically, these 'tables' were made of mahogany and were 4-5 feet (1.2-1.5 metres) wide.

▼ *This library table has an extension at one end, to give more space for reading and writing letters in leisure hours.*

VARIED STYLES

The later half of the 18th century saw a wide variation of styling. One example of 1760 is solid mahogany without a kneehole. Instead, a hinged large flap drops along the back, enabling a researcher to sit at it when opened. Both Chippendale and Sheraton included these extensions in their drawings for pedestal-style tables. Hepplewhite included designs for 'kneehole writing-desks' and thanks to him emphasis changed from simple mahogany to rosewood and satinwood inlay with more restrained lines and less carving.

The greatest flamboyance was shown by a serpentine shape, with concave drawers or cupboards flanking the kneehole. However, Sheraton did produce some exceptional experiments in design, including a kidney-shaped library table and an oval mahogany piece, made for the Duke of York. It had classically reeded pilasters next to the kneehole, and a large cupboard at the back.

It was in the late Georgian period that the French-style library table came into being – a long, rectangular leather-topped piece with four tapered legs. These 'Chippendale' tables had slim, straight legs, either reeded, fluted or subtly turned, ending in plain square feet. Though the carcase was mahogany, the drawers were oak-lined and the brass fixtures finely cast.

The Regency saw the full flowering of the study and its furniture, carrying forward

▶ *A reading table of 1770 with a hinged flap to prop up large volumes. Elaborately carved in mahogany, it was made for Kenwood House in London.*

▲ *The drum table in this modern study has four slim pedestals, a popular variation of the single column which was common in the middle of the 19th century.*

the alternative tradition of the long-legged leather-topped table instead of the pedestal style. The top edges would be cross-banded or plain, but the frieze under the table lip usually contained drawers – some of which were dummy if they continued along the length and width or on both sides.

LONG LEGS, LEATHER TOPS

These tables served a number of purposes – for consulting books and maps, for writing letters and notes, for playing quiet games, and just for sitting at. Indeed there was little to choose between the sofa table and the rectangular library table in the period 1820-1840. The library table was simply fitted with a reading slide instead of end flaps. However, the library table's leather top was quite distinctive, usually in smooth, fine-grained calf or small-grained morocco.

From an early bias toward tables with a single pedestal supported on three or four tripod feet, the fashion changed to a more usual top on two classic curved end supports. Towards the end of the Regency this evolved into two carved legs ending on two rectangular platforms, which were themselves supported on two scroll or claw feet each. The drum table was a popular variation of this design, although round, and continued its reign through the Victorian and Edwardian period.

To accommodate the masculine emphasis, 'library' tables became heavier, the mahogany veneer darker and the carving more elaborate, particularly on the legs and on the side friezes. Byzantine and Gothic taste were much appreciated, complementing heavy chimney pieces and wainscoting.

In smaller country houses, where the smoking room still did practical service as library and study, magazine and newspapers would be spread out on the table – *Punch*, later *The Strand*, and in the Edwardian period, *The Tatler*.

The Drum Table

THE DRUM-SHAPED LIBRARY TABLE WAS THE MOST POPULAR DESIGN IN THE MID-VICTORIAN PERIOD, AND WAS ORIGINALLY DESIGNED TO STORE RENT BOOKS AND PAYMENTS FROM TENANTS.

THIS GEORGE IV PERIOD TABLE IS REVOLVING AND CRAFTED IN BRAZILIAN ROSEWOOD. THE CIRCULAR TOP IS CROSSBANDED WITH REEDED EDGING AND IS FITTED WITH A LEATHER INSERT IN THE CENTRE. THE FREIZE BELOW HAS DRAWERS ALL AROUND IT, SOME OF WHICH ARE DUMMIES.

THE SUPPORTING COLUMN HAS A CARVED LOTUS MOTIF AND RESTS ON THE TRI-CORNERED PLATFORM. THE BASE IS CONCAVE SHAPED AND HAS CARVED REEDING ALL AROUND IT THAT MATCHES THE TABLE TOP.

IT WAS MADE C. 1820 AND WAS PROBABLY DESIGNED TO STAND IN THE HALLWAY OF A RATHER GRAND HOUSE, SINCE IT IS SO FINELY CRAFTED AND ALSO BECAUSE OF ITS SIZE. IT MEASURES 4 FEET (1.2 METRES) ACROSS, WHICH MAKES IT LARGER THAN THE AVERAGE DRUM TABLE.

The Pedestal

THE CONCAVE-SHAPED, TRIFORM PLATFORM SUPPORTS A COLUMN WITH A CARVED, LAPPETED LOTUS MOTIF. NOTE ALSO THE FINELY CRAFTED SCROLL FEET.

1. ROUND, CROSS-BANDED TOP WITH REEDED EDGING AND TOOLED HIDE INSERT.

2. DRAWERS ALTERNATING WITH DUMMY MATCHING DRAWER FRONTS.

3. PEDESTAL DEPICTING CARVED LOTUS MOTIF.

4. TRIFORM PLATFORM WITH REEDING MATCHING TABLE TOP.

5. SCROLL FEET WITH CARVED ACANTHUS LEAF DECORATION.

Regency Rent Table

THIS MAHOGANY RENT TABLE WITH GILT MOUNTS AND TOOLED LEATHER TOP WAS MADE BY J. M. LANE C. 1810.

The earliest drum tables made their appearance in the last decade of the 18th century, and resembled their rectangular cousins in all but shape. The legs were the same, plain and tapering to a narrow peg foot and the mahogany veneer ran horizontally around the frieze. The top was leather and tooled discreetly around the edge.

By the time the Regent was in command, c. 1810, the table had developed its own distinct personality. The four legs had declined to one central pedestal which splayed into four gently curving concave legs. The plain feet were usually encased in brass shoes and castors, which enabled the table to be moved around the room. The leather-lined table top could exhibit elaborate gilt tooling – particularly in the hexagonal or octagonal variations which began to appear. Here the leather could be marked out in six or eight parallelograms encircling a smaller central hexagon or octagon – all executed in gold leaf. The frieze now contained drawers all round.

As the Regency progressed, the styling became more heavy-set and pompous, like the Regent himself. The pedestal was thicker and often mounted on a flat rectangular platform, from which the legs extended in a concave, sabre curve. The top of the leg could be carved with classical heads, leaves or scrolling in wood or brass.

For storage space, there were a variety of options, from bow-fronted wedge-shaped drawers encircling the entire frieze, to two or four drawers with square interiors ranged on opposite 'sides'. Narrow bookshelves sometimes replaced drawers on the frieze, while some elegant examples were surmounted by graduated circles of bookshelves. There were sometimes as many as four, making it taller than the average man.

The prime wood for all these variations was mahogany, the best examples being solid mahogany, although drawers were often oak-lined for strength.

As the reign of the Georges came to its close, the exuberance of Egyptian styles enjoyed a

Library Tables

▶ AN EARLY 19TH-CENTURY TABLE OF FADED BRAZILIAN ROSEWOOD. THE TOP IS SUPPORTED ON A FACETED COLUMN, WHICH STEMS FROM THE CARVED BASE.

PRICE GUIDE 8

▲ WILLIAM IV ROSEWOOD LIBRARY TABLE WITHOUT DRAWERS.

PRICE GUIDE 7

◀ REVOLVING, OCTAGONAL PEDESTAL TABLE C. 1835 WITH FOUR REAL AND FOUR DUMMY DRAWERS. NOTE THE TAPERED COLUMN, QUADRUPED PLATFORM AND BUN FEET.

PRICE GUIDE 8

◀ A RARE EXAMPLE OF A REGENCY FREE-STANDING ARCHITECT'S TABLE WITH AN INNER COMPARTMENT FOR DRAWINGS.

PRICE GUIDE 8

▶ A PARTICULARLY FINE REGENCY TABLE WITH RIBBED MOULDING AROUND THE TOP.

PRICE GUIDE 9

final fulsome expression. Elaborate boxwood stringing and gadrooned lips on the table top, together with heavy cross-banding on the frieze drawers, were all characteristic of pre-Victorian fashion.

By mid-century the solid respectability one associates with the Victorian age was already apparent. The pedestal became more bulbous and turned, the legs more solid — often with heavily carved knees, ending in ball-and-claw or carved paw feet.

It was during this period that the true 'rent table' came into being: a large drum table whose

frieze was deep enough to contain wedge-shaped drawers all round. It was devised to stand in the receiving hall of a large estate house, so that rents could be taken from the tenants and the monies and rent books kept in labelled drawers. Some examples exchanged the central supporting column for a fairly large, square pedestal, capacious enough to hold a cupboard for larger documents. In addition, the table top often contained a lidded inkwell in the centre.

The term 'rent table' has since been extended to cover all manner of round or many-

angled circular library tables, but this was its true derivation. It should not be used in relation to tables with a limited number of drawers or which contain pencil dividers, reading or writing slides. These are traditional library tables and nothing else.

From the 1870s and 80s, the round table took over as the most popular shape, but the new incarnation of the study as 'smoking room' began to rob it of its real purpose. The loo table began to compete for space in this male enclave, and reading and writing was done at a corner desk.

Imitations of earlier tables

continued to be made throughout the Victorian and Edwardian period, however, with figured woods like burr walnut intruding into the mahogany monopoly. Though many of these tables were well proportioned, they lacked the attention to detail, the fine veneers and the delicacy of moulding — particularly on table lips and drawers — that characterized earlier examples. Mass production partnered mass education, and it was the public libraries, reading rooms and civic offices that became the major showplaces for these now unfashionable pieces.

The Card Table

The passion for card games gave rise to the purpose-built card table which, by Victorian times, had become an indispensable item in the drawing room

From the moment of its conception at the end of the 17th century, the idea of a cloth-covered table for playing card games set a strikingly modern problem to designers, for they had to make a piece of furniture for a very specific, yet only occasional, activity. Cabinet-makers of the time would never have settled for today's apologetic solution, a purely functional table, which, like a deck-chair or a camp-bed, folds flat and slides discreetly out of the way. As its surface could not be put to any other purpose, the table-top, when not in use, would have to fold up to protect its covering, and the table would stand as an elegant ornament against the wall. This it did for over two centuries, retaining its fundamental identity from the reign of Queen Anne to the Edwardian era, with its faithful reproductions of earlier styles.

ORIGINS OF THE CARD TABLE

Before the second half of the 17th century, card-playing had been the pastime primarily of soldiers and other idlers in taverns. If they wanted to protect their cards from sticky pools of ale, they simply threw a cloth over the table. In England, cards became fashionable at court during the Restoration and by the reign of William and Mary games like ombre (a three-handed form of whist) were played on small tables with drop-leaves and gate-legs. These were generally of walnut and had no distinguishing features that clearly marked them out as card tables. In fact, they still served other occasional purposes and required a cloth for cards – by now frequently of green velvet. The first stroke of genius was to incorporate the velvet (or a cloth decorated in petit point) in the table itself, the second to dispense with two of the six legs, which, complete with stretchers, must have seriously encumbered the players' legs.

Thus emerged the splendid Queen Anne card table standing on four cabriole legs with a folding top. One or both of the back legs were hinged and extended on a section of the frame to support the flap. This system was more satisfactory on a round table, but the classical shape was a rectangle which opened out to a square, often with rounded projecting corners, which served as candle-stands. Some also had dished wells set in the cloth, where the players kept their stakes.

The Queen Anne card table was nearly always of walnut, but the reigns of George I and II saw the rise to prominence of

▶ Nineteenth-century card tables often displayed the richness of ornament and fine craftsmanship which the Victorians admired.

◀ Inside a Victorian house, the card table might have taken on different guises, since manufacturers followed whatever style was in fashion. Today an ordinary table, 'dressed' for the occasion, will serve the same purpose.

mahogany. The cabriole legs, with only slight variations, remained a permanent feature, many carved on the knee with acanthus leaves, shells or lion-masks, at first with simple pad feet, then the more extravagant ball-and-claw variety. Some card tables were made with a matching uncovered tea-table, and there were even ones with three flaps, which could fulfill both functions in turn. A significant mechanical improvement was a system that allowed the two back legs to be pulled out on a concertina-style frame to complete the frieze round the edge of the table. Around 1750 the friezes became more elaborate with Rococo scrolls or Gothic fretwork, and the legs were straightened in the sturdy four-square Chippendale manner.

In the second half of the century, the lighter neo-classical styles caused even greater changes in the appearance of card tables. Straight, slender, tapering legs, often square with boxed feet, supported a far greater variety of tops: oval, elliptical, D-shaped and serpentine as well as round and square. Lighter woods, especially satin-wood, were in favour, with delicate stringing and marquetry on the frieze and legs and

ment, in which a large number of players competed for tricks with just three cards each, the kind of family game that appealed to populous 19th-century households. Many early Victorian drawing rooms boasted a suite consisting of a loo table and two matching card tables, though in grander houses these might be found in the morning room. In the end, loo tables, despite the continued use of the name, probably witnessed more breakfasts than card parties. Nevertheless, their design had a great influence on the pedestals of card tables in the 1830s and 40s. These had central columns resting on a roughly rectangular, horizontal platform. The sides of the platform were hollowed out to give an X-shaped base, its arms supported by massive scrolled or paw-shaped feet.

In some Regency tables two or four lighter pillars took the place of the central column, and it was this pattern, with the addition of characteristic Victorian ornamentation, that proved most popular between 1850 and 1880. Walnut made its come-back as a base material, largely contributing to the collector's value which many Victorian card tables still hold today. Towards the turn of the century designers abandoned the quest for novel means of supporting the virtually unchanging table-top, and took to reproducing Adam- and Sheraton-style pieces of a century before. Many of these were hand-crafted and some are done with a skill that can easily deceive the semi-tutored eye.

THE CARD TABLE TODAY
Although many are striking expressions of an age of great fantasy and ingenuity, Victorian card tables fell out of favour, even with the Victorians themselves, so there are not as many to be found as one would expect. Today, a characteristically Victorian card table will be less than half the price of a more sought-after Regency table. Higher prices, too, are often paid for Victorian reproductions, both in the highly decorated Louis XV manner and in the English neo-classical style.

beautifully inlaid tops, but the principle of the elegant side-table with a folding top to protect the surface remained the same.

19TH-CENTURY STYLES
By the time of the Regency, card tables had become as essential to English life as teapots, not only among the wilder elements of society like those who gambled their way through Thackeray's *Vanity Fair*, but even among the genteel middle-classes portrayed by Jane Austen. The Regency table has a central column instead of legs, a sensible development one feels, for, when stakes and blood-alcohol levels were high, Adam and Sheraton legs must have taken an awful buffeting. From the base of the column projected four curving splayed legs, which gave the table grace and stability. The most fashionable woods were rosewood and kingwood, often richly inlaid with brass stringing or scroll-work.

The sudden disappearance of the card table's legs was made possible by the invention of the swivel top. Introduced at the end of the 18th century, it dispensed with the overhanging flap and the need for a movable leg to support it. The pattern was

so successful that Victorian furniture-makers were still producing what were essentially variations on a Regency theme well into the 1880s.

Another piece of Regency furniture destined to enjoy a long life was the so-called 'loo table', a solid round centre table, which also rested on a single column. The game of loo was a light-hearted entertain-

◀ An elegant, gilt card table inlaid and veneered with harewood and satinwood. Now in Syon House, it is dated c. 1770.

▲ This George II walnut card table, dated 1735, has cabriole legs and ball-and-claw feet.

The Victorian Card Table

The Swivel Top

① Hinged rectangular table top, opening up to a square, can be turned through 90 degrees.

② A circle of green baize inset into the table top provides a non-slip playing surface.

③ A wooden frame supports the table top in both open and closed positions.

④ Cheval style table base with turned and carved ends and stretcher.

⑤ Carved legs terminating in scroll feet.

INTRODUCED AT THE END OF THE 18TH CENTURY, THE SWIVEL TOP ALLOWED THE TABLE TOP TO REST FIRMLY ON ITS FRAME WITHOUT ANY EXTRA SUPPORT.

ALTHOUGH IN MANY CASES, VICTORIAN CARD TABLES ARE IN FACT REPRODUCTIONS OF PREVIOUSLY POPULAR STYLES, THE MOST COMMON TYPE HAS A RECTANGULAR SWIVEL TOP SECURED TO AN UNDERFRAME. TABLE TOPS ARE MOSTLY IN PLAIN WOOD LIKE WALNUT OR MAHOGANY WITH CARVED EDGES OR ARE INLAID WITH LIGHTER WOODS.

THE FOCAL POINT WAS THE LEG SUPPORT — AS A DEPARTURE FROM THE CENTRAL COLUMN OF REGENCY TABLES, VICTORIAN CARD TABLES BOAST A DIVERSITY OF PILLARS AND CROSS-STRETCHERS DECORATED WITH FINIALS OF VARIOUS SHAPES.

The Card Trolley

THE SWIVEL TOP BECAME A POPULAR FEATURE OF THE CARD TABLE. THIS 20TH-CENTURY ONE DOUBLES AS A SERVING TROLLEY.

After enjoying such a central role in the social life of earlier periods, the card table in Victorian times was considered a somewhat peripheral item of furniture, and as such manufacturers rarely gave close attention to its design. In fact, card tables tended to tag along in the wake of the fashion of the day, adapting themselves as best they could to a succession of styles.

The table-top itself varied little; it was usually a rectangle opening to a square, though other shapes were still made to order. Underneath the top, the hollow frame was divided in two by a bar of wood about a quarter of the way along. The pivot was set in this at the point which, when the top was turned through 90 degrees, allowed it to unfold with its centre exactly above the centre of the frame. The larger compartment in the frame, often lined with baize like the top, acted as a drawer for storing cards and counters.

There was seldom much decoration on the frame and table-top; this was possibly thought superfluous because of the Victorian habit of draping side tables and covering them with ornaments. Some good tables have marquetry tops or cross-banding in a lighter wood round the edge, where cheaper examples have a little rudimentary boxwood stringing or applied mouldings. However, it was to the supports for their card tables that Victorian craftsmen devoted most of their creative energy.

From the simple central column of the Regency table there evolved a splendid diversity of pillars and cross-stretchers, decorated with turned finials in the shape of vases, orbs and spinning tops; in short, Victoriana at its most amusing. The most delicate style was the 'birdcage' of four slender turned

Card Tables

▲ A TYPICAL LATE-VICTORIAN WALNUT CARD TABLE RESTING ON FOUR PILLARS AND FOUR LEGS, WITH CENTRAL FINIAL.

PRICE GUIDE **7**

▲ A DEMI-LUNE CARD TABLE WITH CARVED EDGES AND TAPERING LEGS, FEATURING AN ACCESSORIES DRAWER.

PRICE GUIDE **6**

▲ A WALNUT SWIVEL TOP CARD TABLE WITH DECORATIVE INLAY AND A CLUSTER PEDESTAL.

PRICE GUIDE **7**

▼ A LATE REGENCY ROSEWOOD CARD TABLE WITH BRASS STRINGING, INLAY AND FINIALS AND A SINGLE CENTRAL COLUMN.

PRICE GUIDE **7**

▲ REPRODUCTION CARD TABLE IN CHIPPENDALE STYLE, DECORATED WITH BLIND FRETWORK.

PRICE GUIDE **7**

▲ A 1890s CARD TABLE IN THE SHERATON STYLE, ITS TOP FOLDING LIKE AN ENVELOPE.

PRICE GUIDE **7**

---

pillars surrounding an elaborate finial, popular in the 1850s and 60s. By this time the heavy paws of the late Regency and early Victorian periods had been replaced by longer, curving feet, recalling the original Regency style but more extravagantly carved. In many examples of the same period, the pillars are spread so far apart as to constitute four separate legs, although they are still joined by curving cross-stretchers crowned by a central finial. In others, the pillars have divided into two pairs with a single straight stretcher running between them. Tables of this last kind were

quickly adapted to whatever style of furniture happened to be in fashion: Chippendale, Gothic, ecclesiastical or even Japanese.

The disappointing feature in many Victorian swivel top card tables is the wood employed in their manufacture. In the 1840s a few were still made in rosewood, but most furniture companies were aiming rather more downmarket. 'Mahogany', a name given at various times to any number of tropical hardwoods, enjoyed a revival, but it is not of the same quality as that used a century before.

There followed a vogue for ebonizing deal and other inferior

woods in imitation of the French, but reaction to this, demanding lighter colours and a return to an English tradition, revived the use of walnut. As this aspect of English taste is still very much alive today, mid-Victorian walnut card tables with a good finish are often as much sought-after as the earlier tables in the darker woods of the late Regency style.

POINTS TO WATCH
■ Card tables have usually led a pretty active existence, so be suspicious of one that shows no signs of damage or repair.
■ The baize will have been

replaced several times in the lifetime of a table. Sometimes a new surround will have been substituted at the same time.
■ Card table tops are very susceptible to warping. If the flap does not close properly, the table will be worth much less.
■ On a swivel top table, it is very easy to change the top completely. With plain Victorian tops it can be difficult to judge whether top and bottom are of a piece.
■ The turned finials on mid-Victorian tables are very fragile and may be badly chipped, removed altogether or optimistically stuck back on.

The Pedestal Desk

The pedestal desk was a handsome, sturdy and practical workhorse which would have held pride of place in the essentially male preserve of a Victorian country library

The pedestal desk was a large and imposing item of furniture, usually 4-5 feet (1.2-1.5 metres) in width, and it played an essential role in the activities of the library. Letter-writing, studying and domestic business matters all required an expansive working surface which the pedestal desk provided. Accordingly, it was frequently placed in the centre of the room or in a dominant position, such as the recess of a large bay window.

DEVELOPMENT OF THE DESK
Despite its solid and practical character, the pedestal desk developed out of an essentially feminine piece of furniture. This was the kneehole dressing table, which became popular in the early years of the 18th century, when it could be found in a boudoir or a drawing room. It took the form of a chest of drawers with a central recess, where there was often a small cupboard for such things as slippers. Usually in walnut, the kneehole dressing table was decorative rather than functional, as the aperture was invariably too small to accommodate both knees with any degree of comfort.

With pedestal desks, this difficulty was overcome by making the entire construction larger. The new item of furniture was built up from three separate units rather than one. It was formed of two bulky pedestals, with or without drawers, surmounted by a flat desk top.

The earliest examples of pedestal desks appeared in about 1765 and coincided with the introduction of mahogany into Britain. Walnut had become scarce after the severe frosts of 1709 and ceased to be readily available once its main supplier, France, banned the export of timber in 1720. In its place, the English government encouraged the importation of wood from the West Indies by waiving duty charges.

By 1750, three types of mahogany were in use in England: Spanish (from San Domingo), Cuban and Honduras. The latter was the one most commonly used in the production of the carcases (the basic structures) of pedestal desks. Honduras mahogany was the cheapest and softest of the three varieties, but it contrasted well with the richer Cuban curl wood which was employed in the veneered sections.

The pedestal desk was fully developed during the second half of the 18th century,

when it was popularized by Thomas Chippendale in his *Gentlemen and Cabinet-Maker's Director.*

CHIPPENDALE'S DESIGNS
Chippendale's *Director,* which appeared initially in 1754, revolutionized the working methods of the furniture industry in England. It was a pattern book, the first of its kind in this country, in which the author compiled an exhaustive variety of furniture designs, depicting them in the 161 engraved plates.

The *Director* was not, however, like a present-day catalogue. The idea was that the country gentleman should visit Chippendale's premises in St. Martin's Lane, when he came up to London, and should use the illustrations in the *Director* as the basis for ordering items of furniture that met his own particular needs.

Of course, in practice, this meant that Chippendale's designs were copied or adapted by other cabinet-makers throughout the nation. As so little English furniture from this period carried identifying marks, most of the pedestal desks which conform roughly to the designs in the *Director* are known as Chippendale, even though they probably had no direct connection with his workshop.

One of the most notable exceptions is Robert Gillow's firm in Lancaster, which followed the French custom of stamping the company's name in unobtrusive places, such as the top edge of a drawer. Gillow's were typical of many provincial firms, producing well-made but workmanlike variations on

▼ *A mahogany partners' desk from the Regency period. Desks of this time sometimes had feet with castors. The indented kneehole reflects the desk's evolution from the dressing table.*

◀ The pedestal desk, or the even larger partners' desk, was eminently practical for the man of letters. There was plenty of room on the desk top for piles of books, as well as papers and writing equipment. The drawers provided useful storage space for documents. This portrait is of David Roberts, the Victorian artist, in a corner of his studio.

▶ Full-sized pedestal desks require a large room to do them justice, but smaller models, especially reproduction ones, can fit well into modern rooms. They are both decorative and practical.

▼ A solidly built partners' desk from the reign of George II. It is of carved mahogany with a leather top. It has hidden castors and false drawers at the sides.

the London designs. They were concerned to keep abreast of fashion, however, and, in 1760, several letters were despatched to the capital, asking for copies of Chippendale's most recent drawings, to be used as a source of inspirational material.

STYLES AND MATERIALS

Chippendale was a champion of the Rococo, an ornate style which featured elaborate decorative motifs such as foliage or chinoiserie. He also took the unusual step of collaborating with many of the major architects of the day – James Paine, the

Adam brothers and John Carr. For this reason, some of the grandest examples of pedestal desks have survived in the great country houses. Two of the finest are at Osterley Park and Harewood House; both have charming satinwood inlays, ormolu mounts and striking neoclassical decoration.

This was not typical, however, and by the end of the century the trend was for lighter woods and simpler designs. The pioneers in this field were George Hepplewhite and Thomas Sheraton, both of whom published furniture guides similar in format to Chippendale's *Director*. The importance of these guides can be gauged from the enduring reputation of these two men, even though no surviving items of furniture can be positively attributed to either of them. Indeed, Sheraton's knowledge of the subject appears to have been purely theoretical, as he made his living as a Baptist preacher, bookseller and teacher.

The pedestal desk has never gone out of fashion and the solidity of its design made it particularly well-suited to the heavier styles favoured by the Victorians. Later examples were made out of oak or pine, as well as mahogany, and were adapted to a variety of uses. In 1873, one well-known designer – Owen Jones – even added a mirror and small drawer units to create a dressing table similar to the old kneehole format. The pedestal desk had gone full circle.

The Partners' Desk

THE MOST SALIENT FEATURE OF THE PARTNERS' DESK IS THE PRESENCE OF DRAWERS ON BOTH SIDES, DISTINGUISHING IT FROM THE PEDESTAL DESK. IN MOST CASES, THERE ARE DRAWERS IN BOTH THE FRIEZE AND THE PEDESTALS, BUT THE LATTER ARE OFTEN ENCLOSED BEHIND PANEL DOORS AND DUMMY DRAWERS CAN BE FOUND OCCASIONALLY. BOTH SIDES ARE IDENTICAL.

THROUGHOUT ITS HISTORY, THE MOST COMMONLY USED WOOD HAS BEEN MAHOGANY, ALTHOUGH IT IS STANDARD TO FIND DRAWERS LINED WITH OAK.

SOME PARTNERS' DESKS HAVE MOULDED BRACKET FEET, ALTHOUGH THIS WAS NEVER A WIDESPREAD ADDITION.

LIFTING SIDE FLAPS, WHICH EXTENDED THE WRITING SURFACE, WERE ANOTHER UNUSUAL VARIATION.

① AN EMBOSSED LEATHER TOP.

② A CHAMPFERED EDGE ECHOED IN THE BASE OF THE FRIEZE.

③ THE FRIEZE USUALLY HAS THREE DRAWERS.

④ LOCKABLE DRAWERS MAY BE FOUND ON EACH SIDE OF A PEDESTAL BUT CAN BE REPLACED BY A CUPBOARD ON ONE SIDE.

⑤ PANELLING ON BOTH LONG SIDES OF THE PEDESTAL.

George III Partners' Desk

A FINE MAHOGANY DESK WITH MOULDED LEATHER TOP, THREE FRIEZE DRAWERS AND TWO CUPBOARDS DECORATED WITH FIGURING AND CABOCHON CLASPS.

The Restorer's Work

AN EMBOSSED LEATHER TOP WITH GOLD DECORATION, EXECUTED BY A RESTORER.

THIS NEW BRASS HANDLE AND LOCK PLATE HAVE BEEN ADDED DURING RESTORATION.

A number of variations on the basic design of the pedestal desk can be found. Prominent among these are the library table – a blanket term which includes items with legs instead of pedestals – and the partners' desk.

The partners' desk was a thoroughly practical piece of furniture. The name derives from the matching drawers on either side, from which it is presumed that two colleagues worked together at the same desk, facing each other. It was a logical development, since the pedestal desk was intended to be free-standing. This meant that the back was fully finished and veneered, and it thus made perfect sense to maximize the storage space available.

The use of partners' desks

·PRICE GUIDE·

Pedestal Desks

▼ A MAHOGANY DICKENS' DESK WITH A WRITING SLOPE WHICH HOUSES STATIONERY. THE TOP DRAWERS LOCK AT THE SIDE.
PRICE GUIDE ⑧

▲ A VICTORIAN MAHOGANY PEDESTAL DESK WITH ORIGINAL HANDLES, A WELL-WORN LEATHER TOP, CHAMPFERED EDGES AND CASTORS BENEATH THE PEDESTALS.
PRICE GUIDE ⑧

▲ AN OAK PARTNERS' DESK, MADE IN 1890. THE DESIGN OF DRAWERS AND ROLL-FRONT CUPBOARD IS REFLECTED ON THE OPPOSITE SIDE.
PRICE GUIDE ⑦

▼ DATING FROM 1880, THIS OAK PARTNERS' DESK HAS A GOLD EMBOSSED LEATHER TOP.
PRICE GUIDE ⑧

◀ A VICTORIAN MAHOGANY PEDESTAL DESK TO WHICH GOOD RESTORERS HAVE ADDED A NEW EMBOSSED LEATHER TOP IN PANELS AND NEW BRASS DRAWER HANDLES. THE DUMMY DRAWERS IN THE RIGHT-HAND PEDESTAL FORM A CUPBOARD DOOR.
PRICE GUIDE ⑧

was not confined to the library. In the country, they would commonly have been found in estate manager's offices while, in town, they were often used by businessmen, industrialists or professsional classes.

Chippendale's *Director* and succeeding publications in this vein were targeted at a new type of client. Previously, high-class furniture had mostly been designed for the wealthy aristocracy. After 1750 the demands of an affluent and expanding middle class led to a boom in English cabinet-making. The Industrial Revolution increased the volume of trade, generating an ever-greater need for high quality office furniture.

Most partners' desks echoed the classic pattern of Chippendale's designs but, particularly

around 1800, there was a taste for diversity. Hepplewhite and Sheraton both recommended oval or kidney-shaped desks and these very elegant forms were often complemented by elaborate decoration on the handles and mounts. Desks with serpentine fronts provided a further variation. Styles like these have never gone entirely out of fashion and, especially at the end of the 19th century, there was a craze for marketing reproductions of classical models.

Nevertheless, during the Victorian period, the conventional pedestal format remained the most popular. Partners' desks did not suffer adversely from the introduction of machine-made furniture around 1850, as their angular shape was perfectly suited to it. Most

of the new machinery was very efficient at producing straight lines, but was less able to cope with such refinements as carving and marquetry. The sober and solid design of partners' desks therefore caused no problems.

Mahogany had always proved the most popular material for these desks. The principal exceptions occurred during the Regency, when there was a fashion for lighter, more exotic woods, such as satinwood, and in the late 19th century, when there was a vogue for oak. The latter was very much a nostalgic taste, since oak symbolized for Victorians a pre-Industrial age of craftsmanship. However, this was mostly Slavonian or Austrian oak, a very much paler variety than the oak used in early English furniture.

POINTS TO WATCH

■ Ensure that the three sections of the desk match. If they do not sit solidly, one of the sections may have been replaced or restored.

■ Check the writing panel on the desk top. Synthetic, tooled leather is an obvious modern addition.

■ Handles were frequently replaced. The holes of the originals are often visible inside the drawers.

■ Check that the veneers match, particularly on the sides of the pedestals. New veneers applied to the wrong carcase wood will often lift.

■ Modern mass-produced desks have been veneered to resemble 18th or 19th century pieces; be wary of these, particularly if they are continental.

The Side Table

In workmanlike or decorative designs, the side table nestled against the wall in many rooms, whereas the sofa table proved its versatility within the reception rooms of the house

There were few rooms in a Victorian house without a side table. In the entrance hall, as a visitor furled his umbrella and hung up his hat, an unobtrusive oak table standing against the wall invited him to leave his copy of *The Times*. He met an entirely different breed of furniture in the drawing room. Here side tables were for display. They were curved, polished, turned and carved, with marble or marquetry tops.

In the dining room, elegant but sturdy side tables accommodated the platters and tureens that could not be squeezed on to the dining table at mealtimes.

Below stairs, in the kitchen, a homely pine side table, its top scrubbed white, did a long, unsung day's work with the servants.

A TABLE FOR DISPLAY

Each of these very different tables had one thing in common: they were all intended to be placed against a wall. In many respects, a simple side table – often about 3 feet (1 metre) long by 2 feet (60cm) wide – is like any small table, but close examination generally reveals a few characteristics that give it away.

The table top, for instance, overhangs the front and two sides but not the back, allowing the table to be pushed flush against the wall. The whole table is deliberately oriented outward into the room. Drawers, if any, are fitted in the front only, and the finest decorations are reserved for the three sides that are visible from the room. The front may have an extravagantly carved or inlaid frieze but the back will generally be completely unadorned. The same applies to decorative work on legs and stretchers. Do not waste time on what cannot be seen was the instruction for cabinet makers.

Such tables have their origins in the 15th century, and by Stuart times were to be found in any well furnished house. In the 18th century, skilled craftsmen were particularly attracted to the side table. Its position against the wall made it a natural showpiece for decorative work. The top was frequently a beautiful slab of marble or gilded gesso, but the real attention was reserved for the deep frieze. This often boasted an ornately carved central decoration, featuring shells, masks, flowers, or perhaps a woman's head.

A more restrained style prevailed later in the 18th century, but the side table continued to be an ideal vehicle for fine craftsmanship. Its small size also meant that it could be conveniently made in a number of woods not used for larger tables, including fruitwood, plane and walnut.

THE VICTORIAN SIDE TABLE

The Victorians took to the side table as they did to all tables – with more enthusiasm than

▼ *Elegant but sturdy side tables were to be found in all the public rooms of the Victorian house. Pale woods and graciously curving cabriole legs were especially well-suited to the morning room, where the table housed everyday items.*

discrimination. Their desire to collect and display beautiful (or merely showy) objects made any flat surface valuable. Thus the side table became a natural showcase for clocks, vases and lamps, silver-framed miniatures, potted palms, rare books and wax flowers. The Victorians' love of exuberant and highly-decorated furniture also attracted them to the side table's ostentatious nature. The well-to-do particularly appreciated Regency side tables with built-in mirrors, which accentuated the grandeur of a room by multiplying all the objects within it.

As with so much of their furniture, Victorian designers were better at copying

each suitable for a different room. The 'Elizabethan' oak table in the hall, flanked by matching chairs, gave way to the marble and marquetry-topped tables of the drawing room. The grandest reception rooms would boast a pair of gilt or rosewood pier tables with semi-circular tops. These were designed to stand against the piers, as the wall spaces between windows were called.

Marble-topped console tables, built into the wall so as to be part side table and part shelf, faced each other from the end walls of stately drawing rooms. 'Pier and console tables ought never to be omitted where splendour is an object to be desired and money is not wanting', urged the influential critic Loudon in his *Encyclopedia* of 1836.

At least two types of side table shared the dining room. One was the three-tiered

▲ *Like the piers for which it was designed, the back of a sofa provided a good site against which to set the unfinished edge of a side table. Today, a variety of occasional tables are used in this way.*

and embellishing side tables than initiating new styles. Many 19th-century tables are ostentatious variations on earlier designs. 'Exaggerated domesticity cried aloud from every bulging curve,' lamented one late Victorian critic.

Not all side tables were irredeemably vulgar. One popular design, made of darkened and polished oak, sought to capture the austere spirit of 17th-century furniture, with twist-turned or cup-and-cover legs and simple carving on the frieze. Nor were all drawing-room side tables for display. Some models, often with leather tops, served as writing desks; others could be pulled out into the room and extended for card games.

A TABLE FOR EVERY WALL
Any large Victorian house might have half a dozen quite different types of side table,

▲ *A late-Georgian semi-circular side table. The cream painted surface is decorated with borders of classical motifs and gilding. Elaborately painted roundels feature an Eastern sage and two groups of putti.*

▲ *Dating from the latter years of the 17th century, this table features fine walnut 'oyster veneer' and 'seaweed' marquetry panels, typical of the period.*

The spirally turned oak legs are braced with Y-shaped stretchers around a central oval platform. The oak bun feet are probably a later addition.

sideboard-table, mounted on castors and used as a glorified dinner trolley, 'for the convenience of holding the dessert, the plate, the glasses and other articles in use,' as Loudon explained. Another was more like a sideboard in its function, with a modest gallery for displaying china, but without the drawers and cellarets of the principal sideboard.

Tucked away in the servants' quarters, the pine-topped kitchen side table lacked any ornament whatsoever, but shared with its grander cousins the flat back, which allowed it to rest against the wall. Many of these tables have survived decades of over-work and indifference to become rustic work surfaces in today's servantless kitchens.

The Sofa Table

ALTHOUGH OFTEN NOT OF THE SAME QUALITY AS ITS 18TH CENTURY PREDECESSORS, THE VICTORIAN SOFA TABLE WAS STYLED WITH ELEGANCE, AFTER CLASSICAL MODELS. TYPICALLY IT STOOD ON 'CHEVAL' SUPPORTS — SINGLE UPRIGHTS AT EACH END WITH SPLAYED LEGS AND BRASS-MOUNTED FEET. OFTEN THERE WAS A STRETCHER BETWEEN THE UPRIGHTS, SET CONVENIENTLY HIGH OFF THE FLOOR TO ALLOW ROOM FOR THE USER'S FEET.

DROP ENDS WHICH HUNG FLUSH WITH THE CHEVAL SUPPORTS ALLOWED THE TABLE TO BE EXTENDED, WHILE, IN THE BEST EXAMPLES, DRAWERS WERE CLEVERLY DESIGNED SO THAT THEY COULD BE USED FROM EITHER SIDE, THE DRAWER BACKS BEING CONCEALED BEHIND FALSE FRONTS.

ROSEWOOD AND MAHOGANY REMAINED THE MOST COMMON WOODS FOR EXAMPLES INTENDED FOR THE PUBLIC ROOMS OF THE HOUSE. VENEERS, WHICH WERE BY THIS TIME MACHINE CUT AND THINNER THAN IN THE PAST, WERE OFTEN USED TO DECORATIVE EFFECT IN BORDERS WITH CROSS-BANDING AND STRINGING.

① CHEVAL SUPPORT WITH SPLAYED LEGS AND BRASS-MOUNTED FEET ON CASTORS.

② TURNED STRETCHER SET BETWEEN CHEVAL ENDS.

③ DRAWER OPENING AT ONE SIDE OF THE TABLE. IN FINE EXAMPLES, THE SECOND DRAWER OPENS ON THE OPPOSITE SIDE.

④ CROSS-BANDED VENEER BORDER WITH STRINGING IN LIGHTER-COLOURED WOOD.

The Lyre End

SO-NAMED AFTER THE MUSICAL INSTRUMENT WHICH IT RESEMBLES, THE LYRE END WAS A POPULAR FEATURE OF CLASSICAL FURNITURE DESIGNS AND WAS IMITATED LATER.

Penwork Sofa Table

AN ORNATE REGENCY TABLE WITH A CHAMPFERED RECTANGULAR TOP ON LYRE-ENDED SPLAYED LEGS. THE WHOLE TABLE IS DECORATED WITH CLASSICAL DESIGNS IN PENWORK.

Throughout much of the Georgian era, drawing room tables and chairs remained respectfully with their backs to the wall. During the last decade of the 18th century, however, standing furniture began to move tentatively out into the centre of the room, as if emboldened by the revolutionary spirit sweeping Europe.

ELEGANT LINES

The sofa table was a strikingly successful design. Long, low and narrow, it was developed to provide a convenient working surface directly in front of a sofa or settee.

It was rarely more than 2 feet (60cm) wide or 2 feet 4 inches (70cm) high. Round-cornered end flaps, each supported by two flybrackets, extended its length to 5-6 feet (1.5-1.8 metres). Castors on its feet permitted the ladies to move it effortlessly to the fire or to a seat by the window. They did not have to turn it around, as the

·PRICE GUIDE·

Sofa and Side Tables

▼ AN ELEGANT VICTORIAN SIDE TABLE IN MAHOGANY. DOUBLE STRETCHERS JOIN THE CHEVAL LEGS.

PRICE GUIDE **6**

▼ DEMI-LUNE PINE SIDE TABLE WITH SQUARE TAPERING LEGS, MID-19TH CENTURY. THE HALF MOON DESIGN WAS WELL SUITED TO WALL-STANDING TABLES.

PRICE GUIDE **6**

▲ CROSS-BANDED MAHOGANY SOFA TABLE WITH DROP ENDS AND LYRE-ENDED CHEVAL LEGS. THIS IS A VICTORIAN REPRODUCTION OF A REGENCY DESIGN.

PRICE GUIDE **8**

▼ MAHOGANY SIDE TABLE WITH INLAY ON THE TOP AND TURNED LEGS AND CASTORS. THERE ARE BRASS HANDLES ON THE DOUBLE DRAWERS.

PRICE GUIDE **7**

▲ A MID-VICTORIAN PITCH PINE TABLE WHICH SAW SERVICE IN THE KITCHEN. THE TURNED LEGS TAPER DOWNWARDS.

PRICE GUIDE **6**

▲ A LATE REGENCY OR EARLY VICTORIAN ROSEWOOD SOFA TABLE WITH DROP ENDS, A CENTRE PEDESTAL AND ONE DRAWER WITHOUT HANDLES.

PRICE GUIDE **8**

sofa table had neither back nor front; each side had one real and one dummy drawer.

CHANGING STYLES

Although designed to be useful, no expense was spared to make the sofa table beautiful as well. A plain rosewood top might be bordered by veneer or discreetly inlaid with brass. Areas which were less subject to wear, such as the drawer fronts and even the fly brackets supporting the end flaps, could be yet more intricately decorated.

Regency cabinet makers, who often worked in mahogany, began to lose sight of the sofa table's function and tended to clutter its working surface with decorative inlays. Tables from this period were frequently veneered in woods such as zebra-wood, amboyna and satinwood.

The supports also became increasingly ornate; many later Regency tables stood on gilded lion-paw feet. One particularly popular design, dating from about 1815, incorporated a lyre shape, with brass 'strings' in the uprights at each end.

It was during this period that factory-made sofa tables began to flood the market. Often shorter than their 18th-century proto-types, these mass-produced tables suffered from cost-cutting techniques. Typical symptoms included coarsely turned stretch-ers and thin, poorly applied veneers. Drawers were lined with inexpensive strips of machine-cut pine rather than the traditional oak.

A number of variations on the sofa table to suit it to specialist uses such as writing or games were developed during the first two decades of the 19th century.

A SHORT LIFE

The sofa table had a curiously short life. By Queen Victoria's reign it had lost its end flaps and elegant lines. Perhaps it was spoiled by its own success, for by then drawing rooms were crowded with what had become known as 'occasional' tables. These stood boldly in the centre of the room, arranged beside chairs in what the novelist Fanny Burney described as 'dexterous disorder'.

REAL OR FAKE?

■ Grain should run across the width of the table.

■ Both drawers opening on the same side is not typical of original sofa tables.

■ Cheval supports are some-times taken from Victorian che-val mirrors. The point where the mirror once pivoted will have been carefully concealed.

■ The entire cheval undercar-riage may have been 'borrowed' from another table. Make sure end flaps fall flush with the uprights.

The Canterbury

Whether simple and elegant or elaborately crafted, the canterbury played an important role in the Victorian music room, and still has a place in homes of today

The canterbury was an essential piece of Victorian music room furniture. Smallish, mostly with rectangular framework, and with a number of open partitions, canterburies were designed to stand under the piano when not in use, and could simply be pulled out on their castors when a change of tune was required.

Music played a large part in both Victorian and Georgian life. The popular novels of Jane Austen and her contemporaries emphasized the importance of musical accomplishment for young ladies in the early 19th century, and recount numerous tales of musical evenings in the drawing room. Until Victorian times that was where the piano was usually situated, for a separate room for music was until then a rarity.

18TH-CENTURY BEGINNINGS
The music canterbury seems to have been a late-18th century invention. An example by the famous firm of Gillows has been recorded with a date of 1793. Then, in 1803, Thomas Sheraton used the name 'canterbury' to refer to two different types of movable furniture in his *Cabinet Dictionary*. The first was a supper canterbury – a sort

▶ *If music played any part in a family's life, a good supply of sheet music was essential. Piano playing was a most desirable talent in middle-class girls, and the packed canterbury beneath the piano was a measure of their accomplishment on the instrument.*

▼ *Few people these days use canterburies to hold sheet music. However, they make perfect magazine racks as well as being handsome and decorative pieces of furniture in their own right.*

of trolley designed to hold bottles, cutlery and any other dining implements which might be needed for an informal supper; the second he described as a music stand 'made with two or three hollow-topped partitions, the legs with castors adapted to run in under the pianoforte'.

The origin of the term 'canterbury' has popularly been attributed to the lazy nature of an un-named archbishop who supposedly devised a mobile table to save getting up from his chair unnecessarily, but its real source is likely to remain a mystery. In the last part of the 19th century the word was also used to describe the sort of rectangular piano stool which has storage space for music under its seat, either in a drawer, or in a compartment with a hinged lid.

EARLY DESIGNS
Late-Georgian and Regency music canterburies were very elegant pieces of furniture and their design naturally corresponded with other furnishings. Mahogany was by far the most popular wood used for early examples, although rosewood was not uncommon. The earliest canterburies were

After about 1810, the squarish shape of canterbury was superseded by more ornate Regency designs with Classical decoration and, in some cases, a very different structure. The lower drawer section was retained but the legs were often more elaborately carved, usually with foliate decoration, or they splayed outwards in typical Regency fashion. The partitions on the upper section were often built on the X-frame principle, with two bars forming a cross over-laid in the centre by a large circular moulding. The lyre shape was also a popular pattern for the partitions and sometimes the 'strings' were made in brass.

Canterbury design became far more varied and generally far more elaborate after about 1830, although rather coarse versions of Regency and Georgian styles were still being produced by some makers in the 1850s. These, however, can be distinguished from their earlier prototypes by their fussier and usually clumsier design.

The basic structure of canterburies and their relatively small size made them more difficult to adapt to the rapid succession of historic revival styles which characterized Victorian furniture, although the open partitions provided a marvellous vehicle for carved fretwork. A great many Victorian canterburies were made in that peculiarly curvaceous style which evolved from Rococo and is now referred to as 'naturalistic'. Although usually associated with the middle years of the century, trade catalogues and other documents show that this particular style persisted well into the 1880s, despite the considerably more sophisticated state of public taste.

very simple, with plain upright bars dividing the partition and two horizontal bars at either end. The tops of the partitions themselves were often dipped at the centre to make the music sheets easier to pull out. The four corner uprights continued down to the bottom of the frame to join quite narrow short legs with simple turned decoration and small brass castors. Sometimes the legs and uprights were formed from one continuous piece of timber. A drawer below the partitions provided further storage space and this was finished with small brass knobs. Examples of double-length canterburies of this type, joined end to end, are known, but are very unusual.

Although Classical Greece provided the largest source of design motifs for Regency furniture, the Gothic style was also fashionable. George Smith's influential pattern book *A Collection of Designs for Household Furniture and Decoration* published in 1808, contained designs for rather heavy canterburies with square-sectional legs and Gothic fretwork carving, although the scarcity of surviving examples of this type implies that they were seldom copied.

▼ *The essence of Regency canterburies was simplicity of design. This one, in rosewood, is typical. Restrained baluster turning on the uprights is repeated in profile on the dividing slats, while the brass banding on the base only adds to the beauty of the wood.*

▲ *A mid-Victorian walnut canterbury with lyre-shaped dividers and gallery all richly decorated with typical open fretwork.*

The Table Canterbury

⑤

④

③

①

②

THE FLAT BACK OF THIS CANTERBURY DEMONSTRATES THAT, UNUSUALLY, IT WAS MEANT TO BE PLACED AGAINST A WALL RATHER THAN UNDER A PIANO. THIS IS PROBABLY WHY IT IS LACKING A GALLERY, THE CARVED WOODEN FRIEZE THAT BACKED MOST TABLE CANTERBURIES.

MORE TYPICAL ARE THE ROCOCO FRETWORK SUPPORTS, THE BASE AND TABLE-TOP IN FIGURED WALNUT AND THE COLUMNS EXHIBITING A COMPENDIUM OF TURNERS' STYLES. A DRAWER IN THE BASE OFTEN PROVIDED EXTRA STORAGE SPACE — AS WITH THIS EXAMPLE.

Fretwork Carving

FRETWORK CARVING, WHERE DESIGNS ARE CUT THROUGH A PIECE OF WOOD, COMBINES LIGHTNESS WITH STRENGTH. THE CONVENTIONALIZED FOLIAGE IN THE NATURALISTIC STYLE HARKS BACK TO THE EBULLIENCE OF ROCOCO.

① FIGURED WALNUT VENEER

② DRAWER IN BASE

③ FRETWORK SUPPORTS

④ EXTRAVANGANTLY TURNED COLUMNS

⑤ FLAT BACK FOR STANDING AGAINST WALL

Reproduction Canterbury

THIS MAHOGANY CANTERBURY FROM THE 1950S REPRODUCES A SIMPLE REGENCY DESIGN. VICTORIAN ELABORATION IS TOO COSTLY TO COPY.

By the beginning of Victoria's reign, the music canterbury was a standard piece of middle-class domestic furniture made by most manufacturers, with a variety of designs published in contemporary trade catalogues and designers' pattern books.

One very popular form of decoration that emerged was carved open fretwork on which a number of historic styles were displayed. Fretted panels of Gothic, Renaissance and some-times Classical designs were variously slotted between ornately turned corner uprights ending in small finials. Naturalistic foliate designs were also used and legs were still short and turned, but wider than previously, sometimes bulbous.

NEW MATERIALS

Mahogany, and sometimes rosewood, were still used in Victorian pieces, but the majority were made in figured walnut. New materials were also used but these had limited appeal. Papier-mâché, with painted, gilded and mother-of-pearl decoration on a black ground, was used for some Rococo-style canterburies, and during the 1880s and 1890s some very simple pieces were made in imported bamboo with panels of Japanese lacquer in their sides. At the same time, in line with other fashionable spindled and bracketed 'Art Furniture', some examples were constructed of numerous turned uprights with

·PRICE GUIDE·

Canterburies

▼ A WALNUT CANTERBURY FROM THE 1860S. THIS IS A BASIC DESIGN, WITH BUN FEET TAPERING DOWN TO BRASS CASTORS.

PRICE GUIDE **7**

▲ THIS SPARE, ELEGANT DESIGN IN ROSEWOOD AND MAHOGANY IS TYPICAL OF EARLY CANTERBURIES.

PRICE GUIDE **8**

▲ THIS BAMBOO MAGAZINE RACK DATES FROM THE EDWARDIAN PERIOD.

PRICE GUIDE **4**

▲ ANOTHER WALNUT CANTERBURY FROM THE 1860S. THE ORNATE FRETWORK ON THE DIVIDERS AND THE DRAWER ADD VALUE.

PRICE GUIDE **7**

▲ A SMALL ROSEWOOD CANTERBURY, WITH ITS DELICATELY-TURNED RAILS AND LEGS AND UNUSUAL BOTTOM SHELF, C. 1830.

PRICE GUIDE **8**

▲ A TABLE-TOP WITH GALLERY, FINE FRETWORK, ELLIPTICAL SHAPE AND LOWER DRAWER. IT WAS MADE IN THE 1870S.

PRICE GUIDE **7**

black ebonized finish, while others had simple incised decoration picked out in gold.

NEW STYLES

Victorian canterburies were also made in new shapes and forms. From about 1850 onwards they were often made with an additional upper shelf. A shallow wooden or brass gallery sometimes ran around this table-top to prevent small items from slipping over the sides, and occasionally the top was

designed to lift up to provide a writing slope.

Although on most canterburies the partitions ran from side to side, on some they ran from front to back. The majority remained of rectangular form, but oval and kidney shapes were also popular, particularly for those with Rococo-style fretwork.

Today, of course, music canterburies are not always used for their original purpose, but more usually as magazine racks.

Being very sought after, their prices can seem high in proportion to their size, but not always in relation to the work involved in their making. For this reason the value of decorative Victorian canterburies is sometimes more than that of simpler, earlier ones.

POINTS TO WATCH

■ It is not always easy to distinguish between original pieces and some of the very good reproductions made either

around the turn of the century, or during the 1920s, but the lack of patina and general wear on modern reproductions are easier to detect.

■ Today's copies are invariably of early types as it simply doesn't pay to reproduce Victorian carving.

■ In all cases quality of design is as important as quality of workmanship and a harmonious combination of style and over-all proportion is often the best guide to a piece's worth.

The Upholstered Chair

At first a highly prized speciality, upholstery came to be regarded as essential to seat furniture in the 19th century, lending it colour and pattern as well as comfort

Until recently, little attention was paid to the subject of antique upholstery, yet correctly shaped stuffing and a sympathetic use of fabric and trimmings can make all the difference to the final appearance of a chair or sofa.

Now that upholstered furniture is relatively commonplace, it is hard to imagine that it was once a highly prized possession and that the upholstery cost several times more than the frame it covered. In grand houses all upholstery was supplied with a loose 'case' cover to protect it from dust and light when not in use. This practice continued well into the 19th century, when loose covers provided a form of upholstery in themselves.

EARLY UPHOLSTERY

Fixed upholstery was rare before 1600, with loose cushions being used for comfort. The first example appeared on chairs of state in the late 16th century. These chairs, of folding X-frame construction, were completely covered in a rich fabric held in place with gilt-headed nails.

By 1650 many prosperous households had chairs with fixed padding. The most common type were back stools, literally stools with backs. They were popularly called farthingales, because the gap between the seat and back could accommodate the voluminous farthingale skirts which were fashionable at the time.

From 1700 on, upholstered drop-in seats were slotted into rebates in the frames of dining-chairs and side-chairs. A later alternative was over-stuffing, where the padding and fabric were taken over the frame at the front and sides of the chair before being tacked into place.

TECHNIQUES

Early upholstery was rather crude. Girth-web, a type of webbing used by saddle-makers, was cross-woven and tacked across the seat frame. This was covered with a piece of coarse sacking or hessian, and some form of stuffing was piled in the middle. In better quality chairs, the stuffing was stitched to the webbing.

Stuffing ranged from grass, leaves, rushes and straw to wool, animal hair and various kinds of feathers. Sometimes the stuffing was held in place by bridle ties. The decorative top cover was then tacked into place and the tacks covered with a strip of braid or a fringe which was attached with decorative nails.

From around 1660 on, the front and sides of the seat were usually strengthened with extra stuffing sewn into a 'roll' of canvas or hessian. An additional layer of linen was placed between the stuffing and the top cover to prevent the fibres from working their way through it.

These basic techniques changed very little until the mid-19th century, although more complicated shaping was achieved by employing additional stitching as chair shapes became more complex.

STUFFINGS AND COVERINGS

Horsehair, used for chair backs from the beginning as it stayed in place better than any other material, came to be used in all parts of the chair from the early 18th century. Sometimes two layers of stuffing were present, with vegetable fibre beneath the horsehair. Sometimes the padding was held in place by shallow buttoning – widely spaced metal buttons covered with fabric.

The range of upholstery fabrics varied considerably, though chairs, sofas, settees, stools and firescreens were all usually upholstered in matching fabric.

In the 17th century the grandest chairs

◀ This late 18th-century painted French chair is part of a set of four plus a sofa, all covered in silk and wool Beauvais tapestry. Each back and seat has a different picture in a medallion.

▲ New styles of upholstered seat furniture proliferated in the 19th century. This aristocratic salon has chairs with and without arms as well as several different styles of sofa.

were covered in silk and velvet, which was sometimes brocaded with gold and silver thread. This was imported from France and Italy until the Spitalfields silk industry was established around 1700. The most characteristic finish of this time was perhaps turkey work, where wool was knotted on a canvas ground to provide a pile finish, in imitation of imported Turkish carpets.

In the 18th century, needlework was a popular finish, usually wool over canvas.

▶ The use of upholstered furniture gave new colour options in interior design. Here, the Victorian chairs and sofa have been re-upholstered to co-ordinate with the wallpaper in a very feminine look.

In the 19th century, virtually all fabrics (with the exception of turkey work) were brought into use at one time or another, as was leather. Patterned velvets and damasks were the most popular materials in mid-century, along with plush, a variety of velvet with a long pile much loved by the Victorians. A sombre claret vied with olive green as the most popular colour.

Printed cotton chintzes, previously used for curtains and bed hangings, were popular in both drawing rooms and bedrooms. Chintz covers had several advantages: they gave the room a lighter, more feminine look; they could be used to protect the upholstery underneath from everyday wear, but could easily be removed for social functions; and they covered up old worn upholstery. They fitted the furniture quite closely and had a floor-length valance. A favourite pattern consisted of colourful full-blown roses on a white ground.

This was often executed by the lady of the house and was especially popular for the then newly introduced wing chairs, where the extra surface area was ideal for accommodating biblical and mythological scenes.

Damask became popular in the 18th century and has remained so ever since; early fabrics have large patterns, while later damasks tend to tighter designs. Leather became popular towards the end of the 18th century, at about the same time as tapestry went out of fashion, while woven horsehair was introduced in around 1750 and was particularly used on dining-room chairs as it could be wiped clean.

▶ Made and upholstered in 18th-century style, this chair is in fact 19th century, and the needlework is the work of a talented amateur.

Deep-buttoned Leather Chair

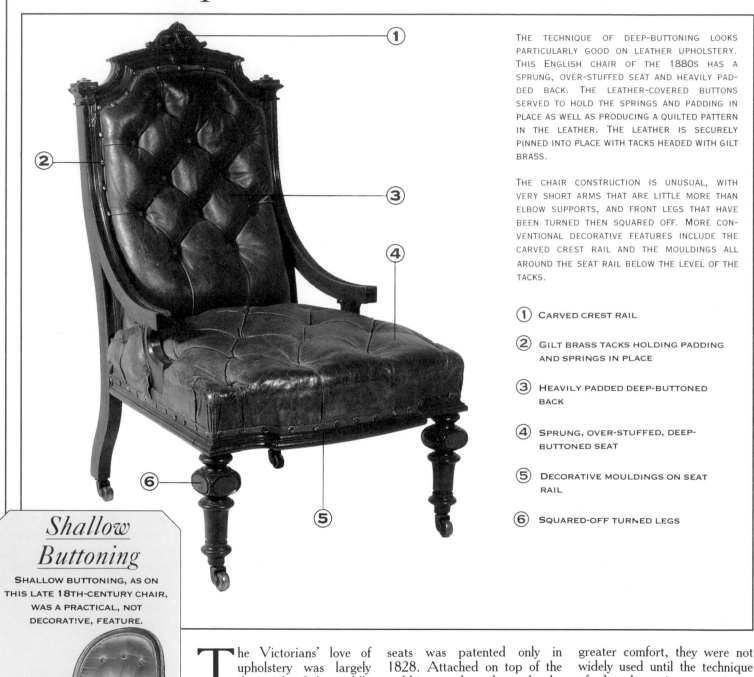

THE TECHNIQUE OF DEEP-BUTTONING LOOKS PARTICULARLY GOOD ON LEATHER UPHOLSTERY. THIS ENGLISH CHAIR OF THE 1880S HAS A SPRUNG, OVER-STUFFED SEAT AND HEAVILY PADDED BACK. THE LEATHER-COVERED BUTTONS SERVED TO HOLD THE SPRINGS AND PADDING IN PLACE AS WELL AS PRODUCING A QUILTED PATTERN IN THE LEATHER. THE LEATHER IS SECURELY PINNED INTO PLACE WITH TACKS HEADED WITH GILT BRASS.

THE CHAIR CONSTRUCTION IS UNUSUAL, WITH VERY SHORT ARMS THAT ARE LITTLE MORE THAN ELBOW SUPPORTS, AND FRONT LEGS THAT HAVE BEEN TURNED THEN SQUARED OFF. MORE CONVENTIONAL DECORATIVE FEATURES INCLUDE THE CARVED CREST RAIL AND THE MOULDINGS ALL AROUND THE SEAT RAIL BELOW THE LEVEL OF THE TACKS.

1. CARVED CREST RAIL

2. GILT BRASS TACKS HOLDING PADDING AND SPRINGS IN PLACE

3. HEAVILY PADDED DEEP-BUTTONED BACK

4. SPRUNG, OVER-STUFFED, DEEP-BUTTONED SEAT

5. DECORATIVE MOULDINGS ON SEAT RAIL

6. SQUARED-OFF TURNED LEGS

Shallow Buttoning

SHALLOW BUTTONING, AS ON THIS LATE 18TH-CENTURY CHAIR, WAS A PRACTICAL, NOT DECORATIVE, FEATURE.

The Victorians' love of upholstery was largely the result of the middle classes' desire for prestige An extravagantly upholstered suite, covered in rich fabrics and appropriately trimmed, was thought to give the appearance – if only superficial – of luxury, comfort and wealth.

SPRINGS AND BUTTONS

Two developments which added to the luxury look in the Victorian period were coiled springing and button backs. Although coiled springs had been in existence for some time, their use for seats was patented only in 1828. Attached on top of the webbing and underneath the conventional layers of stuffing, they drastically altered the outward appearance of upholstered furniture, giving much deeper seats; not only did the springs give depth in themselves, but the layers of padding had to be thicker to stop the springs pushing through the top cover. Beneath, they were supported by strong webbing, sometimes strengthened with cane.

Although springs were designed to allow some movement, and thus to provide greater comfort, they were not widely used until the technique of deep-buttoning was introduced. Deep-set buttons held the springs firmly in place and the resultant pleating of the material became a prized decorative feature in its own right. The metal buttons were always covered in the same material as the top cover.

TRIMMINGS

On some pieces the effect of luxury was enhanced by the use of elaborate trimmings, although narrow, machine-made gimp sufficed for most. Floor-

·PRICE GUIDE· ⟩ _Upholstered Chairs_

▲ A TYPICALLY SHAPED 'GRANDMOTHER' CHAIR OF THE 1860S MADE OF WALNUT AND RE-UPHOLSTERED IN BROCADE.

PRICE GUIDE **7**

▲ THIS LIGHTWEIGHT WALNUT SIDE CHAIR IS ALSO FROM THE 1860S AND HAS BEEN RE-COVERED IN DRALON.

PRICE GUIDE **5**

▲ A FLAMBOYANT WALNUT SPOONBACK IS HERE COMPLEMENTED BY A COLOURFUL FLORAL TAPESTRY.

PRICE GUIDE **7**

▲ THE COVERING ON THIS FRENCH CHAIR, FEATURING LOVE-KNOTS AND ROSES, IS THE ORIGINAL FROM 1880.

PRICE GUIDE **6**

▲ THE HONEY COLOUR OF THIS HIGHLY-CARVED SATIN BIRCH CHAIR HARMONIZES WELL WITH A MODERN DRALON COVER.

PRICE GUIDE **7**

▲ A SOLID MAHOGANY DINING CHAIR FROM THE 1840S COVERED WITH RED LEATHER. THE FRONT LEGS HAVE MODERN CASTORS.

PRICE GUIDE **7**

length fringes with deep lattice-work headings, borders of gathered material edged with twisted cord, and tassels hanging from the facings of arms all added to the expensive look.

In use in the drawing room, many pieces were further adorned with lace-edged anti-macassars and a number of cushions, while Paisley or oriental shawls were draped over their arms.

ROCOCO
The variety of seat furniture increased in the mid-19th century. _Têtes-à-têtes_ and other sofas which accommodated the sitters at various angles became popular, as did fully upholstered chesterfields, ottomans and pouffes. In style, upholstered furniture followed the prevailing fashions, although rococo was undoubtedly the most popular. First introduced around 1840, the swirling curves of Victorian rococo provided the perfect complement to the rich effects of deep buttoning.

DRAWING-ROOM SUITES
Mahogany and walnut drawing-room furniture was usually sold in suites, comprising a sofa or chaise longue, a pair of easy chairs – a large 'grandfather' chair with arms and a smaller 'grandmother' without – and six or more side chairs, usually balloon-backs.

Suites in other styles were similarly composed, but of a more rectilinear shape. Straight, turned legs replaced rococo cabriole legs, while wooden frames were completely covered save for turned uprights on some armchairs and spindle backs on some chaises longues. Interestingly, their basically retangular shapes did not affect the fashion for rounded deep-buttoning.

POINTS TO WATCH
■ To check if upholstery is original, gently tease out a few tacks. As it is impossible to re-use tack holes, any re-covering will have left a tell-tale second set of holes.

■ Removing the original covering can devalue an upholstered chair. Check with an expert before re-covering.

■ Check that the frame is sound. Loose joints can be re-glued, but more serious damage may be expensive to repair.

■ Reconditioning old fabrics such as leather or needlework is a task for a specialist.

The Upholstered Victorian Wing Chair

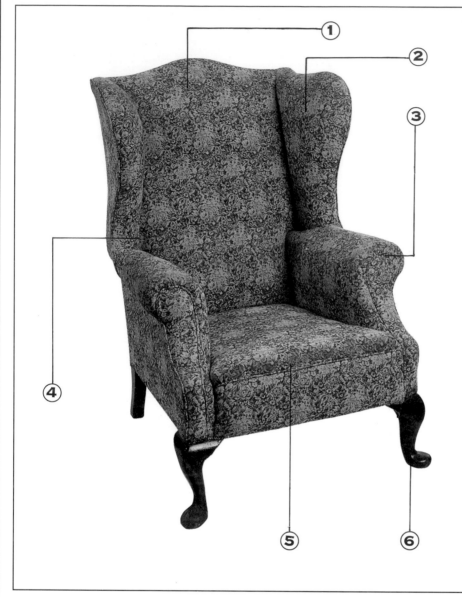

THE DESIGN OF THE WING ARMCHAIR HAS REMAINED BASICALLY UNCHANGED FOR OVER 250 YEARS, BUT CERTAIN MODIFICATIONS WERE MADE DURING THE MID-VICTORIAN PERIOD. COMFORT, WHICH HAD LONG BEEN THE PREROGATIVE OF THE WEALTHY, BECAME AVAILABLE TO PEOPLE EVERYWHERE WHEN MACHINE CARVING WAS INTRODUCED AROUND 1850 AND EASY CHAIRS WENT INTO MASS PRODUCTION. THEY WERE PRODUCED IN ALL SHAPES AND SIZES, BUT THE WING ARMCHAIR WAS ENDURINGLY POPULAR.

IN CONTRAST TO EARLY VERSIONS OF THE WING CHAIR, WHERE THE COVERING WAS DEEMED MOST IMPORTANT, LATER MODELS PLACED GREATER EMPHASIS ON THE STUFFING. THE ORIGINAL MIXTURE OF LINEN WASTE AND HORSEHAIR WAS FOUND TO BE RATHER UNYIELDING, SO IT WAS EVENTUALLY REPLACED WITH A MORE COMFORTABLE MIXTURE OF AMERICAN COTTON, WOOL WASTE AND HORSEHAIR.

THE FRAME, ORIGINALLY MADE FROM WALNUT, ROSEWOOD OR MAHOGANY, WAS LATER MADE FROM CHEAPER MATERIALS, SUCH AS BEECH, ASH AND BIRCH. AN EXPERIMENT WITH IRON FRAMES WAS QUICKLY ABANDONED BECAUSE THE WEIGHT WAS EXCESSIVE.

① WELL-PADDED, TALL, STRAIGHT BACK WITH SLIGHTLY DOMED TOP.

② ROUNDED WINGS SAME HEIGHT AS BACK.

③ ARMS CURVE OUTWARDS, WITH SCROLL FRONT.

④ HARD-WEARING TAPESTRY COVER.

⑤ THICK PADDING OVER DEEP-BUTTONED SPRINGS.

⑥ SIMPLE TURNED LEGS WITH PAD FEET.

Georgian Wing Chair

THE APPEARANCE OF UPHOLSTERY WAS REVOLUTIONIZED DURING QUEEN VICTORIA'S REIGN BY THE INVENTION OF THE COILED SPRING.

THE DEEP-BUTTONING WHICH HELPED TO HOLD THE SPRINGS IN PLACE AND THE THICKER STUFFING THEY REQUIRED, COMBINED TO GIVE AN IMPRESSION OF GREAT COMFORT.

THE WINGS WERE INTENDED TO PROTECT THE SITTER FROM COLD DRAUGHTS.

AFTER 1850, THE WING CHAIR WAS MASS-PRODUCED, WITH A DECLINE IN QUALITY.

Victorian wing chairs were made in a variety of styles although the simplest and most common type had a straight or slightly domed back and round-cornered wings of equal height. The arms curved slightly outwards with just a gentle scroll at the front. The legs were usually turned with simple ring mouldings and ended in brass castors. On better chairs, mahogany was sometimes used, but stained beech was more usual.

Reproduction chairs based on earlier styles, and identifiable by the design of their legs, were made in large numbers from 1860. The upholstered part of the chair tended to remain the same, albeit a little skimpier than previously. Variations included chairs with very narrow wings, those of 'tub' form where the wings were an extension of the back, and chairs where the back and wings were considerably reduced in height. Queen Anne-style chairs, with thin, walnut, cabriole legs, and Chippendale chairs, with similar mahogany legs, were the most common.

In a Victorian house, wing chairs were used in a variety of rooms, both upstairs and downstairs. The covering often reflected their function; leather was popular for libraries and

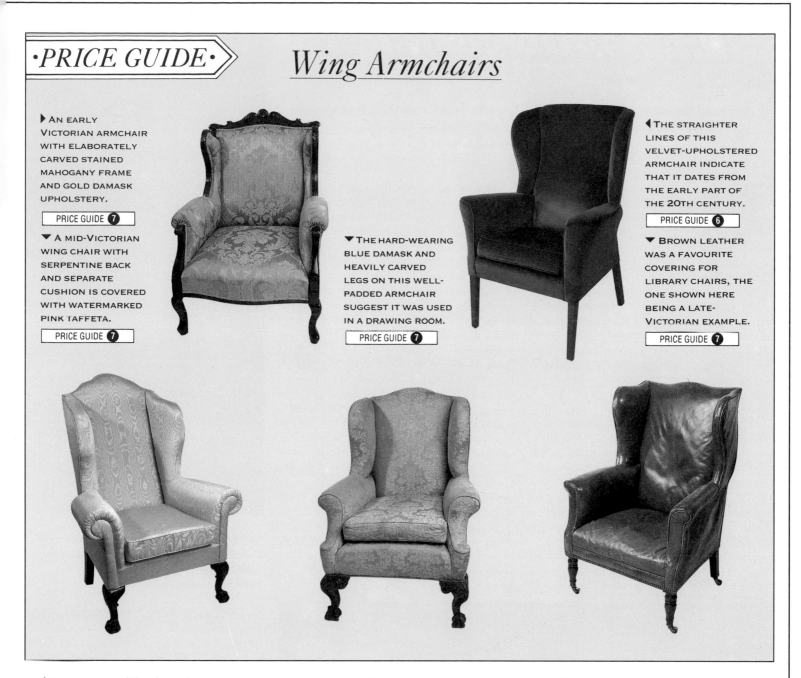

·PRICE GUIDE·

Wing Armchairs

▶ AN EARLY VICTORIAN ARMCHAIR WITH ELABORATELY CARVED STAINED MAHOGANY FRAME AND GOLD DAMASK UPHOLSTERY.

PRICE GUIDE **7**

▼ A MID-VICTORIAN WING CHAIR WITH SERPENTINE BACK AND SEPARATE CUSHION IS COVERED WITH WATERMARKED PINK TAFFETA.

PRICE GUIDE **7**

▼ THE HARD-WEARING BLUE DAMASK AND HEAVILY CARVED LEGS ON THIS WELL-PADDED ARMCHAIR SUGGEST IT WAS USED IN A DRAWING ROOM.

PRICE GUIDE **7**

◀ THE STRAIGHTER LINES OF THIS VELVET-UPHOLSTERED ARMCHAIR INDICATE THAT IT DATES FROM THE EARLY PART OF THE 20TH CENTURY.

PRICE GUIDE **6**

▼ BROWN LEATHER WAS A FAVOURITE COVERING FOR LIBRARY CHAIRS, THE ONE SHOWN HERE BEING A LATE-VICTORIAN EXAMPLE.

PRICE GUIDE **7**

smoking rooms, while damask, plain and patterned velvet, brocatelle and plush, appeared in drawing rooms. Dark green and claret red were favourite colours. Decoration was provided by piping and twisted cord and elaborate tasselled fringes hung to the ground covering the legs.

In drawing rooms, a lot of upholstery was fitted with chintz loose covers with deep gathered valances. These were mostly printed with large floral patterns against a pale background. Since the 17th century, loose covers had been used to protect upholstery while not in use, but Victorian examples were more

permanent. Sometimes they were used only during the summer months and even then were occasionally removed for entertaining. Chintz was also popular for bedrooms, and was used for both loose covers and fixed upholstery.

Below stairs, in the housekeeper's parlour, a wing chair would have looked far less opulent. It would certainly have had a loose cover of cotton or linen, probably plain, but possibly with a floral design. It too would have had a floor-level valance, for reasons of decorum, not decoration. The upholstery underneath would probably have been of patterned plush (a

cheaper version of velvet). The chair may well have been made in one of the lower quality furniture warehouses congregated in London's East End. Much so-called 'commercial' furniture was then sold in retail showrooms, many of which were in Tottenham Court Road, London. Indeed, Shoolbred & Co., the best known Victorian manufacturers of upholstery, had their business there.

POINTS TO WATCH
■ Wings with rounded corners of equal height to the back.
■ Deep-buttoning on back, arms and inside of wings.
■ Well-padded sprung seat,

the covering reaching well down over the front seat rail.
■ Legs turned with simple ring mouldings ending in castors. Edges finished with decorative twisted cord.
■ Scroll-end of arms often had a decorative tassel attached.
■ Elaborate tasselled fringe reached to floor from lower seat rail to cover up legs. Fabrics included, damask, velvet, plush and brocatelle.
■ Upholstery is expensive to replace: a collapsed seat can be repaired or replaced without disturbing the remainder of the upholstery.
■ Avoid a rickety frame — the chair would need stripping.

The Chaise Longue

Designed for comfortable daytime resting, the elegant chaise longue bestowed an air of leisure and luxury on the fashionable Edwardian drawing room

The chaise longue provided the ideal way to relax without the discomfort of a chair or the inconvenience of retiring to the bedroom. It was, of course, an attractive but inessential piece of furniture and as such was found mainly in the homes of those with a leisurely lifestyle.

In Edwardian times, almost every household had its chaise longue. Placed either in the boudoir or in the drawing room, it allowed the Edwardian lady of leisure to relax after dinner, entertain informally, rest between social engagements or simply settle down with one of the popular novels or magazines of the day.

ORIGINS OF THE CHAISE

The concept of the chaise longue – literally a long chair – goes back at least as far as the 17th century. Then, for comfortable daytime resting, the wealthy Jacobean would take to his day-bed. This was a simple bed frame with a panelled headboard, cushion mattress and drapes that reached to the floor for a neat appearance.

But in Jacobean times, there was still no clear distinction between living and sleeping quarters. With the Restoration of Charles II to the throne in 1660, a more gracious lifestyle came in. In rich households, bedrooms were clearly separated from the other rooms of the house. Day-beds became more important. They were now made to be both more attractive and more comfortable.

The Restoration day-bed took the form of a chair with an elongated seat supported on six or eight legs. The legs were twist-turned, following the fashion of the time, and were joined by stretchers. The seat and head were of woven cane. The head followed the style of chairs of the period. For extra comfort, the seat was covered with a thin mattress and the head might be hinged, so that it could be adjusted to a convenient angle.

Day-beds in the form of a single chair continued to be made through to the early 18th century. They might be seen in any room of the house but were especially useful in the library and the drawing room. Seats were covered in tapestry or woven fabric.

▼ *A chaise longue lends itself to more modern use of room space, particularly in this old stone cottage, where it fits perfectly along a wall between windows.*

▲ *The Greek details of this portrait echo a main inspiration for the lines of the early Victorian chaise longue; 17th-century French neo-classicism was much admired.*

The design of day-beds changed with the times and usually followed fashions in chair design. In the early 18th century, day-beds were made with splat backs and curving, cabriole legs in the Queen Anne style.

By now, the French term 'chaise longue' was beginning to be used for day-beds and couches. Chippendale illustrated several designs for them in his *Director* of 1762.

By the turn of the century, the chaise longue was no longer thought of as a variation on a chair. Following a French idea, as its name implies, it was now upholstered and looked more like an asymmetrical settee. The head was either upright or raked, and the back either ran the length of the chaise longue or stopped half way. The basic look of the chaise longue changed relatively little throughout Victorian and Edwardian times.

FRENCH INFLUENCE

The prototype of the Victorian and Edwardian chaise longue was based on a combination of the English day-bed and a French sofa for one. In 18th-century France, this

individual sofa was made by joining together two low armchairs, sometimes with a stool placed in between. The idea was later copied in England, where makers produced a more practical all-in-one version.

The first chaises longues were usually double-ended, with a foot as well as a head. The graceful and decorative effect that they produced matched the elegance of Regency life. The most attractive were made of rosewood inlaid with brass.

Regency chaises longues were made with an outward scroll at the head balanced by a lower scroll at the foot, and a gracefully undulating back. The legs curved downwards and outwards. The fashion-conscious thought of this type as being in the Grecian style. Other fashionable neo-classical details were lion's paws at the feet and lion's heads at the head and foot. Egyptian motifs such as sphinxes were also common.

VICTORIAN TASTES

The vogue for French furniture styles brought the chaise longue back into fashion in mid-Victorian times. But tastes had

▶ *This elaborate brocaded chaise longue, made in the Louis XVI style in France about 1840, reveals the origins of the chaise longue as a combination of two small chairs with a stool between them.*

▼ *In mid-Victorian times, Rococo extravagance replaced the taste for clean neo-classical shapes, and the chaise longue evolved into a more stuffed, padded item of furniture, with ornate carved detail on the frame and legs.*

changed; by contrast to its clean lines in Regency times, the chaise longue was now more scrolling in outline. The idea was to re-create the extravagance of the 17th-century French Rococo, and the effect could be over-ornate.

The typically mid-Victorian chaise longue was single-ended, with a high head and high, exaggerated back. It was either part-upholstered or over-stuffed, sometimes with deep buttoning. The most common material was walnut, with velvet upholstery.

They remained a traditional piece of furniture and, into Edwardian times, continued to be produced by commercial manufacturers.

The Edwardian Chaise

THE GALLERIED CHAISE LONGUE — WITH EITHER A ROW OF TURNED WOODEN SPINDLES OR ART NOUVEAU-STYLE STRUTS SUPPORTING THE BACK — WAS THE MOST TYPICAL EDWARDIAN CHAISE.

FURNITURE OF SUCH SIMPLICITY AND LIGHTNESS WELL COMPLEMENTED THE NEW PALE COLOURS OF THE EDWARDIAN INTERIOR. THE UPHOLSTERED SEAT AND BACK — STUFFED WITH HORSEHAIR OR FLOCK — THE TURNED LEGS AND THE CASTORS ARE ALSO CHARACTERISTIC OF THE PERIOD. WHILE MUCH IN EDWARDIAN TIMES WAS FORWARD-LOOKING, THERE WAS A TRADITIONAL SIDE TO EDWARDIAN TASTE; SUCH FURNITURE REFLECTED THE PREFERENCE FOR COMFORT AND GOOD DESIGN OVER RADICAL INNOVATION.

① CARVED SCROLLED STRUT TO GALLERY.

② MACHINE-TURNED, STRAIGHT LEGS ON CASTORS.

③ DEEP-UPHOLSTERED SEAT AND BACK.

④ PADDED STRAIGHT ARM-REST.

⑤ LIGHTER-TONED UPHOLSTERY.

Victorian Chaise Longue

AN IMPOSING MID-VICTORIAN CHAISE LONGUE OF ROCOCO STYLE, IN WALNUT WOOD WITH CABRIOLE LEGS C. 1860

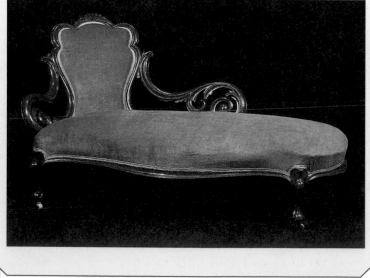

By late Victorian times, chaises longues were being made in large numbers, as demand dictated, for hardly a drawing room was complete without its chaise longue and almost every household had one or more.

By this time also, the dark, cluttered and over-decorated interiors of the Victorian era were beginning to look old-fashioned. There was a marked preference for more sparsely furnished interiors. Reflecting this, furniture became less massive and overpowering and more dainty and delicate.

The design of chaises longues moved with the times. Out went Rococo curves and buttoned upholstery; in came the lighter style of the Edwardian era.

Chaises longues now had straight turned legs, set on castors, and were of solid, plain

·PRICE GUIDE·

Chaises Longues

▲ Velvet-covered chaise longue of stained mahogany, with gilded shell detail, in the fashionable neo-classic Regency style.

PRICE GUIDE **7**

▲ Spindle back, light wood detail and machine-turned straight legs on castors typify simpler Edwardian chaises longues.

PRICE GUIDE **6**

▲ Mid-Victorian mahogany and buttoned black leather chaise longue with ball-and-claw feet.

PRICE GUIDE **7**

▲ Cream damask silk, painted and gilded beechwood chaise longue in Louis XIV style, made about 1900.

PRICE GUIDE **7**

▲ Mahogany chaise longue with original bolster cushion, button-backed but made on classical lines in the Regency period.

PRICE GUIDE **8**

▲ Mahogany chaise longue with deep-buttoned, heavy-padded upholstery and curved feet of mid-Victorian ornate styling.

PRICE GUIDE **6**

construction with a simple backward-scrolling head. The part-upholstery was often velvet or leather, real or imitation.

Later Edwardian chaises longues were made with outward-curving legs. This reflected a brief fashion for earlier French styles. Fully upholstered chaises longues, covered with patterned fabric, also became popular. Some were in fact made as sofas, with a hinged arm at one end that could be lowered to transform the sofa into a chaise longue. A late Edwardian type looked right back to Jacobean times. It was an almost complete re-creation of the Jacobean day-bed, although it was mistakenly thought of by the Edwardians as being in the Elizabethan style. The fashion for Art Nouveau was sometimes reflected in the heart-shaped motifs, discreet scrolls and carved galleries that commercial manufacturers some-times added to chaises longues.

In the furniture emporiums of the time, chaises longues could be purchased either singly or with a set of chairs to match. With the chaise longue came six side chairs and two armchairs. Furnishing a room with a match-ing suite of furniture was quite common at the time. Nowadays sets are frequently dispersed, but rooms are smaller, anyway.

POINTS TO WATCH

■ Check that the legs are firmly joined to the rails.

The webbing underneath should not be worn out.

■ Look out for serious wear and tear on the upholstery; this means that the whole piece will need re-covering. Unless it is irretrievably worn, original upholstery is worth preserving as it adds to the authenticity of the piece.

The Ottoman

The ottoman, with its eastern allure, greatly appealed to the
Victorians who soon adopted it for a multiplicity of decorative and
practical purposes

Ottomans varied greatly in size and they were suitable for both Victorian cottages and mansions. In large reception areas it was common to see three or four, set among the armchairs and sofas. In the most lavish interiors, they would be upholstered in the same fabric as the chairs. This versatile piece of furniture, in a variety of designs and fabric finishes, could be found almost everywhere in the Victorian house, from the reception rooms to the study and smoking room, as well as on staircase landings and in the bedrooms.

ARRIVAL OF THE OTTOMAN

Ottomans designed in Europe were developed from the richly upholstered benches, covered with cushions, that were used in the Ottoman Empire.

In essence the ottoman is an upholstered seat for one or several people, with little or no visible wood. In the box ottoman the seat is hinged, opening to reveal a storage space.

Ottomans became common in Britain in the early 19th century. George Smith, upholsterer and cabinetmaker to the Prince of Wales, popularized them with the publication, in 1804, of his *Collection of Designs for Household Furniture and Interior Decoration.*

REGENCY DESIGNS

Covered in broadly-striped fabric, most of the Regency versions resembled a mattress supported on a low wooden plinth. They had no backs, but in the centre they often had large, sturdy cushions propped against each other, forming a back rest with seating on two sides.

Ottomans were frequently used in public places, such as picture galleries, as, placed against the walls, they prevented people from touching the pictures. Ottomans were also convenient for the empty areas in the centre of a room, and large, circular ones were sometimes built around a central statue or a display of plants.

Both round and rectangular designs were used in the Regency period. They were often upholstered in striped cotton or silk and the fabrics were often thin. The stuffing was frequently held in place by tightly drawn threads which were prevented from pulling through the fabric by silk tufts. These tufts dotted the fabric's surface. Around 1820, it became more usual to use buttons covered with the upholstery fabric,

in place of silk tufts. Until the middle of the century this style of buttoning remained fairly shallow.

In 1828 Samuel Pratt registered a patent for coiled springs, and these springs were soon used in the thickly padded upholstery of the best designs. In the 1830s and 40s, completely upholstered furniture, without

▲ *The ottoman was derived from the luxuriously upholstered benches used in Turkey and throughout the Ottoman Empire. In this painting, Lord Byron is seen reclining on one such bench. The ottoman quickly proved itself to be a most versatile piece of furniture. The padded top with the addition of a cushion or back rest made it ideal to lounge upon.*

any show wood, was popular. The ottoman became steadily more complex, sometimes having a padded arm and an upholstered back rest.

VICTORIAN OTTOMANS

Throughout the Victorian period it was acceptable for men to lounge in public and for women to recline. Comfortable, well upholstered furniture was therefore in vogue and the informality of the ottoman was ideally suited to this fashion. Those covered with velvet, brocade and thick wool were often deep-buttoned, sometimes with springs under the buttoning. Other designs relied for comfort on layers of horse hair and padding – all that was necessary for the shallow-buttoning which became fashionable again after 1880.

Smoking rooms were often decorated in Moorish or Turkish style, with plenty of cushions to set the scene. Carpet-topped ottomans with quilted velvet sides provided just the right luxurious feel, as did those entirely covered in Turkey-style carpet. Some were divan-shaped, with matching cushions that could be laid against the wall to form a sofa.

Embroidery-topped ottomans in the smoking room often featured medieval-type scenes, coats of arms or geometric patterns. In general, a pale-coloured surrounding fabric tends to date a piece before 1850. After this period, dark greens and reds were most popular.

Berlin woolwork was the most popular form of embroidery. It was taken up in the Regency period and by 1850 women's magazines featured hundreds of designs for all sorts of household items. In the smoking

room, examples could be found on everything from ottomans and smoking caps to carpet slippers.

THE OTTOMAN TODAY

Box ottomans remain one of the cheapest and simplest forms of storage, as interesting fabric can transform a crude frame into an acceptable piece of furniture. Large mattress-types are now constructed from foam rubber and upholstered in hard-wearing woollen fabrics, often to match a sofa or a suite. Buttoned leather ottomans have remained in production throughout this century, as they are versatile and luxurious. Antique examples needing renovation can often be purchased quite cheaply at house sales or in junk shops.

▲ *This small, richly-covered needlepoint ottoman serves as a useful footstool in this comfortable traditionally-decorated room. The storage space within can be used for slippers, magazines, sewing utensils or any number of small items.*

▼ *Many ottomans were designed with attractively curved sides which not only enhance the visual appearance but serve a practical purpose too. They enabled the wide-skirted Victorian ladies to sit more comfortably!*

▼ *This mid-19th century ottoman has been designed in the popular Gothic style – in place of upholstery the sides have attractive wood panelling. The seat is padded and covered with English needlework, while the ottoman box itself is fitted with a small lock and key.*

The Box Ottoman

THE BOX OTTOMAN WAS ONE OF THE MOST VERSATILE PIECES OF FURNITURE IN THE VICTORIAN HOUSE. GOOD-QUALITY RICHLY UPHOLSTERED EXAMPLES COULD BE USED IN ANY ROOM IN THE HOUSE FROM THE PARLOUR TO THE SMOKING ROOM.

THIS EXAMPLE WITH ITS ATTRACTIVE CURVED SIDES DATES FROM THE 1850S AND IS UPHOLSTERED ON TOP WITH RED NEEDLEPOINT. THE HINGED LID AND PLINTH ARE TRIMMED WITH ROSEWOOD.

① ROSEWOOD TRIM AROUND THE SEAT TO PROTECT THE UPHOLSTERY FROM UNNECESSARY WEAR.

② PADDED FABRIC LINING USED TO DISGUISE THE WOODEN CARCASE OF THE OTTOMAN.

③ BRAID TRIM TO PROVIDE A NEAT, DECORATIVE FINISH TO THE TAPESTRY EXTERIOR FABRIC.

④ SMALL CASTERS FIXED TO ROSEWOOD FEET, MAKING MOVING EASY.

Trimmings

ATTRACTIVELY-SHAPED HANDLES IN BRASS MAKE TRANSPORTATION EASIER.

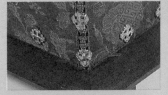

BRASS UPHOLSTERY STUDS IN A CROSS DESIGN HOLD THE FABRIC IN PLACE.

William IV Ottoman

THE SHAPE OF THE OTTOMAN CHANGED LITTLE AFTER ITS INTRODUCTION TO BRITAIN. THIS WILLIAM IV TAFFETA OTTOMAN IS VERY SIMILAR TO LATER VICTORIAN EXAMPLES.

As ottomans were generally completely covered with fabric the carpentry was often rudimentary, and may indeed have been carried out by the upholsterer rather than a skilled carpenter. Any available wood was used for the box, as strength rather than elegant craftsmanship was required. So simple was the basic design that home-made versions are frequently found, their tops covered with a thin layer of padding and the interior lined with cheap cotton or even wallpaper.

Circular or bow-fronted versions are almost invariably the work of professional carpenters, as are those made to fit into a bay window or an awkward alcove. The more elegant parlour ottomans with curved sides are obviously cabinetmaker's pieces. They sometimes have

·PRICE GUIDE· Ottomans

▲ LARGE OTTOMAN SET ON AN INVISIBLE PLINTH COVERED WITH RED, CREAM AND BLUE-PATTERNED CARPETING WOVEN WITH AN EASTERN DESIGN.

PRICE GUIDE **5**

▲ LONG OTTOMAN UPHOLSTERED IN MAROON PLUSH WITH A PATTERNED NEEDLEPOINT SEAT, C 1880.

PRICE GUIDE **6**

▲ SQUARE OTTOMAN WITH MAHOGANY PLINTH AND FEET AND FITTED WITH A SMALL LOCK. THE SEAT IS UPHOLSTERED IN PAISLEY CLOTH.

PRICE GUIDE **6**

PRICE GUIDE **6**

▲ SQUARE OTTOMAN FITTED WITH A SMALL LOCK. IT HAS A MAHOGANY PLINTH AND FEET, AND A NEEDLEPOINT SEAT.

▲ SMALL OTTOMAN WITH MAHOGANY PLINTH AND FEET, AND UPHOLSTERED IN BLUE WITH A FLOWER-PATTERNED NEEDLEPOINT SEAT, C 1860.

PRICE GUIDE **6**

◀ LONG OTTOMAN, C 1860, WITH SHAPED SIDES TRIMMED WITH CORD. IT HAS A GEOMETRIC NEEDLEPOINT PATTERN.

PRICE GUIDE **6**

mahogany show wood on the inside of the hinged lid and around the top of the sides.

The manufacturer's or retailer's name is occasionally found inside the lid or on the base, though the vast majority are unmarked and are valued purely on the quality of their construction.

Better examples were fitted with carved or bun feet, with brass or china castors. Cheaper versions stood on simple square supports or on a wooden plinth which protected the upholstery. On more expensive designs a protective wooden moulding was sometimes used at the edges, again to save the rich and carefully worked fabric from damage.

Some ottomans have a solid wooden carcase (like a box). Most, however, have a lighter wooden framework. Webbing was stretched across the frame and covered with hessian to support the stuffing.

The interiors were lined with dark linen or cotton, the top edges of which were neatened with a simple braid or cord. The exterior fabric was tacked to the outside edges of the lid and box and was trimmed with decorative braid or ornamental brass tacks embellished with attractive patterns.

POINTS TO WATCH
■ Original upholstery is most desirable; new fabric should be in period style.
■ If the springing and webbing is defective it can be expensive to remedy if you want to keep the original covering.
■ Reproduction deep-buttoned ottomans are fairly common. Look underneath to check the originality of the frame and any maker's mark.

The Edwardian Buffet Sideboard

The sideboard, often known as the buffet, was an essential part of Edwardian breakfast and dining room furniture. It came in a great range of styles, reflecting the changing tastes of the era

Although a variety of tables and cupboards had been in use for displaying plates and for serving food since medieval times, it was during the late 18th century that the sideboard developed into a more recognizable and familiar form of furniture. At each end of a long table, cabinet maker Robert Adam stood a small urn mounted on a short pedestal; the table was used for serving food, and the urns for cutlery, perhaps, or cold water. This was such a useful arrangement next to the dining table that it was not long before the pedestals and urns had turned into cupboards and the separate parts had become united into the now-familiar form of the sideboard. Since this piece of furniture could combine a range of very different elements, from wine cooler, or cellaret, to plate-warmer, it is hardly surprising that sideboards have always been very variable in appearance.

THE DESIGN REVOLUTION
Victorian furniture to a large extent was ostentatious and wildly decorative. Pieces were not so much designed with their use in mind but rather as decorative objects in their own right. This was particularly true of sideboards, which were made to display the owners' wealth of glass and silver.

After the Great Exhibition in 1851, often regarded as the showcase of excessive Victorian design, furniture styles gradually became more restrained. Even so, it was to take a design revolution to fundamentally change the style of the sideboard. This revolution came not from within the trade – although the more imaginative commercial makers were to adopt it later – but from a series of highly skilled individual craftsmen and artists.

The resulting 'Gothic Revival' of Pugin and Burges marked a return to medieval principles of simple design, although the furniture produced could, in fact, be as ornate as earlier Victorian pieces on occasion. The Gothic principles of genuine craftsmanship and unostentatious decoration carried on into William Morris's activities, although Morris himself probably never designed any furniture. Pieces produced by

his firm were made by colleagues such as Philip Webb, who designed large tables, notable for their unconcealed joinery – in marked contrast to more usual Victorian pieces, where the construction was always well hidden.

CHARLES EASTLAKE
The work of Morris and others evolved into the Arts and Crafts Movement towards the end of the century, but other influences were also at work. In 1868 Charles Eastlake published his influential book, *Hints on Household Taste* which sold in large numbers in England and America. Its clear, easy-to-grasp philosophy of honesty in design was shared by many of his contemporaries. 'To fulfil the first and most essential principle of good design, every article should at first glance proclaim its real purpose', he wrote, going on to suggest that some furniture makers 'seem to think it betokens elegance when the purpose is concealed'.

Eastlake's approach has been termed 'Reformed Gothic'. He favoured straight lines and rejected curves, and did not approve of sideboards having mirrors, which had become very fashionable but were perhaps not relevant to the piece. He

▲ *At the beginning of this century, furniture design turned away from the heavy, imposing lines of Victorian times. Sideboards, showed greater simplicity and interiors were generally more informal.*

◀ *Today, the sideboard is still an essential and practical item of furniture in the breakfast or dining room.*

▲ *In reaction to the flow of cheaply-made furniture, designers such as Bruce J. Talbert created fine pieces like this gilded sideboard, c. 1866.*

▼ *Designed as an exhibition piece by George Jack for Morris & Co in 1886, this mahogany sideboard already hints at the Art-Nouveau styles to come.*

was hard on machine-made ornament and artificial lustre, recommending that pieces be decorated with elaborate relief on lower panels which might also include surface texture and colouring. Charles Eastlake's furniture showed simple and well-made joints yet retained an air of classicism, sometimes with a Latin inscription at the top of pieces. His ideas owe much to Jacobean and Elizabethan cabinet makers in skilfulness and deceptive simplicity.

Eastlake's work led on to that of Godwin, who incorporated Japanese influences to produce furniture with strong vertical and horizontal lines, foretelling the main lines of 20th-century design.

'JACOBETHAN' STYLES

Around the end of the century a varied group of designers, united under the banner of the Arts and Crafts Movement, were continuing the revival of traditional skills and craftsmanship. They advocated working with craftsmen from many different disciplines, so materials such as stained glass, leather and pewter were incorporated into their furniture designs, usually in a decorative context.

The re-establishment of Jacobean and Elizabethan skills, much embellished by these other influences, led to the production of furniture which has been termed 'Jacobethan'. Characteristics typical of that earlier time were incorporated – a frequent feature, for example, was the presence of twist-turned columns and legs.

TYPES AND STYLES

Jacobethan was by no means the only style of sideboard furniture available in the early years of this century. The highly ornate Victorian styles were still available, though declining in popularity, and the Victorian influence was still felt in contemporary pieces – with the inclusion of large mirrors, for instance. In other sideboards, tall backs were disappearing and sideboards were even available in forms closely resembling the original Adams style. Medieval, Gothic-style pieces were much in evidence, and the influence of Art Nouveau with its sinuous designs in inlay and carving was apparent in some pieces. The simple styles of the Arts and Crafts Movement became a major influence on commercial manufacturers who included features like leaded lights and bronze panels.

All Edwardian homes had a sideboard in their breakfast rooms, and perhaps another in the dining room. People could choose from a variety of styles. These reflected different influences, several of which could be seen in the one piece of furniture.

The Edwardian Sideboard

EARLY 20TH-CENTURY SIDEBOARDS, DESPITE THE FLUIDITY OF DESIGN AND VARIETY OF INFLUENCES, HAD A SET OF RECURRING FEATURES. THEY WERE GENERALLY MADE OF OAK, CONSIDERED TO BE THE MOST TRADITIONAL OF MATERIALS.

SIDEBOARDS USUALLY HAD AN UPPER MIRRORED BACKBOARD SUPPORTED BY ROWS OF COLUMNS WHICH RESTED ON A FLAT SERVING SURFACE. UNDERNEATH WERE DRAWERS FOR CUTLERY AND CUPBOARDS, OFTEN WITH METAL HANDLES IN A GOTHIC STYLE.

SQUARED PANELLING WITH ART NOUVEAU STYLE DOCORATION WAS COMMON AS WAS THE USE OF INLAYS.

A PEDESTAL PLINTH REPLACED THE SIX LEGS OF VICTORIAN SIDEBOARDS.

① STRAIGHT, CARVED LINES ON PEDIMENT

② ART NOUVEAU-STYLE FRETWORK

③ BAS-RELIEF PANELLING ON CUPBOARD DOORS

④ PEDESTAL PLINTH IN PLACE OF THIN LEGS

Columns

MOST EDWARDIAN SIDEBOARDS INCORPORATED PILLARS OR COLUMNS WHICH RANGED FROM THE WIDELY-USED VICTORIAN SPINDLES TO NEO-CLASSICAL 'GREEK' SHAPES.

The Buffet

A STAINED OAK 'JACOBETHAN' SIDEBOARD.

The creativeness and innovation of the furniture makers and designers of the late 19th century was, in many ways, a response to the unimaginative nature of the commercial furniture business. But once their important new ideas had developed, the designers wanted to influence the trade. Many of the new makers spoke of producing simple, utilitarian furniture for ordinary people, and tried to achieve this by making the new furniture generally available. Trade and public alike were influenced through the designers' own publications. This was true of Eastlake, of course, and also of his contemporaries. Bruce Talbert, for instance, had published *Gothic Forms, applied to Furniture, Metalwork, etc, for Interior Purposes* in 1867. Exhibitions, which were very popular at the time, were another area of influence.

The trade could not afford to ignore the trend towards the new simpler designs. They started to incorporate the new ideas in their products, to employ and commission the innovators, and to exhibit their own work. In 1893 major makers like Howard and Sons and Gillows, Collinson and Lock participated in the Arts and Crafts Exhibition.

Unfortunately, the trade's participation was not always beneficial. Some largely untalented designers simply incorporated obvious mannerisms of the Arts and Crafts designers in their own work. Thus evolved the 'Quaint Style', an unintentionally inelegant and tasteless mockery of contemporary design which abused Art Nouveau, Gothic, and Arts and Crafts alike.

More conscientious and creative commercial designers adopted various of the new thinkers' principles in the way they were intended. One of the most effective entrepreneur designers of the time was Sir

·PRICE GUIDE·

Edwardian Sideboards

◀ THIS LATE VICTORIAN MAHOGANY SIDEBOARD FEATURES BACK MIRRORS AND AN ELEGANT GALLERY.

PRICE GUIDE 6

▶ THIS SMALL EDWARDIAN SIDE-BOARD IN THE AESTHETIC STYLE FEATURES INLAID PANELS.

PRICE GUIDE 7

▼ TYPICAL EDWARDIAN SIDEBOARD AFTER ELABORATE VICTORIAN STYLES, C. 1900.

PRICE GUIDE 6

◀ SIDEBOARD-CUM-DISPLAY CABINET IN THE AESTHETIC STYLE, C. 1900.

PRICE GUIDE 6

▶ SIDEBOARD WHICH SHOWS BOTH ARTS & CRAFTS AND ART NOUVEAU FEATURES.

PRICE GUIDE 6

Ambrose Heal. Many of his pieces are fine examples from the Edwardian era. The wood is often traditional oak. It is sometimes beautifully, though modestly, inlaid with other woods or mother-of-pearl. The lines are straight and modern, with Gothic trim in the handles.

The makers' catalogues were the routes by which ideas reached the buying public. In their *'Dining Room and Living Room Furniture'* of 1910, Heal and Sons illustrated 'inexpensive and unpolished oak' products which were simple and utilitarian in design. They also figured

walnut and polished chestnut, and steel was starting to make an appearance.

In about 1910 Heal's published a delightful book titled *Workmanship*, which rebuked those who believed that craftsmanship was a thing of the past and who said that all was machinery and competition. 'In the production of the best modern furniture the machine is sedulously kept in its proper place' asserts the text, allowing that machines are speedy in sawing and planing, but cannot produce acceptable chamfers, ornamentation and carving.

Other makers' catalogues, too, suggested the principles behind the designs of furniture as well as illustrating them. Wylie and Lochhead of Glasgow sold 'Simple, well-made, artistic and inexpensive furniture, suitable for small flats and villas, etc., designed by our own artists and made in our own workshops'.

In the days before television, catalogues and exhibitions brought the ideas of the new designers to the public quickly and effectively. It was not long before the characteristic forms of the 20th century were to be

found in the ordinary home.

POINTS TO WATCH

■ Look for quality wood – oak is most typical.

■ Look for interesting design features like 'Jacobethan' twist-turned legs and square panels.

■ Look for well executed decoration in the panels such as bas-relief or painting.

■ Be careful of Edwardian reproductions that are passed off as 'genuine' older pieces.

■ Watch out for staining and varnishing on Edwardian pieces. Most were left unstained to show the natural wood.

The Roll-top Desk

The roll-top desk, with its elaborate compartments stuffed full of secrets,
and its solid traditional look, was the pride of the gentleman's study

Modernist notions about furniture design and interior decoration were not greeted with universal enthusiasm when they first became fashionable in the 1920s: many of the rooms in the average home continued to display a love of what was traditional and conservative. Nowhere was this more evident than in the gentleman's quarters: studies and billiard rooms were a last bastion, in design terms, against post-War modernism.

In fact gentlemens' rooms often had a positively romantic feeling about them, with their nostalgic collections of prints, medals in glass cases, racks of pipes, and yellowing collections of comics or magazines. The roll-top desk, with its hidden drawers and secret compartments, often stuffed full of unpaid bills, old diaries and other mementoes, was the perfect symbol of this private world of retreat.

ORIGINS OF ROLL-TOPS

The very first desks had their origins in the Middle Ages in the writing boxes with sloping lids carried by monks, knights or merchants as they went on their travels. The surface was often covered with a woollen cloth, called *bure* in French, which eventually gave rise to the word bureau. Later on this came to signify any desk compartment, and in the USA more particularly a chest of drawers. The drum shaped roll-top sometimes attached to it was known as a 'tambour' – a cabinet maker's term denoting a flexible shutter or fall, made of narrow moulding or reeds of wood with their flat sides glued together with a canvas or linen backing.

EARLY EXAMPLES

The earliest examples of roll-top desks were made in France during the reign of Louis XV. The German-born cabinet-maker Jean François Oeben, who worked for the King together with his pupil, J.H. Riesener, made a famous 'bureau de Louis XV' which launched the fashion. Particularly elaborate are the rococo pieces of Louis XVI's reign, with complicated marquetry made by Roentgen. They were much admired in England by Sheraton, who wrote 'this style of furniture is somewhat elegant being made of satinwood, crossbanded and varnished'. Hepplewhite described a 'tambour writing table' as 'a

▲ *The early 20th century roll-top desk was well-suited to either home or office use. The carcase was commonly made in honey- or dark-stained oak, while the interior housed a variety of small compartments and drawers, often in a contrasting-coloured wood.*

very convenient piece of furniture, answering all the uses of a desk with a much lighter appearance'.

The simple desk-table shape was often altered in the 18th century by filling in the desk area below with sets of drawers, leaving a kneehole space between, or by

adding a bookcase above to make a tall 'secretary' or 'secretaire'. A 'bureau tallboy' was an early Georgian variation. This form increased in popularity from 1860 onwards due to a craze for letter writing.

Other rounded-top desks had a solid 'cylinder fall' that slid into the back of the piece as a leather-covered writing surface was pushed forward. The cylinder itself was not flexible, being made of segments of pine or mahogany glued together and covered with a sheet of veneer. The lid was raised by a pair of knob handles. Such a design in mahogany was featured in Sher-

▶ *Dating from the last quarter of the 18th century, this Louis XVI cylinder desk made in acacia wood features fine brass mounts and inset stringing.*

▼ *A George III mahogany roll-top desk with cylinder tambour top. The elegant tapering legs complete with original castors are typical of the more feminine style desks produced at this time.*

Victorian pedestal desks, with two sets of drawers on either side, were often made with roll tops. A particular feature of the best examples of the period are the complicated inside 'fit-ups', flat compartments for letters, small drawers for valuables, paper-clips and buttons, open vertically divided sections for grouping correspondence, inkwells, pen-trays, and so on. Satin walnut was a popular choice of material for the finest fit-ups, and the brass furniture was at times very handsome. Half-pedestal desks – with drawers on only one side – were also made with roll tops and elaborate fit-ups.

A CLASSIC DESIGN

During the first two decades of the 20th century, the roll-top desk proved to be an enduring classic. Styles from older periods were much copied, including the marquetry and veneer work and slender-legged pieces by Sheraton and Hepplewhite. These obviously decorative or more feminine versions of roll-tops may feature cabriole or straight tapered legs with castors. Numerous other variations were made, some with metal or brass galleries, or a wooden gallery intended as a bookshelf. Some have a foot rail, others do not have the panel at the back covering the kneehole. It is also possible to find a Victorian chest of drawers altered to make up a desk with a roll-top.

drawers, and curved motifs, such as the trefoil, on the slope frame.

Some Victorian variations have an 'S-shape' tambour, enclosing the work area, without a pull-out surface. As with all tambour top desks, these are prone to deterioration and are difficult to put right once the slats of the tambour have become warped, wrenched or splintered due to their sticking in the guiding grooves on the inner sides of the desk.

aton's *Cabinet Dictionary* of 1803, and has the appearance of a barrel laid sideways, with the lid descending below into the curved lower half of the shape as the desk area slides forward. Some furniture makers altered desks, replacing tambour tops with this solid, cylinder fall type, but these alterations have not lasted well.

POPULAR STYLES

The roll-top was one among many styles of desk that continued in popularity and was developed in the later part of the 18th and then the 19th centuries, others being the Davenport desk, the Carlton House desk, and variations on the French *bureau plat* or flat-topped desk like the bonheur du jour. Late in the 19th century the roll-top bureau found some great exponents in America: particularly fine are the oak 'gothic' desks inspired by the designs of the Englishman Charles Eastlake. Such examples have panelled sides, incised decoration on the

▶ *The small pigeonhole compartments, drawers and shelves which comprise the interior fit-up of the roll-top desk make it ideally suited to storing the paraphernalia of the modern study. This is a typical Victorian mahogany roll-top.*

The 1920s Roll-top Desk

THE ROLL-TOP DESK WAS AN ENDURING CLASSIC OF THE INTER-WAR PERIOD; MADE AS EXACT COPIES OF EARLIER PIECES, OR IN MODERN, UTILITARIAN DESIGNS, OFTEN IN LIGHT OAK WITH MATCHING WOODEN HANDLES.

SHAPES OF REPRODUCTION PIECES CAN VARY FROM PEDESTAL AND HALF-PEDESTAL TO FRENCH ROCOCO OR EARLIER NEO-CLASSICAL DESIGNS IN THE SHERATON OR HEPPLEWHITE TRADITION. COPIES OF VICTORIAN PIECES MAY BE IN MAHOGANY OR OAK, WALNUT OR ROSEWOOD.

KNOWN AS A TAMBOUR, THE ROLL-TOP WAS USUALLY MADE OF SLATS OF WOOD GLUED TO A FABRIC BACKING FOR FLEXIBILITY, AND HELD IN POSITION BY GROOVES ON THE INNER SIDE PANELS. SEMI-CIRCULAR GROOVES HOUSED THE CYLINDER SHAPED TAMBOUR WHILE S-SHAPED GROOVES WERE COMMON ON VICTORIAN VERSIONS, GIVING A CHARACTERISTIC SERPENTINE TOP.

Top Variations

THE SERPENTINE TAMBOUR IS TYPICAL OF VICTORIAN ROLL-TOPS. THE SEMI-CIRCÚLAR TOP SOMETIMES APPEARS IN SOLID FORM (RIGHT); THE RESULT IS A CYLINDER DESK.

① PANELLED INFILL BEHIND KNEEHOLE
② PIGEONHOLE COMPARTMENTS
③ FILING DRAWERS
④ PEDESTAL WITH DRAWERS

The Bureau à Cylindre

THE BUREAU A CYLINDRE IS THE EARLIEST FORM OF ROLL-TOP DESK. IT ORIGINATED IN FRANCE DURING THE LOUIS XV PERIOD (1723-1774).

Not all 1920s versions of the roll-top were slavish copies of earlier period pieces. Innovative French designers produced some very finely-made examples, because the roll-top style challenged cabinet making skills and encouraged ingenuity: Emile-Jacques Ruhlmann made an exquisite macassar-ebony roll-top desk on slender tapering legs, featured in his pavilion at the 1925 Paris exhibition.

'Edwardian Sheraton' pieces can be very fine, but they sometimes display a tendency to over-do the elaborate marquetry or ormolu decoration. Particular care should be taken with these pieces as poorly-made veneers do not last well and can deceive an untrained buyer into thinking the piece is of an earlier date and therefore more valuable.

GOOD WORKMANSHIP

As with Victorian or Edwardian pieces, the value of a 1920s roll-top desk is defined by the fineness of the 'fit-up' inside the desk top, and by the quality of the workmanship in general. Inlay or grooving on desk drawers will enhance

·PRICE GUIDE·

Roll-top and Cylinder Desk

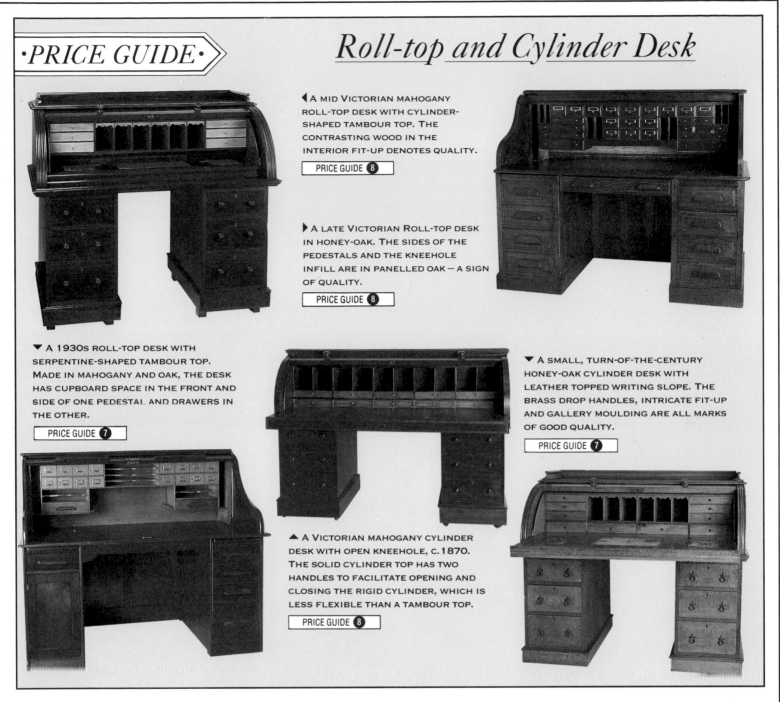

◄ A MID VICTORIAN MAHOGANY ROLL-TOP DESK WITH CYLINDER-SHAPED TAMBOUR TOP. THE CONTRASTING WOOD IN THE INTERIOR FIT-UP DENOTES QUALITY.

PRICE GUIDE **8**

▶ A LATE VICTORIAN ROLL-TOP DESK IN HONEY-OAK. THE SIDES OF THE PEDESTALS AND THE KNEEHOLE INFILL ARE IN PANELLED OAK — A SIGN OF QUALITY.

PRICE GUIDE **8**

▼ A 1930s ROLL-TOP DESK WITH SERPENTINE-SHAPED TAMBOUR TOP. MADE IN MAHOGANY AND OAK, THE DESK HAS CUPBOARD SPACE IN THE FRONT AND SIDE OF ONE PEDESTAL AND DRAWERS IN THE OTHER.

PRICE GUIDE **7**

▼ A SMALL, TURN-OF-THE-CENTURY HONEY-OAK CYLINDER DESK WITH LEATHER TOPPED WRITING SLOPE. THE BRASS DROP HANDLES, INTRICATE FIT-UP AND GALLERY MOULDING ARE ALL MARKS OF GOOD QUALITY.

PRICE GUIDE **7**

▲ A VICTORIAN MAHOGANY CYLINDER DESK WITH OPEN KNEEHOLE, C. 1870. THE SOLID CYLINDER TOP HAS TWO HANDLES TO FACILITATE OPENING AND CLOSING THE RIGID CYLINDER, WHICH IS LESS FLEXIBLE THAN A TAMBOUR TOP.

PRICE GUIDE **8**

value, as will panelling, carved detail, or any other distinctive design feature. Bear in mind that many Edwardian and 1920s desks were made up from earlier pieces of furniture. As with all desks a way to check authenticity is to examine the inside wall of the drawer sections. A difference in wood may reveal that the piece is a reconstruction. Similarly, a light tone to the interior wood may indicate a cheap copy with a thin veneer, or a new veneer laid on a poor bleached oak original.

Age can be indicated fairly clearly by the quality and style of the leather panel on the writing surface inside the desk. Lifting veneer is sometimes a sign of a reproduction piece, with the veneer applied to the wrong carcase wood.

BEWARE ALTERATIONS

Roll-tops themselves are not easy to replace, and a desk with the original in good working order is a real find. Check that the glue of the tambour is not so brittle and cracked that a few pushes of the lid will end its life forever. Unfortunately, since many dealers have found the flat-topped pedestal desk easier to sell, especially if the piece was smaller, many roll-tops have been dismantled to give desks a more Georgian appearance.

Brass furniture is also a guide to quality; matching drawer handles, fine detailing inside the desk lid, original and working locks are all highly desirable. Some roll tops feature a pierced ormolu gallery along the top of the desk lid. Apparently 3ft 2ins is the optimum width for a desk. Anything narrower will be more expensive, as it is more in demand for our smaller modern interiors, while larger versions are difficult to place.

POINTS TO WATCH

■ Check the roll-top slides well and will not jam. Roll tops are difficult to repair.

■ Look for working locks and matching drawer handles. Examine drawers for holes from removed handles.

■ Examine veneer carefully for blistering, or other suspicious deterioration indicating a fake or reconstructed piece. Very thin veneer is a sign of a later, Edwardian make.

■ Look for elaborate and well-made fit-ups inside a roll-top. With luck you may find a secret compartment!

The Pine Chest

The box chest – one of the oldest and most basic forms of furniture –
served the Victorian and Edwardian schoolboy, sailor and servant-girl
alike for storing or hiding their personal possessions

◀ *Going off to a new school was always an ordeal. A travelling chest carried the boy's clothes plus a few treasured possessions and a term's supply of provisions.*

century. Horizontal rails were tenoned or pegged into four corner posts, or stiles, which were extended down to make narrow legs. This frame was filled with flat panels to complete the chest.

A common fitting in these chests was a shallow box inset just under the lid, usually on the left-hand side. Here candles were kept, not just because it was a handy storage space, but because the candles acted as a deterrent to moths and other insects which were discouraged by the faintly unpleasant odour of tallow candles.

19TH-CENTURY CHESTS

Increasing prosperity in the 18th and 19th centuries helped create a diversity of furniture types. From the mule chest, a large chest with two drawers fitted below the main body of the piece, evolved the chest of drawers. The one great drawback with a lidded chest is that anything put on top of it has to be removed before it can be opened, while it is impossible to put anything at all on top of a coffer.

However, the simple chest was still produced in large quantities, albeit for a poorer clientèle. In the 19th century every servant had their own chest or box. These plain pine boxes, very similar to the school trunk, are commonly seen today.

Every seaman, whether an officer or a sailor, also had a chest. These are quite distinctive; 3 feet 6 inches (106cm) long, 2 feet 6 inches (75cm) deep and 2 feet (60cm) high, the sides sloping inwards slightly so that the top is smaller than the base. At each end was a stout wooden block through which a rope handle was spliced, though today it is rare to find this original handle surviving.

DECORATIVE STYLES

Chests and coffers, with their large flat surface, have always lent themselves to decoration, particularly painting and carving. Nearly all medieval chests were painted, though little remains to be seen on the rare surviving examples. Heraldic emblems were a common motif and carved scenes were also coloured.

Originally made from tree-trunks hollowed out by fire, chests or coffers are among the earliest items of furniture made by man.

Chests made from hollowed-out logs with lids hinged with wrought iron straps were superseded in the Middle Ages by the plank or board chest. Five planks were nailed together to form a basic rectangular box, with the short sides extended downwards to make feet. A sixth plank made the lid, which lifted on pin hinges – interlocking loops of metal set into the back and lid. Chests intended for money or valuables were known as coffers, and often had a curved or domed lid. Later, any chest with this sort of lid came to be known as a coffer.

Plank chests varied considerably in size, from about 24 inches (60cm) to well over 6 feet (2 metres) long, all the planks being of one piece. Such chests were common by the first part of the 17th century and were still being made in the 19th.

CHEST CONSTRUCTION

The next stage in the history of the chest was the introduction of joined or framed construction around the middle of the 17th

Most carving on chests was abstract in form. Semi-circular lunettes, guilloches and other decorative shapes predominated. In 17th-century England, carving was often asymmetrical. It would seem that people were not overly concerned if, for example, the lunettes running along the top rail of a joined chest did not fit exactly, leaving only enough room for one-third of a lunette at one end.

Among the earliest, and today one of the most sought-after, carved decorations was the linenfold panel. First used in England around 1480, it remained popular for around a century, and is, therefore, rarely found on 17th-century chests. The Victorians, though, were particularly fond of this drapery pattern and many old chests were recarved with linenfold in the 19th century, an industry centred in the Wardour Street area of London's Soho.

Inlaid decoration was another option, most famously in the so-called Nonesuch chests. These were made by Dutch and German immigrant craftsmen, most of whom lived in Southwark, just south of London Bridge, during the late 16th and

▶ *A pine chest is not only a useful place to tidy away toys or to store extra bedding but, with its overtones of buried treasure, the sea and mystery, can be a valued plaything in its own right.*

▼ *An early framed coffer in oak. The carved decoration is carried across frames and panels, uniting them in a single design. A serpentine band of guilloche forms the frame, while a carved seraph's head balances a massive iron lock-plate.*

▼ *The ancient lineage of the chest made it an ideal subject for the Arts and Crafts Movement's attempts to re-establish old craft values. This coffer, attributed to William Morris's circle, is of silverwood and dates from 1888. Inside, it is painted red while the exterior is a pastiche of medieval styles.*

early 17th centuries. These fanciful chests were decorated with a representation of an extravagant Tudor building resembling Henry VIII's Renaissance palace of Nonesuch in Cheam, Surrey (destroyed in the 17th century).

Split turnings are occasionally seen. These are turned columns or spindles that have been split along their length, then glued to the front of the chest. Unusual in Britain, they are a common form of decoration on American Colonial furniture.

Early coffers are sometimes found bound with wrought-iron straps. These were functional rather than decorative, applied to lend security to chests meant to hold money or particularly valuable items, though to our eyes the blacksmith's work certainly adds to the attraction of the chest, and purely ornamental ironwork was added to later examples.

OAK AND PINE

The timbers used for making chests were varied. Pine was by far the most common in the 19th century, while before this oak was the favoured wood. Elm was also used from the 17th to the 19th century, as were fruitwoods, yew, cedar and – especially in the 19th century – teak.

Cedar was popular for lining chests intended for storing clothes, due to its splendid scent. In the same way, cypress linings were sometimes used because of the belief that moths disliked the timber and therefore did not attack the clothes or blankets stored inside.

But beware, many chests were produced in the 'medieval' style during the 19th century.

A Painted Blanket Chest

LARGE, SOLIDLY-BUILT CHESTS LIKE THIS BECAME KNOWN AS BLANKET CHESTS IN THE 18TH CENTURY. THIS EXAMPLE FROM THE 1880S HAS A BASIC FRAME CONSTRUCTION, WITH A SOLID PLINTH, AND RETAINS ITS ORIGINAL PAINTED DECORATION. THE WOOD HAD A PAINTED GRAIN SIMULATING PALE OAK AND IS OVERPAINTED WITH A STENCIL DESIGN IN BLACK, SIMULATING EBONY INLAY. ON THE INSIDE OF THE LID A MORE EXOTIC WOOD, PERHAPS BIRD'S-EYE MAPLE, IS MIMICKED. A CANDLE BOX IS IN ITS TRADITIONAL PLACE ON THE TOP LEFT AND THE PIECE IS FINISHED BY A PAIR OF BLACK METAL DROP CARRYING HANDLES.

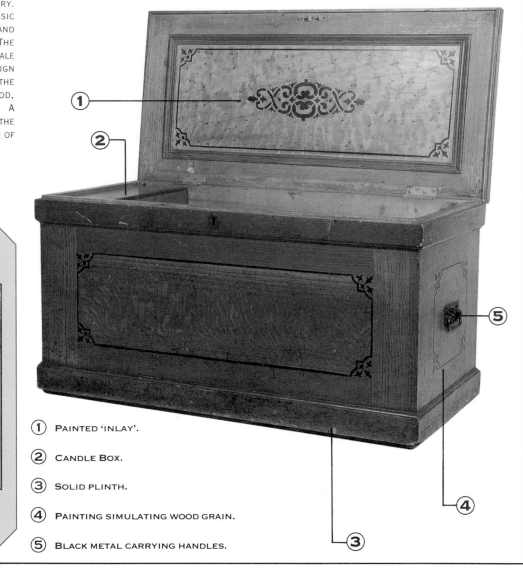

Candle Boxes

CANDLE BOXES OUTLIVED THE AGE OF CANDLES. TWO GLASS-HANDLED TRINKET DRAWERS HAVE BEEN ADDED HERE.

(1) PAINTED 'INLAY'.

(2) CANDLE BOX.

(3) SOLID PLINTH.

(4) PAINTING SIMULATING WOOD GRAIN.

(5) BLACK METAL CARRYING HANDLES.

Victorian Miniature

THIS MID 19TH-CENTURY PINE COFFER, JUST 18 INCHES (48CM) LONG, IS COVERED WITH ANIMAL HIDE AND GILDED BRASS STUDS. IT WAS PROBABLY USED FOR JEWELLERY.

The chest was a common item in servants' quarters, children's rooms and special work areas in the late 19th and early 20th century. Servants, mostly female at this date, kept their spare clothes and what few personal belongings they had in chests that were typically made of pine and covered with leather-cloth.

New children's chests often had padded, cloth-covered tops so they could be used for seating as well as for storing blankets and toys. Children's rooms were the final repository of old furniture, and 17th- and 18th-century chests may be seen in some photographs of Victorian and Edwardian nurseries.

The chest remained an important piece of everyday furniture in the workplace. Every tradesman kept his tools in a box or a substantial, though more or less portable, chest. Carpenters' and joiners' tool chests in particular often had splendid inlaid and compartmentalized interiors masked by plain and battered exteriors.

PAINTED CHESTS

Cheap 19th-century chests were always painted, often in a single colour with contrasting linings to the top and sides. Sometimes

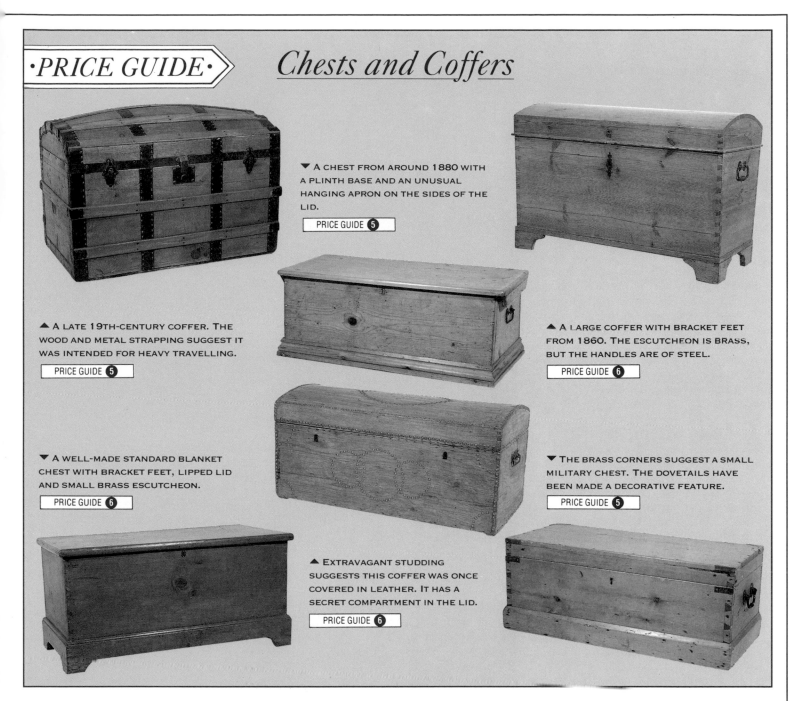

Chests and Coffers

▼ A CHEST FROM AROUND 1880 WITH A PLINTH BASE AND AN UNUSUAL HANGING APRON ON THE SIDES OF THE LID.

PRICE GUIDE **5**

▲ A LATE 19TH-CENTURY COFFER. THE WOOD AND METAL STRAPPING SUGGEST IT WAS INTENDED FOR HEAVY TRAVELLING.

PRICE GUIDE **5**

▲ A LARGE COFFER WITH BRACKET FEET FROM 1860. THE ESCUTCHEON IS BRASS, BUT THE HANDLES ARE OF STEEL.

PRICE GUIDE **6**

▼ A WELL-MADE STANDARD BLANKET CHEST WITH BRACKET FEET, LIPPED LID AND SMALL BRASS ESCUTCHEON.

PRICE GUIDE **6**

▼ THE BRASS CORNERS SUGGEST A SMALL MILITARY CHEST. THE DOVETAILS HAVE BEEN MADE A DECORATIVE FEATURE.

PRICE GUIDE **5**

▲ EXTRAVAGANT STUDDING SUGGESTS THIS COFFER WAS ONCE COVERED IN LEATHER. IT HAS A SECRET COMPARTMENT IN THE LID.

PRICE GUIDE **6**

they were grained, but the result was often splendid naivety rather than an accurate rendition of an expensive wood. Unfortunately few of these original finishes survive, most having fallen victim to the fashion for stripping pine.

LEATHER-CLOTH

Leather-cloth or American cloth appeared in the latter half of the century. Real leather, velvet, sharkskin and even fur had been used to cover chests in the past but the new material, a product of the machine age, provided a cheap and much-used alternative.

Pine chests were often sold by the large department stores such as Whiteley's in Bayswater or the Army & Navy Stores in Victoria. These shops had mail-order catalogues through which people could make purchases, a special boon to those living in the colonies.

The cabinet-makers who produced the chests were known as garret masters, and made the furniture in the room in which their families lived and slept. At the end of the week they hawked their products around the big stores.

It is possible to find pine chests with scenes painted on them;

cattle, hot air balloons and especially ships are the favourite subjects. These are almost always modern paintings on old pieces. Seamen's chests did, it is true, sometimes have ships painted on them, but only on the inside of the lid, never on the outside where the painting would be damaged.

Older-style chests were also re-produced in the late 19th century.

POINTS TO WATCH
■ Check that the hinges are original, particularly on older pieces.
■ Check that the candle box is still inside; if one has been

removed, there will be tell-tale grooves in the wood inside the chest at the top left.
■ Make sure that the feet are original. A little wear is acceptable, but chests with split or unevenly worn feet should be avoided.
■ If the chest has been stripped, check for coarse grain, possible scorch marks and caustic deposits caused by bad stripping.
■ Many oak chests were recarved in the 19th century. Looking at good original pieces in museums and country houses is the best way to acquire an eye for original work.

The Pine Chest of Drawers

Today's vogue for stripped and waxed pine has made collectable pieces
of chests of drawers that were mass-produced as cheap, utilitarian
furniture in the late 19th century

During the 19th century the mechanization of various sections of the furniture industry meant that furniture of all types could be bought more cheaply than ever before. Employers could make sure that their domestics were equipped with at least the bare essentials in terms of furniture and if a maid was lucky, as well as a chest of drawers, she would have had a chair and washstand too, possibly of a matching design. The ordinary pine chest, so popular with buyers today, would not have been regarded as at all elegant and would probably have been either stained to look like a more expensive wood or painted in a plain and practical colour.

17TH-CENTURY ORIGINS

The chest of drawers as we know it today developed around the mid-17th century from the simple coffer. This was at first a deep, long box with a hinged lid which eventually came to incorporate one long drawer in the lower part. These coffers are variously described as 'mule chests' or 'dowry chests'.

By 1680 the whole of the chest was taken up by drawers below a flat fixed top, with a pair of cupboard doors underneath enclosing further interior drawers. From then on it took on its familiar form, with either flights of three or four long drawers, or two short drawers set above three long ones. Most of these early chests were made of oak with coffered panels, or of a simple carcass with decorative veneer or marquetry finish. Other distinguishing features of the period were metal drop handles and bun feet.

Until around 1800, when large wooden knobs began to be fitted, nearly all chests of drawers had brass loop handles of some sort. Many had solid backplates, at first cartouche-shaped but after 1780 elliptical or circular. Then from around 1840 onwards swan neck handles with a simple loop attached to two small circular plates became the most popular type.

The 18th and 19th centuries saw the basic chest of drawers develop into various specialized types including the gentleman's 'bachelor's chest', chests on stands, tall double chests known as 'tallboys' and the popular Wellington and military chests. Standard, flat-fronted designs were popular in the early Georgian era then again in the Regency period. Some 18th-century models

included a 'brushing slide' which pulled out from above the top drawers on two tiny handles and was described by Sheraton as 'an additional table top on which to work.

CURVE-FRONTED CHESTS

The bow-fronted and more sophisticated serpentine-fronted chests were both Georgian inventions. Some serpentine models had fitted top drawers to accommodate toilet accessories; often they contained several lidded compartments and even fold-away hinged mirrors. These curve-fronted chests were mostly made of expensive hardwoods such as mahogany, although later in the century there was greater use of lighter woods and veneers on cheaper pine and oak carcasses.

THE RISE OF PINE

Pine chests of drawers as such were not made until the end of the 18th century. Until recently British furniture makers have considered pine to be a very second-rate wood and consequently it was mostly used for the carcasses of veneered furniture or for the simplest functional pieces. In the 18th century chests made entirely in pine were generally made for use in country cottages and farmhouses. Although similar in style to better pieces of furniture, their construction was often cruder – drawer linings were coarser and the joints less well made – but these early construction methods can now give useful clues to dating.

Because they were principally utilitarian,

▼ *While British makers used paint to disguise pine, their continental counterparts used it decoratively. This French piece in the Louis XVI style, with its gaily-painted swags and flowers, dates from 1850.*

▲ *Stripped of its layers of paint and varnish, then waxed to a soft, honey-gold shine, Victorian pine chests of drawers make attractive and functional furniture for the modern bedroom.*

most were of simple rectangular shape. Their feet were either of bracket type, with decorative shaping on the inner edges, or splayed gently outwards. Often there was a shaped apron running along the front.

CHEAP AND ADAPTABLE

As hardwoods became ever scarcer, the 19th century saw a much greater use of pine for carcass furniture. Increasing demand from a growing middle-class market meant that style and appearance often scored over the desire for quality. Pine was cheap and adaptable. As well as the use of veneers, Victorian furniture manufacturers favoured the application of thick treacly coats of varnish or stain to all kinds of woods, including pine.

Most of these stains were intended to simulate oak or mahogany, although they were sometimes grained to look more like exotic woods. The practice was largely confined to manufacturers catering for the cheaper end of the market, which was the main supplier of furniture for servants' accommodation. By the 1870s and 1880s straightforward pine chests were being turned out, with the help of mechanical processes, in huge numbers.

Five-Drawer Pine Chest

THE MASS-PRODUCED VICTORIAN PINE CHEST OF DRAWERS WAS A CHEAP, FUNCTIONAL PIECE, WITH A SIMPLE FOUR-SQUARE DESIGN AND VIRTUALLY NO DECORATION SAVE FOR THAT PROVIDED BY PAINTS, STAINS AND VARNISHES. THESE FINISHES WERE SUBJECT TO WEAR, AND MOST HAVE SINCE BEEN REMOVED.

THE FIVE-DRAWER STYLE, WITH TWO SHORT DRAWERS ABOVE THREE LONG ONES, WAS TYPICAL. MOST HAD SIMPLE KNOB HANDLES IN WOOD OR WHITE PORCELAIN.

THE CHEST TOP LIPPED OVER, AND HAD A MOULDED EDGE, WHILE THE FEET WERE ROUNDED, REMINISCENT OF BUN FEET. AS AN ADDED REFINEMENT, THE KEYHOLES WERE INSET WITH BRASS TO CUT DOWN ON WEAR IN THE SOFT WOOD.

(1) SIMPLE, FOUR-SQUARE DESIGN.

(2) MOULDED, LIPPED-OVER EDGE.

(3) WHITE PORCELAIN KNOB HANDLES.

(4) BRASS INSETS ON KEYHOLES.

(5) SHORT, ROUNDED, TURNED FEET.

Regency Chest

THIS LATE REGENCY PINE THREE-DRAWER CHEST HAS TYPICAL BRACKET FEET AND ELLIPTICAL BRASS HANDLES.

While better quality Victorian bedroom furniture made in mahogany and other hardwoods was usually in an identifiable historic style, simple pine suites were generally completely plain. Very few chests of the period had any form of carved decoration, although occasionally they were made with split-columns applied on either side of the drawers. Instead of metal handles they had either wooden knobs or rather clinical white ceramic ones. The top of the chest usually had a simple moulded edge but was sometimes completely plain.

VICTORIAN FEATURES

The overall proportion of Victorian pine chests differed from earlier examples. They were either slightly squatter and had two short drawers above two long ones of equal depth, or were conversely taller than before, still with four flights of drawers, but with the drawers made deeper than previously. The elegant bracket feet of the 18th century were replaced by heavy turned feet which were easy to mass-produce and required less skill to fit. Occasionally the legs were replaced by a solid plinth and sometimes this was shaped to form a

PRICE GUIDE · Pine Chests of Drawers

▲ CONTINENTAL MAKERS WERE MORE INCLINED TO CARVE PINE THAN BRITISH ONES. THIS GLASS-HANDLED CHEST IS FRENCH AND DATES FROM 1860.

PRICE GUIDE 6

▲ A LATE-VICTORIAN FOUR-DRAWER CHEST WITH PLAIN BRACKET FEET AND STEEL DROP HANDLES. IT HAS BEEN PAINTED TO IMITATE OAK.

PRICE GUIDE 4

▲ A FIVE-DRAWER GEORGIAN CHEST, WITH SHAPED BRACKET FEET, BRASS DROP HANDLES AND OAK COCK BEADING AROUND THE DRAWER FRONTS.

PRICE GUIDE 7

▲ A VICTORIAN VERSION OF THE FIVE-DRAWER CHEST, WITH WOODEN KNOB HANDLES AND A DECORATIVELY-SHAPED APRON AROUND THE BASE.

PRICE GUIDE 7

▲ AN UNUSUAL FOUR-DRAWER CHEST WITH A FANCIFUL, SCROLLED GALLERY TOP. THE FRONTS OF THE TOP DRAWERS ARE SHAPED SO THEY CAN BE OPENED WITHOUT HANDLES.

PRICE GUIDE 5

▲ NEW PAINT FINISHES MAKE FOR AN INTERESTING ALTERNATIVE TO STRIPPED PINE. THIS LATE-VICTORIAN CHEST HAS BEEN GIVEN A BRAND NEW LIVERY.

PRICE GUIDE 6

decorative apron at the base.

Throughout Queen Victoria's reign bedroom furniture was increasingly sold in suites. Most consisted of a chest of drawers, a washstand, a small occasional chair and a narrow wardrobe. Towards the end of the century the chest of drawers was popularly combined with the washstand by the addition of a shaped splash-back which extended from the back forwards along the sides. Dressing chests, where the chest of drawers had a mirror set between small drawers for trinkets, were another variation, but these are not all that common in pine — perhaps an indication of the low status of the wood.

STRIPPED PINE

We are so used to seeing pine furniture stripped of its original finish that it is easy to forget that the lovely natural honey colour was not originally intended to be revealed. As well as various wood finishes, towards the end of the century some pieces were painted, mostly in white, which was thought to be the most hygienic colour, or in green. Just after 1900 the progressive furniture designer Ambrose Heal successfully marketed a range of very simple bedroom furniture painted in a variety of colours.

POINTS TO WATCH

■ Less reputable dealers strip off damaged veneers on inferior 18th-century pieces to sell the revealed pine carcass.

■ A particularly elaborate piece with a serpentine front and ornate apron for example, is quite likely to have started life with a layer of veneer.

■ Hand-cut dovetails inside drawers suggest an early date of manufacture.

The Washstand

In their two hundred year history, washstands went from a genteel
luxury to a mass-produced commodity, reflecting changing tastes and
social attitudes on the way

Throughout the 18th and 19th centuries, before the widespread introduction of bathrooms, the washstand was an indispensable item of bedroom furniture. Prior to this time, there was no such object as a separate washstand. This is not to suggest that people did not wash, just that a simple table on which a jug and basin were placed was considered sufficient.

CHIPPENDALE WASHSTANDS

It was towards the middle of the 18th century that custom-built washstands first made an appearance. They were invariably made of mahogany, then the most fashionable wood. The earliest published English designs for washstands are those illustrated by Thomas Chippendale in his *Gentleman and Cabinet-maker's Director*. These were merely tripod stands in mahogany and there was a hole in the top in which a bowl could fit and two small triangular drawers set halfway down. These drawers helped keep the washstand rigid and provided storage for such things as a toothbrush and tooth powder. Occasionally a turned wooden sphere is found fitted to the top of the drawers to hold a soap-ball.

Chippendale also illustrated a more elaborate example of cabinet work which he called a shaving table. This was a small cabinet fitted with numerous drawers. The top opened out sideways to reveal a basin, smaller dishes for soap recessed into the woodwork and a mirror frame which could be pulled up and held on a catch. The mirror itself canted forward for ease of shaving.

LATE 18TH-CENTURY STYLES

By the time Hepplewhite and Sheraton published their pattern books at the end of the 18th century, the two Chippendale designs had merged. The outcome was the corner washstand. In contrast to the sweeping Rococo style used by Chippendale, these late 18th-century washstands exhibit the much straighter, simple lines typical of the period. Decoration, if there was any, was usually confined to veneered inlay.

These new washstands could vary a great deal in complexity from the basic type. Still usually made in mahogany, this had a shelf halfway up and a wooden top with one large hole for the basin and two or three smaller holes for various dishes. A splashback, also in mahogany, was fitted at the rear to protect the covering of the wall against which the washstand stood from splashes and spillages.

More elaborate versions could be fitted with a 'night convenience' – a chamber pot. A further neat adaptation was illustrated in a book by Thomas Sheraton. This washstand featured a quadrant-shaped splashback that could be folded down neatly to act as a lid.

The quality of design and workmanship lavished on washstands of this period stems from the different patterns of use of rooms in the 18th century. Bedrooms were used as much for sitting in as for sleeping in. In Sheraton's view the washstand ought to be able to 'stand in a genteel room without giving offence to the eyes'.

VICTORIAN DEVELOPMENTS

By the time Victoria ascended the throne in 1837 the final form of the washstand had begun to evolve. Much larger than the 18th-century versions, washstands were now wider than they were tall. In fact larger versions somewhat resembled a sideboard. They were often made to match *en suite* a wardrobe and dressing table. The mahogany tops and splashbacks of earlier times were replaced, at first by marble, then later by tiles, as notions of hygiene took hold.

As the size of the washstand expanded, so did the range of china it was intended to

hold. Beside the basin and soap dish, there was a sponge bowl, water bottles, tooth-glasses, large jugs to fill the basin and often a china bucket to fill the jugs. These buckets and jugs were lugged up and down stairs by the housemaids. Although the technology existed to connect running water to houses, it was still an expensive option, and servants were cheaper.

CAST IRON

The 19th century was the age of cast iron, and more and more domestic applications of this material were discovered in the course of the century. It lent itself admirably to the manufacture of washstands, and was increasingly used for them, especially in the second half of the century. Cast iron was strong, took decoration easily and, above all, was sanitary. It was much easier to keep clean than wood in an age that was for the first time becoming aware of the importance of hygiene.

After 1880 running water was fitted into most new houses and bathrooms began to be built in. However, the painted wooden washstand was still a common fitting in houses well past World War I.

◀ *The designer William Burges specialized in medieval fantasies. He created Castell Coch, the 19th-century 'castle' built for the Marquis of Bute near Cardiff. His pastiches of medieval styles included washstands. This one in gilded and painted oak inset with mirrors and mother-of-pearl and with marble basins, is typical.*

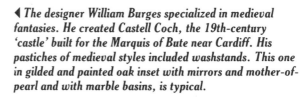

▲ *The Arts and Crafts designers also looked to the past. This solid oak stand with massive strap hinges was made for Liberty's around 1894.*

◀ *While the master bedroom would have had a magnificent mahogany or satinwood washstand, more modest quarters made do with smaller, pretty pieces in painted pine.*

▶ *The appeal of a Victorian washstand can be greatly enhanced by the addition of a collection of contemporary china. Matching sets would have included graduated jugs and bowls as well as dishes for soap and sponges.*

Art Nouveau Washstand

VICTORIAN WASHSTANDS WERE MADE TO SUIT EVERY TASTE. THIS PRETTY STAND, MADE IN THE LAST TWENTY YEARS OF THE 19TH CENTURY, SHOWS A STRONG ART NOUVEAU INFLUENCE, ESPECIALLY IN THE FLOWING, SINUOUS CARVED TENDRILS FRAMING THE SPLASHBACK AND IN THE CURVED LINES OF THE SHELF-FRONTS. THE TOP IS A SOLID PIECE OF BLACK AND WHITE MARBLE, A COLOUR SCHEME WHICH, UNUSUALLY, IS NOT REFLECTED IN THE TILES OF THE SPLASHBACK.

OTHER UNUSUAL FEATURES ARE THE PANEL-FRONTED CUPBOARD WITH BRASS HANDLE AND HINGES THAT IS SET IN THE CENTRE OF THE LOWER SHELF, AND THE NARROW SHELF ABOVE THE TILES ON THE SPLASHBACK. THIS DISTINCTIVE AND STYLISH STAND IS SET OFF BY ITS ATTRACTIVE TURNED LEGS AND MATCHING SHELF SUPPORTS.

① ART NOUVEAU CARVING

② NARROW TOP SHELF

③ TILED SPLASHBACK

④ MARBLE TOP

⑤ MATCHING TURNED LEGS AND SUPPORTS

⑥ PANEL-FRONTED CUPBOARD

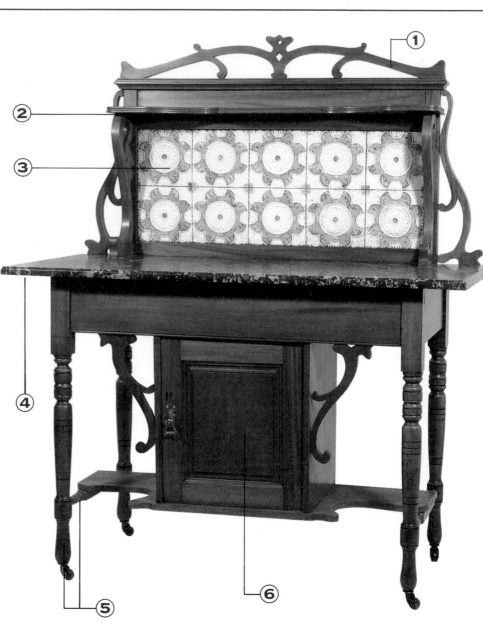

Night Convenience

THIS COMPACT WASHSTAND WITH A RECESS FOR A CHAMBERPOT IN THE DRAWER DATES FROM THE REGENCY.

Queen Victoria's long reign was marked by a succession of stylistic movements, and even a basically utilitarian piece of furniture like a washstand did not escape their influence.

The Gothic taste influenced washstands from the 1840s to the 1860s. It ranged in its effects from a complete painted pastiche of what the Victorians thought a medieval washstand would have been like, to a mere suggestion in the tiles used to cover the top and splashback.

For those with a little more money, and perhaps a little more taste, Arts and Crafts luminaries such as Morris and Robert Edis began producing unfussy, good-looking washstands in English woods from c.1870 onwards.

The Japanese style had a brief vogue in the 1870s, when washstands appeared decorated with lacquer work. However, the most popular style in the late 19th century was Georgian Revival.

Neo-Classical motifs could easily be applied to the large, sideboard-like washstand, which made it simple to incorporate in a complete suite of bedroom furniture.

London's growing legions of the middle class could go to Tottenham Court Road, where there were many furniture shops, or the new department stores such as Whiteley's in Bayswater, and buy a total 'off the peg' look for their bedrooms in a variety of styles at a price to suit their pocket. It was the same in Manchester, Birmingham, Glasgow or any other large city.

The materials used were, at

Victorian Washstands

▲ THE EXTRAVAGANT BARLEY-TWIST LEGS MAKE THIS MAHOGANY STAND ESPECIALLY DESIRABLE.

PRICE GUIDE 6

▲ THIS PINE STAND WITH ITS NARROW TURNED LEGS AND SLOPING WOODEN SPLASHBACK HAS BEEN PAINTED TO RESEMBLE BEECH.

PRICE GUIDE 5

▲ A TWO DRAWER WASHSTAND FINISHED IN SATINWOOD WITH AN ATTRACTIVE TILED SPLASHBACK.

PRICE GUIDE 6

▲ A SIMPLE, UNADORNED DESIGN, PURELY FUNCTIONAL, GIVES THIS MASS-PRODUCED STRIPPED PINE STAND A MODERNIST LOOK.

PRICE GUIDE 5

▲ THIS MAGNIFICENT SATINWOOD STAND WITH EBONY BEADING TAKES THE SHAPE OF A KNEEHOLE DESK.

PRICE GUIDE 7

▲ MAHOGANY AND MARBLE CHARACTERIZED THE BEST WASHSTANDS OF THE MID-19TH CENTURY

PRICE GUIDE 6

least in part, dictated by price. Better-quality washstands designed to appeal to the wealthy were made of mahogany or occasionally walnut.

Less expensive was beech, particularly favoured if the washstand was to be japanned or lacquered, while bamboo was in vogue from 1880 through to 1914. Sometimes beech was turned to simulate bamboo.

PINE WASHSTANDS

The rapid growth of towns and cities during the 19th century made for a huge increase in the demand for cheap furniture in general, and improving standards of cleanliness made for an increased demand for washstands in particular.

The cheapest, and thus by far the commonest, timber used for washstands was pine, which was invariably painted. Using paint to simulate the grain and texture, skilled makers could disguise their softwood washstands as mahogany, walnut, or any other exotic wood. By using stains, they could make them look like satinwood.

Sadly, many of the splendid painted finishes have been taken off in recent years as a result of the fashion for stripped pine.

The pine washstands were at first topped with marble, but again the increased demand from the new cities was for a cheaper, more adaptable material and tiles were used instead. Necessity was turned to advantage and these became the main decorative feature of later washstands.

POINTS TO WATCH

■ Try to preserve any original finish as in the future such pieces will be difficult to find.

■ If the washstand has been stripped, check that all the caustic soda, which shows up as a white powder, has been removed.

■ Avoid pieces with wide gaps in the grain of the wood, caused by poor stripping.

■ Marble and tile tops and splashbacks should be checked for chips; top and splashback should be in the same style.

■ If there are any drawers fitted, check inside to make sure that the handles are the original fittings.

The Wooden Bed

Almost forced off the market in the 1830s by the introduction of iron and
brass bedsteads, the wooden bed came back later in the century in a
variety of guises

In the furnishing of her new flat, the independent Edwardian woman, with progressive views and a modest income, looked for affordable furniture which conformed to Arts and Crafts principles and which, in the bedroom at least, was designed on hygienic lines. Her choice of bed was therefore a simple wooden bedstead, devoid of canopy and drapes, consisting of a frame supported by a plainly designed headboard and footboard.

STATUS SYMBOLS

In its design and lack of pretention, this early 20th-century bed had more in common with the relatively plain, unadorned sleeping platforms of ancient times than with its immediate predecessors. From medieval times to the end of the 19th century this essentially practical piece of furniture became the symbol of a household's wealth.

The familiar four-poster of Elizabethan times consisted of the bed frame itself, the bedhead, the canopy or tester and two columns, all made of wood, usually oak. With its bedhead panelled and embellished with richly carved inlays and with bulbous columns supported by pedestals, this was a massive, magnificent piece of furniture. As one of the most expensive items in a wealthy household, it was a prized possession bequeathed in wills from heir to heir. Few of such beds have survived intact but an example such as the Bed of Ware shows how splendid such pieces were.

In the 17th century, richly embroidered drapes (always a feature of early beds, for warmth and privacy) all but obscured the wooden framework, which was now worked in walnut and beech as well as oak. This was also the age of the state bed, frequently set on a throne-like dais, taller and more extravagantly carved than its predecessor and enveloped in rich textile 'furniture' topped with coloured plumes. Throughout the 18th century, a range of four-posters appeared, along with angel or half-testers, French dome beds, tent and couch beds, all constructed in a variety of woods and with surfaces veneered, lacquered, japanned, gilded or painted.

DECLINE OF THE WOODEN BED

The brass and iron beds that made their first appearance in the 1830s virtually ousted the wooden bed for several decades.

In the unhealthy living conditions engendered by the Industrial Revolution, metal beds were deemed more hygienic than wooden beds with their dusty curtains. Although broken up and discarded, many of the posts and panels from these venerable pieces reappeared later in the century as manufacturers vied with each other to offer reproductions of Queen Anne or Early Georgian beds 'in which genuine old posts are employed.'

Although metal beds continued to be produced in countless numbers throughout the century, the wooden bed was gradually reinstated from about 1850 and in a greater variety of styles than ever before. A series of exhibitions from 1851 onwards had educated the prosperous middle classes in the decorative styles of the past; they liked what they saw and not least was their appreciation of the bed's former role as a symbol of wealth and status. Perfectly happy to accept reproductions of what was deemed right and fitting for their forbears, the public created a new demand and the trade willingly obliged them by offering representations of period bedrooms in catalogues and showrooms.

▶ *The Edwardian style is an attractive and accessible style for today's bedrooms, lending lightness and charm even to small rooms.*

▼ *This Regency rosewood bed in the Classical style was made for Lord Stuart at the beginning of the 19th century. The architectural design is enhanced by ormolu ripple moulding outlining the panels, by the free-standing columns and the scrolled finish to the headboard and baseboard. The cover is ivory silk.*

◀ *Progressive young women often looked to France for stylistic ideas. White-painted, wooden-framed beds were an integral part of the French look.*

▶ *Made of walnut and with ormolu Egyptian motifs, this French lit en bateau is contemporary with Napoleon's North African campaigns.*

Retailers such as Gillows, Heal's (established 1810) and Shoolbred's all produced catalogues advertising their respective interpretations of so-called Grecian, Gothic, Elizabethan, Italian Renaissance and French Rococo styles.

MODERN FOUR-POSTERS
The 'Elizabethan' four-poster was popular as early as the 1830s; its enduring appeal lay, according to one critic, in its 'indis-

putedly British' nature – 'it was rich without being vulgar and its coarse vigour did not overtax the somewhat limited finesse of the average British carver'. As late as 1911, Liberty's were offering one in their catalogue, retailing for £90. Shoolbred's medieval half-tester bed, illustrated in their 1876 catalogue and available in 'oak, American ash or Kawrie pine' is largely inspired by the work of Gothic revivalist and architect, A. W. N. Pugin, whose State Bed for the Speaker's House in the Palace of Westminster it faintly resembles.

Gillows showed Adam-style furniture at the Paris Exhibition of 1878, prompting *The Cabinet Maker* to remark (in 1881) 'How admirably the Adam's style lends itself to the chaste decoration of bedroom furniture'.

Heal's, who sold only bedding and bedroom furniture until the 1880s, were in the forefront of the styles race. Although their 1852 catalogue illustrates no fewer than 67 patterns of iron and brass beds, the same catalogue was largely devoted to mahogany four-poster and half-tester bedsteads in an astonishing variety of styles. One example, a half-tester in 'Renaissance' style, stands 9ft (2.7m) tall 'with carved stumps, handsomely carved foot board and cornice' and sold for £14.

For those with aspirations to the heights of grandeur, and a purse to match, Heal's staged a set of bedroom furniture at the International Exhibition of 1862 in South Kensington, especially designed by J. Braune in the Louis-Seize style. With mahogany furniture enamelled a soft shade of cream including gilded ornament carved in lime wood, and a magnificent half-tester with embroidered satin and cerise silk hangings, it cost a staggering £2000.

Sheraton Revival

BEDROOM SUITES REVIVING CLASSIC FURNITURE STYLES WERE MADE IN THEIR THOUSANDS IN THE EDWARDIAN PERIOD. HIGHLY MECHANIZED WORKSHOPS ATTEMPTED TO RECREATE HAND-CRAFTED PIECES WITH VARYING SUCCESS. THIS METAL-FRAMED MAHOGANY BED HARKS BACK TO THE ERA OF THOMAS SHERATON, AT THE BEGINNING OF THE 19TH CENTURY.

THE BOW END IS A TYPICAL REGENCY FEATURE, AS ARE THE SQUARE, TAPERING LEGS. THE BED IS VENEERED IN WALNUT WITH BOXWOOD STRINGING OUTLINING THE PANELS. THE MACHINE-CUT MARQUETRY WORK IN THE CENTRE PANELS ADDS TO THE ATTRACTIVENESS OF THE PIECE, AND WOULD HAVE BEEN CARRIED THROUGH ON THE REST OF THE SUITE.

1 SQUARE-SECTIONED TAPERING LEGS

2 BOW END

3 MACHINE-CUT MARQUETRY PANELS

4 METAL FRAME SCREWED TO END-BOARDS

Modern Conversion

MASSIVE VICTORIAN BEDS ARE TOO BIG FOR MODERN BEDROOMS. THIS MAHOGANY BED HAS BEEN SCALED DOWN BY REPLACING THE HEADBOARD WITH THE BUTTONED-VELVET TAILBOARD.

The reproduction beds produced for the wealthy middle-class market in the second half of the 19th century were only marginally influenced by the work of leading designers such as A. W. N. Pugin and William Burges, whose pieces were specially commissioned by aristocratic clients or made for a few important exhibitions. Although the Arts and Crafts Movement, initiated by William Morris, championed a revival of natural materials and hand craftsmanship, by the turn of the century even their artistic creations, conceived to counter commercialism, were being commercially produced and marketed by progressive firms such as Heal's and Liberty's.

AMBROSE HEAL

Liberty's were producing bedroom suites in the Anglo-Japanese style made fashionable by designers such as E. W. Godwin and C. F. A. Voysey while at Heal's the head of the firm, Ambrose Heal (1872-1959), had begun designing furniture himself. Described by one critic as 'the only man in the retail trade of that time who had any real interest or knowledge of design', Heal successfully married Arts and Crafts ideals with commercial know-how. While

·PRICE GUIDE·

Wooden Beds

▼ MADE ENTIRELY OF BEECH, THIS SPANISH BED OF AROUND 1900 HAS A LIGHT FRAME AND NO CASTORS.

PRICE GUIDE **6**

▲ THE RAILS AND FRAMING OF THIS PINE BED FROM 1840 HAVE BEEN TURNED AND STAINED TO IMITATE BAMBOO.

PRICE GUIDE **7**

▼ A FRENCH BED FROM THE 1880s IN THE GRAND MANNER, MADE OF WALNUT AND WITH SHORT CABRIOLE LEGS.

PRICE GUIDE **7**

▲ THIS METAL-FRAMED MAHOGANY BED HAS A SIMPLE SLATTED CONSTRUCTION WITH BOXWOOD STRINGING.

PRICE GUIDE **6**

▼ PART OF A SUITE, THIS BED, PAINTED TO RESEMBLE LACQUER WORK, IS A 1920s VERSION OF A LATE-VICTORIAN THEME.

PRICE GUIDE **7**

▲ A RAIL-END FROM SPAIN IN STAINED BEECH. LIGHT WOOD-FRAMED BEDS WERE POPULAR.

PRICE GUIDE **7**

the elegant, ebonized and inlaid beds produced by Morris & Co were inaccessible to the masses because of their high cost, Heal brought good design at more affordable prices to his Tottenham Court Road store.

PLAIN AND SIMPLE

Heal's first designs were illustrated in his 1898 catalogue, *Plain Oak Furniture,* and in *Simple Bedroom Furniture* published the following year. He named his plain oak furniture after English seaside towns – St Ives, Newlyn – and despite the indebtedness of some of it to Morris and Voysey, it has a freshness and simplicity wholly

lacking in other commercially produced bedsteads.

In keeping not only with 'art' styles but also the views of sanitarians, the beds were generally uncanopied with plain, almost austere head boards and feet. In 1900, Heal won a Silver Medal at the Paris Exhibition for a bedroom suite of lightly fumed oak, wax polished and inlaid with ebony and pewter. The twin beds with hangings designed by Godfrey Blount show considerable individuality in design and also Heal's excellent cabinet making, a feature praised by *The Architectural Review* as a 'triumph of craftsmanship'.

By about 1904 Heal was beginning to enjoy public recognition and commercial success. His simple, stylish furniture was particularly suitable for the growing number of suburban villas and houses in the new garden cities. His cottage bedsteads and later painted beds show the same simple design principles coupled with expert craftsmanship. Heal himself wished to be remembered as a man who revived the true craftsmanship of which 'that man of genius William Morris was the inspiration'. He succeeded, for, almost singlehanded, he brought good design at modest prices to the high street.

POINTS TO WATCH

■ Genuine early oak four-posters are rare and very expensive. Most are of fine quality and have a good provenance.

■ Many apparently 'early' beds are made up of old posts and panelling from various unlikely sources. Look carefully for keyholes and the like in unusual places.

■ Reproduction beds in period styles were produced in vast numbers in the second half of the 19th century; all were machine made.

■ Reproduction early 'oak' beds can be found made entirely of plastic, so check carefully before buying!

The Octagonal Table

Since the 16th century, octagonal versions of many different types of table have been produced, from work tables and card tables to large centrepieces for fashionable rooms

A large octagonal centre table of the Edwardian period was likely to be made in the fashionable reproduction 18th-century style. The best examples were made of glossy, dark mahogany, to quite a plain design with only a restrained amount of decoration. Such a piece looked well in a gentleman's smoking room or study. While its symmetry was pleasing to the eye, the sobriety of its design suited masculine taste. This, together with the table's comparatively unusual shape, gave a distinguished and dignified look to a room.

Octagonal tables are less common than their round, square or rectangular counterparts. Being in essence a variant of conventional tables, they do not form a specific group, nor were they made for one specific purpose. Indeed, they were made to suit almost as wide a range of functions as other tables, from the general – as in the case of a centre table, useful for any need and every purpose – to the particular – as in card and work tables.

17TH CENTURY AND EARLIER

Octagonal tables have been known in England at least since the 16th century. Rare and precious examples, inlaid with marble and standing on a pedestal base, were prized in Renaissance times. From the 17th century, more workaday eight-sided tables, made of solid oak, were not infrequently seen in the English home.

Like much other Jacobean furniture, these early octagonal tables were sturdily constructed. A boldly carved and arcaded frieze ran round the eight sides below the table top. The eight legs, often turned or fluted, were joined by a solid ground-shelf fixed a few inches above floor level.

Very like the round tables of the time, these octagonal tables measured just three feet (90 cm) across. Variations were made with a centrally hinged top and gateleg, and could be folded and placed flush against a wall. The Jacobean octagonal table probably served no distinct purpose and must have been equally ideal for reading or writing, for taking a solitary meal, or for sharing a jug of ale.

18TH-CENTURY ELEGANCE

The octagonal tables of the 18th century, on the other hand, tended to be made for specific purposes, and varied accordingly in their size and design. Heavy oak and sturdy

centre tables stood on four rather than eight legs; these were slender and tapering and ended in elegant pad feet. The frieze below the table-top was now plain, and the folding top and gateleg system became increasingly uncommon.

In later Georgian times, after the mid 18th century, the octagonal shape was applied overwhelmingly to tripod tables, standing on a twisted stem and three outward-curving feet. The octagonal top was also frequently applied to the newly created work table, standing on four tapering legs and fitted with a drawer and sometimes a work bag for needlework hanging below. In both tripod and work tables, the shape of the table-top was often elongated, making it more of a rectangle with cut corners than a regular octagon.

REGENCY SPLENDOUR

By the beginning of the 19th century, Regency fondness for symmetry saw a return to the perfectly octagonal table top. The form was now favoured for quite large centre tables; the most ornate were decorated with cross-banding in a contrasting wood, and were supported on four outward-curving legs ending in brass paw feet set on castors.

The octagonal pedestal table was another characteristically Regency type. Decoration, both to the table-top and the legs, could be extravagant. The table-tops were splendidly inlaid with contrasting slabs of coloured Italian marble. The rosewood

frieze below was often inlaid with brass, and the supporting pedestal embellished with three-dimensional gilt chimerae, swags and other neo-Classical motifs.

Smaller octagonal marble-topped tables of the period were, typically, supported on four legs that began in the shape of gilt lion's heads and ended in gilt paw feet. The decorative value of such pieces probably outweighed their practical usefulness. Such splendour was not to be seen again until mid-Victorian times.

VICTORIAN STYLES

Octagonal versions of practical centre tables, as well as smaller work tables, writing and card tables, continued to be made into early Victorian times. The shape was also convenient for tables in which the top was deep enough to contain drawers — one at each facet of the octagonal frieze.

Revivalist styles dominated. Octagonal tripod tables in 18th-century style were made in large numbers. Octagonal pedestal tables, their supports adorned with neo-Rococo motifs, became quite ornate. A nostalgic revival of 'Olde Englishe' furniture styles encouraged a return to heavy oak.

It was, however, the Gothic revival led by A. W. N. Pugin, and put into practice by William Burges and others, that promoted the popularity of some of the most highly decorated octagonal tables. Their interest in Gothic, as well as oriental and Moorish shapes and designs, in which the octagon is a central feature, resulted in finely inlaid and intricately carved eight-sided centre tables.

The vogue for octagonal tables was continued in a plainer, more manageable and certainly more practical version of Pugin's Gothic revival designs. Typical versions stood on a pedestal or four legs joined by cross-stretchers. Their sturdy, 'honest' construction was also at one with hand-crafted furniture promoted by Morris and the Arts and Crafts Movement. Nevertheless, into the Edwardian era, revival styles drawn from the 18th century were by far the most commercially successful.

◀ *An unusual octagonal table, with eight legs joined by stretchers and no central column, forms the centrepiece of this picture of a Georgian revival interior, painted just before World War I.*

▲ *An early 19th-century oak octagonal library table in the master bedroom of West House, Chelsea. Oak was seldom used for fine furniture by this period – its coarse grain makes it difficult to carve.*

construction had been swept out of fashion – the Georgian taste was for more refined furniture mostly in walnut and, later, mahogany.

As a more gracious lifestyle evolved, so furniture became more specialized. The octagonal shape was applied to centre tables as well as to writing tables, work tables and little 'occasional' tables, such as card tables.

By comparison with its heavy oak predecessors, the early Georgian octagonal table was refined and delicate. Octagonal

▲ *This George III mahogany tripod table exhibits a typically understated elegance.*

▶ *A. W. N. Pugin was at the forefront of the Gothic Revival. This rich table, its inlaid walnut top resting on ogee arches, was made in 1847.*

Edwardian Octagonal Table

THIS ELABORATELY CARVED AND INLAID MAHO-GANY TABLE IS A COMPENDIUM OF THE EDWAR-DIAN CABINETMAKER'S DECORATIVE TECHNIQUES. THE SPLENDIDLY SCROLLED LEGS, FINISHED WITH CARVED LEAVES, INLAID BELLS AND BRASS CASTORS, ARE JOINED TO THE CENTRAL SHELF BY FRETWORK SUPPORTS, GIVING THE TABLE LIGHT-NESS AND STRENGTH.

THE OCTAGONAL TOP IS INLAID WITH A FLORAL MARQUETRY PATTERN ON A WALNUT GROUND EDGED WITH SATINWOOD, WHILE THE SATINWOOD APRON IS FINISHED WITH A STRIP OF WALNUT WHOSE GRAIN IS SET AT RIGHT-ANGLES TO THAT OF THE SATINWOOD, A TECHNIQUE KNOWN AS 'CROSS-BANDING'.

① ORNATELY CARVED AND INLAID LEGS.

② PIERCED SUPPORTS FOR LIGHTNESS AND STRENGTH.

③ BRASS CASTORS.

④ INLAID TOP.

⑤ DECORATIVE CROSS-BANDING.

Faded Glory

COLOURED VENEERS FADE WITH TIME. WHEN FIRST MADE, THIS TOP HAD VIVID SHADES OF GREEN AND RED.

Islamic Style

THIS SMALL MIDDLE-EASTERN OCTAGONAL TABLE IS INLAID WITH TEAK, EBONY AND OTHER EXOTIC WOODS PLUS MOTHER-OF-PEARL.

The octagonal table continued to be seen in the home into late Victorian times in both progressive or revival styles. Most examples were by now in the form of medium-sized centre or occasional tables as the demand for fussy little card and work tables began to fade.

REVIVAL STYLES

For popular taste, there was the commercially produced centre table in simplified 18th-century style. Proportions were slender and the wood most often rose-wood or mahogany. The thinly cut table-top, with bevelled edges, was supported on eight tapering legs joined by stretchers radiating from a central column. An arcaded apron joined the legs a foot or so below the top.

The taste for 18th-century revivals continued beyond the turn of the century and into Edwardian times. The 18th-century style octagonal table of the 1910s and 1920s was ele-gant yet of solid construction. Gadrooning was a favourite form of decoration around the rim of the top. The system of eight radiating stretchers was retained; in typical revival examples of the Edwardian period, these were pierced and fretted in 'Chippendale' style.

Small octagonal tripod tables of the type made so profusely during the 18th century were another characteristically Edward-ian type of revival furniture. Although they were almost exact replicas of their 18th-century prototypes, their octag-onal tops were larger in propor-

Octagonal Tables

▼ THIS PINE GYPSY TABLE OF THE 1880S IS OF A TYPE USED BY SHOWMEN AND TRAVELLERS. ITS LEGS UNSCREW FOR EASE OF TRANSPORTATION.

PRICE GUIDE **5**

▲ A WALNUT TRIPOD TABLE FROM THE 1880S WITH AN ELABORATE MARQUETRIED TOP DISPLAYING A STAR MOTIF.

PRICE GUIDE **6**

▼ AN EDWARDIAN MAHOGANY TABLE WITH A SCOLLOPED TOP AND APRON AND CARVED ACANTHUS LEAVES AT THE TOP OF THE LEGS.

PRICE GUIDE **5**

▲ A LATE VICTORIAN TABLE MADE OF THUJA WOOD, OR ARBOR VITAE, A CONIFER SIMILAR TO CYPRESS, POPULAR WITH VICTORIAN CABINETMAKERS.

PRICE GUIDE **6**

▼ THIS TABLE TOP IS VENEERED WITH ROSEWOOD AND INLAID WITH SATINWOOD. THE TURNED LEGS, DELICATE GALLERIED SHELF AND ORIGINAL BRASS CASTORS ALL ADD VALUE TO THE PIECE.

PRICE GUIDE **6**

▲ THIS SIMPLE, ELEGANT, EDWARDIAN MAHOGANY TABLE HAS WALNUT CROSS-BANDING AND STRINGING.

PRICE GUIDE **5**

tion to the stem and tripod.

The pleasing symmetry of the octagonal shape was not confined to reproduction furniture, however. The eight-sided table-top also featured both in Art Nouveau designs and in furniture made by craftsmen working in the tradition of the Arts and Crafts Movement.

ART NOUVEAU

Octagonal tables in Art Nouveau style, made by members of the Glasgow school, for example, tended to have eight legs arranged in symmetrical pairs. Art Nouveau decorative motifs, inlaid into the wood, were usually restricted to the legs and frieze.

Octagonal tables made in the Arts and Crafts tradition tended to be larger than Art Nouveau-style examples. Decoration was kept to a minimum and the frieze below the table top reduced to a purely functional feature. The ground shelf was dispensed with altogether. In keeping with the aim for simplicity, the stretchers were

also quite plain. One of the most important craftsmen working in this tradition was Ernest Gimson, of the Cotswold school of furniture makers.

Both Art Nouveau and Arts and Crafts furniture, including octagonal tables, came to be made commercially. Traditional furniture was the overwhelmingly popular choice, however. For all the novelty of Art Nouveau and the 'honest craftsmanship' of the products of the Cotswolds school, among others, an octagonal table in

18th-century style, factory-made in dark mahogany, appealed to the serious good taste that characterized the conservative aspect of the Edwardian era.

POINTS TO WATCH

■ Make sure veneer has not split, peeled or blistered.

■ The weakest point of tripod tables is where the legs join the stem. Most have metal strengtheners.

■ Check for cracks in curved legs where the grain is weak.

The Gateleg Table

The gateleg table, with its traditional design, was a popular reproduction
piece in many conservative, middle-class Edwardian homes

Until the late 18th century, dining rooms with massive central tables were not at all common. Early tables either came in two parts, top and bottom, or they folded up. A great deal of use was made of trestles. One of the earliest references to a folding table came in a will of 1502 when one John Coote of Bury St Edmunds mentions 'the best faldyn table' in the hall.

EARLY GATELEGS

The gateleg is an essentially 17th-century solution to the problem of supporting the top of a folding table. The flaps of a gateleg are supported on a frame which is fixed to the bottom stretcher and to the underframe and swings out like a gate. So obvious is the resemblance that it comes as a surprise to find that the term 'gateleg' was not applied to this sort of table until the 19th century.

The earliest use of the gateleg was on side-tables with a single, semi-circular drop leaf. By the 1640s, this had developed into a free-standing table with two leaves and six legs – two of them on gates. English gateleg tables of this period had round or oval tops; Dutch versions were often rectangular, sometimes square.

A CENTURY OF FASHION

The heyday of the gateleg's popularity ran from the middle of the 17th century to the middle of the 18th century, and they continued to be produced as 'country' furniture for a further 100 years.

The reason for their decline in popularity in fashionable households lay in changing eating habits. The 17th-century custom was for people to eat at several small tables in a large room; a party of 10 or 12 people in the 1670s would be accommodated in small groups at two or three gatelegs. By around 1750, this had changed to everyone being seated at one large, solid table. This explains both why 17th-century gatelegs are still relatively common and also why large examples are rare.

Although gateleg tables went out of mainstream fashion, a variation, more suited to use as a light occasional or side table, became popular. In the mid-18th century appeared the drop-leaf table, a close relation of the gateleg but distinguished from it by the lack of bottom stretchers. Made of mahogany, or oak and mahogany, it had only four legs, two of which were hinged

from the middle of the frame to swing out and support the flaps, making a four-legged circular or oval table. On early versions the legs were of cabriole form, later they were square with the back chamfered off.

VARIATIONS

Gateleg tables came in a variety of guises. The finest were the large double-gate (that is, with two gatelegs on each side) tables of the last half of the 17th century. The accounts at Windsor Castle record one in 1686 as an 'Ovall Wanscott table 6 ft 6 ins long and 4 ft 6 ins broad, with a Turned Frame (the Table made to fould)'.

At the other end of the scale, there were also variations for small occasional use. One type had an oval one-piece top that hinged up vertically when not in use and was set on

▲ *Although 17th- and 18th-century gatelegs were used as dining tables, Edwardian reproductions were often on a smaller scale and intended for side or occasional tables. They helped lend a traditional 'Jacobethan' touch to many different kinds of rooms in both country cottages and town houses.*

two cruciform gates that folded flat. Another small table had two trestle ends joined at the top and bottom with two gates fitted to swing outward from the middle; a variation on this theme was to replace the trestle ends with a single turned support.

SIMPLE CONSTRUCTION

The construction of a gateleg table was fairly straightforward. A frame of four legs joined by stretchers and an underframe was

◀ *This George I table is made of yew-wood, a favourite of country furniture-makers. It has a rich honey patina, column-turned legs and a typical brass drop-handle.*

▼ *Tables with double gatelegs are an unusual but impressive variation of the standard gateleg form. This one from 1690 is 6ft 3ins (1.90 metres) long with the flaps up.*

oped in the 1840s and proved very successful. What is so noticeable about Sutherland tables is the narrowness of the top when the flaps are both folded down; it is no more than 9 inches (23 cms).

The narrow top is held up on two, sometimes four, turned end supports, while the deep leaves rest on gates that, like the drop-leaf table, have no bottom stretcher. Sutherland tables were invariably fitted with castors.

Highly-figured walnut veneer was the preferred finish for the tops of Sutherlands but they were also made of plain mahogany, ebonized beech or plainer, less-figured walnut, which was often enhanced with inlaid decoration.

pegged and tenoned together. On early examples, the top was also pegged and glued into place. After 1700 it was often fixed by hand-cut screws. The gate usually had a wooden hinge; holes were drilled in the stretcher and the underframe, and the gate slotted in so that it could pivot freely.

Early gateleg tables, before 1670, had tongue and groove joints where the flaps were hinged to the main part of the top. Later examples had a rule joint to the flaps, which swung on metal hinges – butterfly-shaped wrought-iron ones on early examples, oblong on later ones.

At first, legs were simple and square in section, but very soon they came to be seen as an excellent opportunity for the turner to show his art. Boldly-turned legs became a distinctive decorative feature At first, single twists were fashionable; around 1680 double barley-sugar twists first appeared, while by 1700 baluster turnings were the most common. A long narrow drawer was commonly fitted into the frieze at one end of the table below the top, and the frieze itself could also be shaped.

Oak was the most commonly used wood, sometimes with an elm top, while solid walnut was favoured for the best quality tables. Yew was also used, as were fruitwoods such as apple and cherry, in country versions.

Inlaid decoration was rarely used. Because the tables were generally made of solid wood and not veneered, the top of a gateleg rarely has much figure to it, though good tables acquire superb patination and colour over the centuries.

THE SUTHERLAND TABLE

In the 19th century gatelegs were still made, but were generally considered provincial curios, though reproductions of earlier styles had their adherents. A variation of the gateleg, the Sutherland table, was devel-

▶ *A genuine old gateleg table makes an attractive centrepiece. Fully extended, it can seat six comfortably and the rich, dark patination of old oak complements most colour schemes.*

Edwardian Gateleg Table

THIS IS A TYPICAL MASS-PRODUCED LATE-VICTORIAN OR EDWARDIAN VERSION OF THE GATELEG TABLE. ALL EIGHT OF THE LEGS HAVE BEEN MACHINE-TURNED TO IDENTICAL BARLEY-SUGAR TWISTS. THE INSIDE OF THE GATELEG HAS BEEN NOTCHED TO CORRESPOND WITH A SIMILAR NOTCH IN THE BOTTOM STRETCHER, SO THAT THE GATE FITS FLUSH WHEN THE FLAPS ARE FOLDED DOWN. EACH LEG ENDS IN A MODIFIED BUN FOOT.

THE OVAL TOP IS EDGED WITH THUMB MOULDING. THE TABLE WAS TREATED WITH A DARK STAIN WHEN NEW TO SIMULATE AGE, BUT USE AND ASSIDUOUS POLISHING HAVE WORN AWAY THE FINISH, REVEALING THE LIGHT WOOD BENEATH, PARTICULARLY ON THE LEGS AND AROUND THE EDGE OF THE TOP.

① THUMB MOULDING AROUND EDGE

② LIGHT WOOD SHOWING THROUGH STAIN

③ MACHINE-TURNED BARLEY-SUGAR TWISTS

④ NOTCHED LEG AND STRETCHER

⑤ MODIFIED BUN FEET

Corner Table

THIS HIGHLY CARVED EDWARDIAN CORNER TABLE HAS A SINGLE BOBBIN-TURNED GATELEG TO MAKE IT A SQUARE SIDE TABLE.

Moulded Join

THE THUMB MOULDING IS CARRIED THROUGH AROUND THE EDGE OF THE FIXED TOP SO THAT IT SHOWS WHEN THE FLAPS ARE NOT IN USE.

Furniture in Victoria's reign was dominated by stylistic revivals. The Sutherland table was one of only a few new forms of furniture developed.

The main reason for this was the Romantic movement and a tendency to look backward to a sentimentalized past rather than face up to the somewhat harsh realities of rapid industrialization. Gothic was the main revival style in the 1840s and 1850s, but by the 1860s a new generation of designers had transferred their allegiance to the more recent styles of Queen Anne, associated with the advent of elegance and simplicity.

SWEETNESS AND LIGHT

Houses of the Queen Anne Revival, or 'Sweetness and Light' as it was sometimes called, were typified by those of the architect Richard Norman Shaw. His large, handsome, well proportioned red-brick houses can still be seen today in the Bedford Park area of west London.

Furnishing such houses in the correct style called for a choice between original antique furniture and reproduction. At this time, antique furniture was simply regarded as old, and it was relatively cheap.

This made it attractive to the young middle-class people with artistic leanings but a lack of funds, who formed the backbone of the movement. Much of our present-day interest in antique furniture has its roots in the Queen Anne Revival, and this is the reason why pictures of late Victorian rooms show gateleg tables and similar furniture.

At first, there was more than

Gateleg Tables

▼ THE SIMPLE, SQUARE GATELEGS AND THE MASSIVE UNDER-FRAME OF THIS EDWARDIAN OAK TABLE ARE BOTH UNUSUAL FEATURES.

PRICE GUIDE **6**

▲ A CARVED TOP USUALLY INDICATES A LATE VICTORIAN OR EDWARDIAN TABLE. THIS COMPACT OAK TABLE DATES FROM 1900.

PRICE GUIDE **5**

▼ AN EDWARDIAN TABLE IN UNSTAINED LIGHT OAK. THE CUT CORNERS AND PIE-CRUST MOULDING ON THE TOP HELP TO ADD INTEREST.

PRICE GUIDE **5**

▲ THIS VICTORIAN TABLE IS VENEERED IN WALNUT. UNUSUAL FEATURES INCLUDE A WIDE FRAME AND DIFFERENT TURNINGS ON THE GATE.

PRICE GUIDE **7**

▼ HERE THE GATELEG IS ADOPTED FOR AN EDWARDIAN TABLE WITH ARTS AND CRAFTS INFLUENCES. NOTE THE INLAID LEGS AND TOP.

PRICE GUIDE **6**

▲ AN EDWARDIAN SUTHERLAND TABLE IN STAINED OAK WITH FOUR TYPICAL SPINDLE END SUPPORTS AND A SINGLE TURNED STRETCHER.

PRICE GUIDE **5**

enough genuine old furniture to go around but, as the historical look became more popular, re-productions filled the gap in the market. Besides, not everyone liked the idea of second-hand items. Reproduction gatelegs became a very popular piece of furniture in their own right in the late Victorian and Edwardian periods and were still being made in the 1930s.

REPRODUCTIONS

Reproduction tables are gene-rally easy to recognize. They were darkened to simulate the deep, rich patination of age, and close inspection will reveal that the colour – close to black in many cases – is only on the surface. On the edges the colour will have worn off, revealing unstained timber. Many tables were made in Virginia walnut, a naturally dark wood that does not take a polish.

Modern machine-made screws and hinges also indicate reproductions, but most telling of all are the turnings of the legs and gates, invariably rather skimpy and effete in comparison with the bold, robust work found on earlier pieces. All turning was done on machine-lathes, giving a uniformity to the legs that is simply not seen on earlier hand-turned examples.

Reproduction was not the only option. Sadly, it was just as popular to adapt – some would say mutilate – genuine old pieces of furniture.

Gateleg tables suffered badly. New tops were married to old bases and, worst of all, carving was added to the top in the strange belief that it would make the table look more genuinely old.

POINTS TO WATCH

■ Look underneath the table. Pieces aged by staining will be all one colour, while original old tables will vary.

■ Make sure top and bottom match in colour and style.

■ Look at screws and hinges to see if they have been dis-turbed in any way.

■ Avoid 'carved-up' tables which have added decoration on the top.

■ Check that the feet are original. Early gatelegs stood on stone floors and oak feet wore down and broke easily.

Cane and Wicker Furniture

Lightness, durability and comfort were the hallmarks of well-made cane
and wicker furniture and such qualities made it ideal for use in the
Edwardian conservatory

The Edwardian conservatory was not a place for formal occasions or for the family's most expensive and heavyweight furniture. It was far rather a room for relaxation, for loafing around, for taking tea on return from the beach or from a walk in the countryside. Attractive cane and wicker fitted the requirements very well and although popular in all sorts of other situations, it particularly suited Edwardian conservatories. These were well-stocked with a range of chairs, tables, cake stands and flower baskets which were often as decorative as they were practical.

AN ORIENTAL IMPORT

Cane and wicker furniture can be made from a variety of materials including willow, rush, even spun wood-pulp fibre, but the most usual is rattan. Canework first became popular in Britain during the reign of Charles II when the thriving East India Company brought canes from rattan palms back to Britain from the Malay Peninsula. The split canes, long, thin and flexible, were fixed to wooden frames and interwoven to form an attractive, fine mesh in a number of patterns.

The Great Fire of London in 1666 contributed greatly to the success of cane. After the Fire, there was such a demand for cheap, readily available furniture that cane manufacturers could hardly cope. Traditional furniture-makers complained, and even petitioned – unsuccessfully – for restrictions on cane furniture.

Nevertheless, cane soon became accepted as a standard furniture material with the backs of seats of all types of wooden furniture being embellished with decoratively woven inserts. In the 18th century, Sheraton advised the use of cane for anything where lightness, elasticity and durability ought to be combined. As the years passed, more and more uses were found for this versatile material, with items ranging from bed steps, to bed ends, and even babies' cribs.

BENTWOOD FURNITURE

Canework continued to be popular throughout the 19th and well into the 20th century. The innovative German designer, Michael Thonet, was responsible for significant developments in the range of cane furniture in the second half of the 19th century. He

▲ *Versatile cane and wicker was extremely popular with the Victorians and Edwardians who used it both inside and out.*

established the techniques of bending wood for furniture frames, and expanded the established methods of bending veneers. Thonet's bentwood furniture became one of the most abundant and popular styles of the century, and because his styles and methods frequently used cane in chair backs and

seats, they influenced canework furniture makers all over the world.

A VOGUE FOR WICKER

The shaved bark of rattan canes was not the only part used in furniture-making. The flexible inner core offered its own possibilities too and, together with willow and reed, it spawned an enormous quantity of lightweight wicker furniture in the 19th century. Basket-making, from which wickerwork furniture is descended, is probably the oldest craft in Britain, and certainly predates the Romans. In contrast to canework, where the strands are woven together into a mesh, wickerwork is dependent upon stiff but flexible rods, around which the osier is woven. Plaited straw and osiers made the most comfortable medieval chairs, and wicker remained common for furniture through the ages.

The Victorian period saw wicker furniture become particularly elaborate. Exoticism of all kinds had a strong appeal and a whole range of fanciful shapes, cobweb-like patterns often incorporating oriental motifs, were made from both rattan and willow. Curvaceous lines and scrollwork edgings framed intricately woven palms, fans, feathers, hearts and sunbursts. First popular for the porch or the garden, wicker pieces were soon brought inside the house to the parlour, bedroom and nursery.

By Edwardian times the most ornate styles had virtually disappeared with important designers leading the way towards new sturdy, practical-looking designs. Simple beauty and skilful weaving became the order of the day. Cane furniture continued to be popular and the variety of both cane and wicker ware available to the Edwardians was remarkable. Nursery furniture, tea waggons, lemonade stands, log-baskets all appear in catalogues alongside the more conventional solid-wood chairs and tables. Because they were light, cane and wicker pieces could be moved around the conservatory and out into the garden without too much effort.

▼ *Woven cane was also used to make highly sophisticated furniture. This fine Regency sofa has a cane-filled seat and back set into an elaborate, carved-mahogany frame.*

▲ *The simple charm of antique wicker gives an attractive period feel to today's conservatories, while contemporary pieces look good alongside.*

▼ *One of a pair of ebonized wood chairs designed by George Walton with cane seat and back c.1896; the lightness of the cane perfectly complements the elegant, slender shape.*

Edwardian Wicker Chair

WICKER HAS BEEN IN USE SINCE ANCIENT TIMES — INITIALLY IN THE CRAFT OF BASKET-MAKING, AND LATER IN THE MANUFACTURE OF FURNITURE. THE LIGHTWEIGHT YET STURDY QUALITIES OF WICKER WORK MADE IT IDEAL FOR SEATING, AND IT WAS ENTHUSIASTICALLY TAKEN UP BY THE VICTORIANS AND LATER THE EDWARDIANS.

MANY DESIGN IDEAS WERE BROUGHT BACK FROM THE EMPIRE AND THEY RANGED FROM THE MERELY FANCIFUL TO THE OUTLANDISH. IN FACT, THE VERSATILITY OF WICKER WORK WENT SOME WAY TOWARDS APPEASING THE ALMOST INSATIABLE VICTORIAN APPETITE FOR NOVELTY. FOR THE MOST PART, HOWEVER, DESIGNS SUCH AS THIS PAINTED EDWARDIAN EXAMPLE WERE PRACTICAL AND USED TRADITIONAL BASKET-WEAVING TECHNIQUES. CHAIRS WERE EXTREMELY COMFORTABLE — CRAFTSMEN MADE SURE THAT THE OSIER WAS CLOSELY WOVEN AND THE END OF EACH PIECE WAS CAREFULLY WRAPPED IN. AROUND THE TURN OF THE CENTURY WICKER FURNITURE BEGAN TO BE MADE IN MATCHING SETS WHICH INCLUDED CHAIRS, SETTEES, TABLES, OCCASIONAL TABLES, EVEN ROCKING CHAIRS. EVERY HOME WOULD HAVE HAD SOME USEFUL AND AESTHETICALLY PLEASING ITEMS.

1. INTRICATE WEAVING ON PARTS THAT REQUIRE THE GREATEST STRENGTH

2. STOUT CROSS-MEMBERS FOR STABILITY

3. DECORATIVE REINFORCEMENTS

4. OPEN-WORK BACK

5. SIMPLE, CIRCLE-PATTERNED SEAT

6. PAINTED SURFACE ON ALL BUT SEAT CENTRE

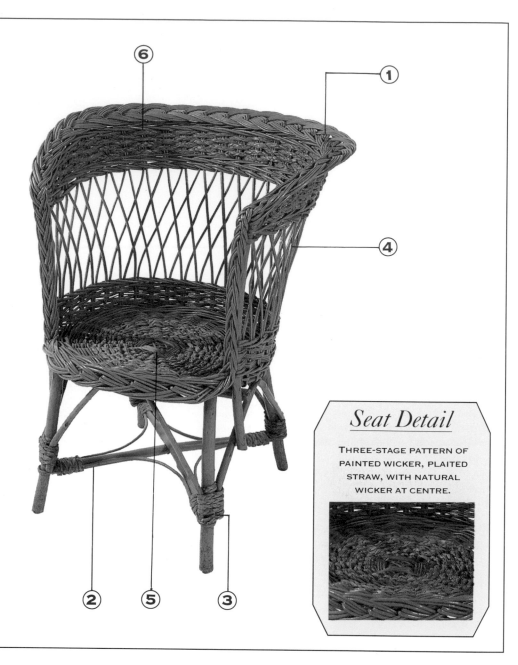

Seat Detail

THREE-STAGE PATTERN OF PAINTED WICKER, PLAITED STRAW, WITH NATURAL WICKER AT CENTRE.

Dryad Chair

A CLASSIC BRITISH DESIGN BY HARRY PEACH AT THE DRYAD CANE WORKS (C.1910).

By the first decade of the 20th century cane and wicker was arriving in Britain from all corners of the world. Not only was it available in a variety of styles but buyers could choose from a good range of colours. A great deal of furniture, however, was supplied in its natural colour, and it was common practice to paint it. The colour most often used was white – an inheritance from the hotter parts of the Empire, where items had to be white to avoid damage from the intense sunlight.

Apart from the Empire, cane and wicker came to Britain from both America and Europe, and Britain itself had its own industry centred in Leicester.

HOME PRODUCTION

Dryad, established in 1907, were one of the major manufacturers of the time and their craftsmen, trained at Leicester School of Art, were taught that 'the art of making cane chairs lay not in the decoration put on them, but in the soundness of their construction and fitness for their purpose'. Dryad also emphasized the importance of good frames, which were usually hardwood or cane, and of good finishing.

Dryad designs, although influenced to a certain extent by products from Austria and Germany, emerged as unmistakably English classics. Rounded back chairs were typically expansive and big scaled with their flaring arms and many had full-length skirting.

AMERICAN WICKER

On the other side of the Atlantic, Gustav Stickley produced a

Cane and Wicker

▲ EDWARDIAN TWO-SEATER SETTEE MADE OF HOOPED CANE WITH CHECK-PATTERNED SEAT AND BACK

PRICE GUIDE **5**

▲ EDWARDIAN WICKER THREE-SEATER WITH CURVING, FULL-LENGTH SKIRT AND DIAMOND INSETS

PRICE GUIDE **5**

▼ EDWARDIAN WICKER ARMCHAIR WITH ATTRACTIVE CURVILINEAR SHAPE.

PRICE GUIDE **4**

▼ EDWARDIAN CANE TABLE, PART OF A SET WITH FOUR MATCHING CHAIRS IN EXCELLENT CONDITION.

PRICE GUIDE **8**

▲ BLACK-PAINTED VICTORIAN ARMCHAIR WITH WOVEN SEAT, BACK AND ARMRESTS WITH LOOPED INSERTS.

PRICE GUIDE **5**

▲ ATTRACTIVE, SQUARE-BACKED CHAIR DATING FROM THE EARLY PART OF THE 20TH CENTURY.

PRICE GUIDE **4**

line of striking new-look wicker called Craftsman. Stickley shared Morris' reverence for honest craftsmanship and his quest for simple beauty resulted in sturdily built pieces which were both practical-looking and reasonably priced. His designs were a strong reaction against the earlier Victorian curvaceous fantasies and were distinctly boxy and masculine in their appearance.

American wicker, generally, was extremely successful in Britain. When the two largest companies, Heywood Brothers and Wakefield Rattan Company merged in 1897, one of their first steps was to open warehouses in London and Liverpool. Inexpensive and fashionable imported pieces, ranging from rocking chairs to office chairs, were sold in their thousands.

EUROPE'S CONTRIBUTION

The influx of imported wicker was increased by high quality German and Austrian products. Generally angular in structure, these pieces were as modern as any conventional wooden furniture of the period. Austrian wicker was particularly stylish, often incorporating novelty patterns and leather upholstery.

Whatever else, wicker was always made to be practical and not simply as high-craft furniture; the best-made pieces have survived from the 19th and 20th century in surprisingly good condition.

POINTS TO WATCH

■ Cane and wicker items needing only simple renovation can frequently be picked up at very low prices.

■ Always inspect items carefully for signs of woodworm infestation. Furniture that has been used outdoors is particularly susceptible.

■ Look out for weakened or cracked strips of cane, especially in chair seats.

■ Painted cane or wicker can be smartened up by repainting but be aware that this is likely to affect the value of some items of furniture, so ask advice first.

■ Modern cane and wicker continues to be popular so inspect the feet of items for authentic signs of wear.

The Bergère Chair

With its clean and simple lines, the classic Bergère chair was both
comfortable and serviceable. It was useful in almost any room but was
most often seen in the library, parlour or boudoir

Essentially a slender, lightweight
armchair with a low back and
downward-curving arms, a typical
bergère had the back, seat and space below
the arms filled with woven cane. Sometimes
the seat was padded and often a loose,
shaped cushion was fitted in to it.

Bergère chairs were popular from the
18th century through to the 1930s and
beyond. Although fashions in ornament
changed, bergère chairs generally retained
their simple lines. They were always
pleasing to the eye and, with their elegant,
unobtrusive shape, harmonized with the Art
Deco designs with which the most fashion-
conscious woman chose to decorate her
boudoir.

THE FRENCH STYLE

The bergère chair originated at the court of
Louis XV in the middle of the 18th century
as a low, round-backed armchair which the
ladies of the court found particularly convenient, as it amply accommodated their
fashionably extravagant petticoats. Like
other chairs and sofas of the time, the early
French bergère was not caned, but richly
upholstered with tapestries. The woodwork, including curving cabriole legs, was
waxed, painted or gilded.

ENGLISH ADAPTATIONS

The low armchair was soon introduced into
England, at a time when many new and
stylish forms of furniture were being made.
The bergère was anglicized as a 'birjair',
'burjair' or 'berjair' by cabinet-makers and
designers such as Thomas Chippendale and
Thomas Sheraton.

These 18th-century bergères were either
upholstered or caned, with woodwork in
mahogany or walnut. Like the French
prototype, they had low, arched backs and
low seats. In one version, the back was
straight and set at right angles to the arms;
in another, the back curved around to join
the arms in a single flowing line.

Ornately upholstered chairs had their legs
and exposed woodwork carved with beading, fluting, husks or leaves, and the arms
ended in elegant scrolls. According to
fashion, the wood might also be japanned or
painted. The upholstery might be of coloured leather, silk or damask. Thomas
Chippendale made a number of these
luxurious upholstered bergères as commis-

sions from his wealthier, fashionable clients.

The 18th-century caned bergère was a
less exuberant piece of furniture. Caned
furniture had been popular in the 17th
century, and Thomas Sheraton was largely
responsible for bringing it back into fashion
around 1785. Although based on an
upholstered prototype, the caned bergère,
round or square-backed, with a mahogany
frame, was essentially a new, classic style of
furniture.

During the Regency, bergère chairs took
on an exotic form as the classical styles of

▲ *With its classically simple lines and pure
geometric shape, a bergère chair could happily
harmonize with any room decorated in the Art
Deco style. This one sat in the lounge of fashion
designer Paul Poiret's riverboat.*

ancient Rome, Greece and Egypt captured
the imagination of furniture designers. The
most extravagant chairs in the new style had
prominent curved backs, massive armrests
in the shape of chimeras or lion's masks, and
legs ending in bold paw feet. Additional
ornament sometimes took the form of stars

and leaves. The most striking caned bergères had ebonized frames set off with gilding or brass inlay.

After about 1815, bergère chairs regained their 18th century simplicity; now, however, the back legs often swept outwards and the chair was set on castors. Some had frames carved and painted to simulate bamboo.

VICTORIAN REVIVALS

Early Victorian taste looked back to the playful curves of the Louis XV period. The Victorian Rococo bergère retained its plain caned seat and arched back but the woodwork of its frame was scrolled and curved. The front of the seat curved outward in the centre and in again at the sides, and the legs were turned into S-shaped cabrioles that ended in paw feet; this fashion lasted through the 1840s and 1850s, but had run its course by 1880.

By this time, most furniture was mass-produced. The firm of Morris, Marshall, Faulkner & Co, founded by William Morris to recreate traditional crafts, included among its hand-made furniture a simple square-backed bergère with a discreetly turned frame. Like most Arts and Crafts products, however, a hand-made bergère was beyond the budget of most households.

Late Victorian mass-produced bergères returned to the simpler, classic lines of the late 18th century. The main differences were that the seat was now set lower and the back now rose higher. The woodwork was typically waxed or gilded.

▲ *The Art Deco ideal of co-ordinated design is expressed in this bergère painted and upholstered to pick up the floral theme and the colourways of the wallpaper and bedspread.*

▼ *Gilt wood was also used in the bergères of the 1920s and 1930s, but with more restraint. In this French chair, most of the decorative value is in the vivid upholstery.*

◀ *Regency bergères were opulent gilt fantasies. This one has chimera heads, animal legs and feet, stars and Egyptian winged sun motifs.*

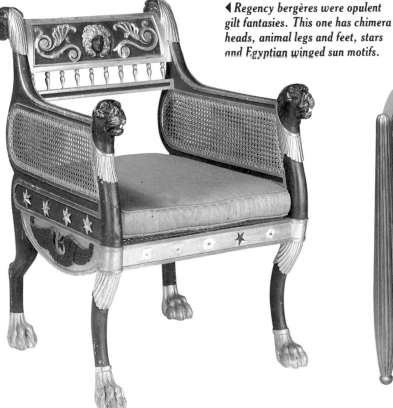

The Upholstered Tub Bergère

AS WELL AS THE STANDARD CANE BERGÈRES, 1930S DESIGNERS PRODUCED UPHOLSTERED VERSIONS WITH A DEEP SEAT AND A LOW, CURVED BACK WHICH WAS CONTINUED THROUGH THE ARMS IN A SINGLE SWEEPING LINE.

THESE TUB BERGÈRES HAD A SIMPLE, LIGHT WOODEN FRAME, WITH NO CARVING OR TURNING. RIBBED PANELS OF EBONIZED WOOD WERE TYPICALLY USED BENEATH THE ARMS OF THE CHAIR INSTEAD OF CANE INFILL.

THE LOW, PADDED, SPRUNG SEAT WAS COVERED WITH A THICK FITTED CUSHION UPHOLSTERED IN THE SAME FABRIC — NEVER A COMPLEMENTARY OR CONTRASTING COLOUR. THE DEEP LOW SEATS MEANT THAT TUB BERGÈRES WERE SELDOM MADE WITH LEGS; THEY EITHER SAT STRAIGHT ON THE FLOOR OR, AS HERE, ON SHORT, BROAD FEET.

① PLAIN WOODEN FRAME WITH LIGHT WOOD VENEER FINISH

② SIDES FILLED WITH PANELS OF RIBBED, EBONIZED WOOD

③ CURVED ARMS CONTINUING THE LINE OF THE LOW, CURVED BACK

④ SHAPED, SPRUNG, UPHOLSTERED CUSHION SET IN A DEEP, LOW SEAT.

⑤ SHORT, BROAD FEET

Art Deco Bergère

THIS TUB BERGÈRE IS ATTRIBUTED TO JACQUES EMILE RUHLMANN, DOYEN OF FRENCH ART DECO DESIGNERS. IT MIXES A SIMPLE, EVEN SEVERE, DESIGN WITH SUMPTUOUS, LUXURY MATERIALS.

The cane-backed bergère was a popular piece of furniture in the first 40 years of the 20th century. It looked well in the less cluttered interiors of post-Victorian Britain and was included among the traditional factory-made furniture for which there was a continuing demand.

The design of bergère chairs was not greatly affected by the avant-garde Edwardian fashion for Art Nouveau or the later vogue for Art Deco. Following conservative taste, bergère chairs were made in 'Jacobethan' and other revivalist styles.

'Jacobethan' bergères were square-backed, with a solid oak frame and bobbin-turned arms and legs. The addition of a bobbin-turned stretcher between the front legs added to the Jacobethan look. Such pieces were considered the perfect furnishings for the Tudor-style houses of the 1920s and 1930s.

Bergères imitating 19th-century styles had a more graceful appearance and were usually made of mahogany. Some were based on Regency bergères and had gently downward-curving arms. The rear legs curved back and out and the front legs were decorated with discreet carving. They were supplied by Heal's and Liberty's among others.

·PRICE GUIDE·

Bergère Chairs

▲ A 20TH-CENTURY CANED BERGÈRE IN THE STYLE KNOWN AS JACOBETHAN, SHOWING A CARVED OAK FRAME.

PRICE GUIDE **6**

▲ NOT A BERGÈRE; THE HIGH BACK AND WINGS ON THIS 20TH-CENTURY OAK CHAIR MARK IT OUT AS A COMPOSITE STYLE.

PRICE GUIDE **6**

▲ THE WOODEN INSET PANEL IN THE BACK ALLOWS FOR A DECORATIVE CIRCULAR WEAVE IN THE CANE.

PRICE GUIDE **5**

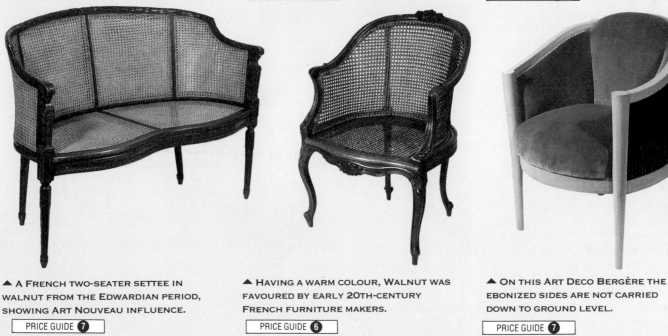

▲ A FRENCH TWO-SEATER SETTEE IN WALNUT FROM THE EDWARDIAN PERIOD, SHOWING ART NOUVEAU INFLUENCE.

PRICE GUIDE **7**

▲ HAVING A WARM COLOUR, WALNUT WAS FAVOURED BY EARLY 20TH-CENTURY FRENCH FURNITURE MAKERS.

PRICE GUIDE **6**

▲ ON THIS ART DECO BERGÈRE THE EBONIZED SIDES ARE NOT CARRIED DOWN TO GROUND LEVEL.

PRICE GUIDE **7**

A third revivalist style popular in the 1920s and 1930s was based on the designs of George Hepplewhite and Thomas Sheraton. The frame was carved with neo-classical motifs and painted, and the cane in the back of the chair was often inset with a small round or oval painted panel. Satisfying the demand for suites of furniture, increasingly popular after 1900, manufacturers also made revivalist bergères in sets of two or more with matching settees.

Although most bergère chairs were very solidly made, their cane back, seat and arms and their light wooden frame – the very features that give these chairs their distinctive look – also work to their disadvantage. The cane tends to weaken the construction of the chair, and is itself subject to considerable strain, wear and tear.

Furniture in the Art Deco style was not produced in great quantity. Only those with the most radical tastes – and the financial resources with which to indulge them – would take the dramatic step of furnishing their homes in the new, angular style. Most households, even in those adventurous times, continued to buy pieces of traditional, practical furniture, of which the bergère was a typical example.

POINTS TO WATCH

■ Check that the legs are firmly attached to the seat rail, and that the back and arms are equally secure.

■ Make sure the canework is taut and securely attached to the frame.

■ Try to preserve any original paint, padding or upholstery.

■ Worn or damaged cane is best replaced rather than mended.

The Three-Piece Suite

Adding a master touch of comfort and luxury to the middle-class living room, the three-piece suite came to symbolize the advantages of suburban life

Although three-piece suites have been made since the 18th century, their popularity is essentially a 20th-century phenomenon. The classic suite of two padded and sprung armchairs and matching settee was developed in response to the increasing number of middle- and working-class families who wanted, and could afford, the luxury of comfortable, upholstered furniture, but who lived in houses with relatively small rooms.

The rise of the three-piece suite was helped by falling prices that resulted from the development of mass-production techniques in furniture-making and from the introduction of new, often synthetic, materials, particularly towards the end of the 1920s.

DESIGNER INFLUENCES

Art Deco, the set designs of Hollywood movies and an intellectual infatuation with mass-production techniques – even in one-off pieces – all affected the look of 1930s designer furniture. Art Deco designers produced pieces for a very small market, a wealthy and fashion-conscious avant-garde who sought out furniture that was self-consciously modern and, as far as possible, totally rejected traditional principles.

The new International Style designers, including de Stijl in Holland, Gropius and the Bauhaus group in Germany and leading architect-designers such as Le Corbusier and Mies van der Rohr were at the centre of the evolution of modernist design.

They saw furniture as the perfect medium for the expression of functional design principles. As a result, much of the furniture they designed is more concerned with making a point about the fundamental nature of furniture than it is with its comfort and practicability.

THE ART OF THE MACHINE

A keystone of the theoretical approach of avant-garde designers was a belief in the values of the machine. They broadly shared the principle that their designs should be egalitarian in nature, capable of mass production and have the simple, unfussy shapes, clean lines and streamlined surface simplicity of the machine-made.

Despite this principle, many of the top Art Deco designers produced pieces that could be afforded only by a wealthy elite. These pieces, ranging from chairs in plywood – then a relatively new material much

valued for its flexibility – to elaborate sofas and outrageously sumptuous bedroom furniture, may have had the simple lines modernist thinking required but were never seriously intended to be mass produced for use in ordinary homes.

This was not always the case. The furniture company Thonet, for example, employed Le Corbusier to design tubular steel furniture, and the British firm PEL used the work of Wells Coates.

ACCESS TO THE MASSES

In the 1930s, mass production was more a matter of economics than aesthetics. British manufacturers catered for the mass market by producing furniture that married economical manufacturing techniques with stylistic flourishes adapted from the work of the leading designers.

The result of this compromise was a hybrid style that combined mainstream Victorian flamboyance with the leaner,

▶ *Many 1930s three-piece suites have survived into the 1980s where they have become popular additions to modern interiors. Most prized are those with their original upholstery — usually a durable woven fabric, moquette, leatherette, leather, or, as here, a combination of these. Worn pieces can easily be re-covered.*

◀ *The 1930s three-piece suite was designed with both style and comfort in mind. The distinctive geometric lines and often small dimensions of typical suites were perfectly suited to the modern interiors of the new suburban semi-detached houses and compact town flats of the period.*

▲ *With the introduction of new mass production techniques in the 1930s, aesthetics gave way to functional considerations.*

more functional look of the 1930s. At its worst, the style produced ranges of thoroughly banal, utilitarian furniture. At its best, it was represented by well made, comfortable and stylish pieces that harmonized well with the Deco ideal of integrated interior design.

NEW MATERIALS

The process of translating advances in design into mass-produced furniture was aided by the introduction of new materials. Chromed tubular steel frames replaced wood as the basis for many different types of furniture. Foremost in popularizing this style in Britain was the firm PEL (Practical Equipment Ltd.), a subsidiary of Tube Investments formed to make furniture inspired by Le Corbusier's designs for Thonet.

Upholstered furniture achieved a new frugality of style in the products of such manufacturers as Parker-Knoll and Bowmans, who incorporated wooden armrests and bases.

Expensive traditional coverings like wool, leather and hide were replaced by cheaper materials like calico and the synthetic, rexine. This could have a dramatic effect on price. An upholstered easy chair in hide cost around £25 in 1934; the same chair in a cheaper material cost around £7.

SURFACE STYLES

Three-piece suites tended to conservatism in their design. In the typical 1930s middle-class living room, pure Art Deco may have existed in the design of small tables, mirrors and vases, while the three-piece suite was still of an essentially mainstream shape, but

given the surface appearance of Art Deco by the use of modernist fabric designs such as geometric shapes in bold, primary colours, or motifs drawn from Modernist schools of painting or tribal art.

In the later 1930s and the 1940s, three-piece suites tended to adopt more simple shapes but reverted to plainer styles and colours as used by designers such as Sir Ambrose Heal and Gordon Russell.

Much of today's furniture owes a heavy debt to the 1930s. Some of it is a deliberate attempt to recreate Art Deco styles, but much more follows the design principles and production techniques of over 50 years ago.

▼ *One of the leading Art Deco craftsmen was Maurice Dufrène, known for his lavish designs, as reflected in this sumptuous four-piece Beauvais tapestry and giltwood salon suite*

DESIGN IN FOCUS

The Two-Seater, Drop-End Sofa

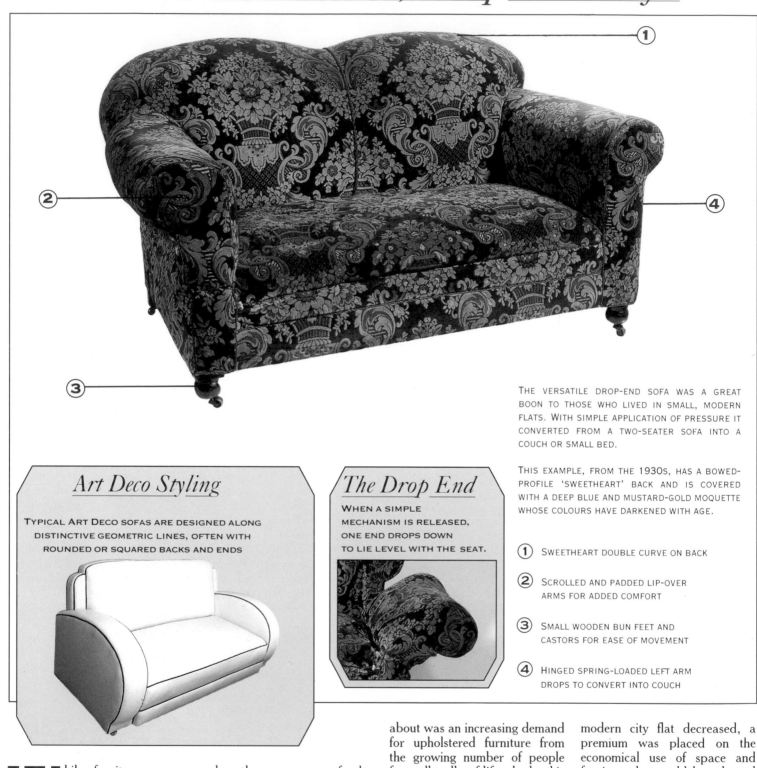

THE VERSATILE DROP-END SOFA WAS A GREAT BOON TO THOSE WHO LIVED IN SMALL, MODERN FLATS. WITH SIMPLE APPLICATION OF PRESSURE IT CONVERTED FROM A TWO-SEATER SOFA INTO A COUCH OR SMALL BED.

THIS EXAMPLE, FROM THE 1930S, HAS A BOWED-PROFILE 'SWEETHEART' BACK AND IS COVERED WITH A DEEP BLUE AND MUSTARD-GOLD MOQUETTE WHOSE COLOURS HAVE DARKENED WITH AGE.

① SWEETHEART DOUBLE CURVE ON BACK

② SCROLLED AND PADDED LIP-OVER ARMS FOR ADDED COMFORT

③ SMALL WOODEN BUN FEET AND CASTORS FOR EASE OF MOVEMENT

④ HINGED SPRING-LOADED LEFT ARM DROPS TO CONVERT INTO COUCH

Art Deco Styling

TYPICAL ART DECO SOFAS ARE DESIGNED ALONG DISTINCTIVE GEOMETRIC LINES, OFTEN WITH ROUNDED OR SQUARED BACKS AND ENDS

The Drop End

WHEN A SIMPLE MECHANISM IS RELEASED, ONE END DROPS DOWN TO LIE LEVEL WITH THE SEAT.

While furniture generally took on a less ornate, more functional look in the early part of the 20th century, upholstered furniture such as the two-seater sofa often retained the basic style set in the Victorian era, with padded lip-over arms, although more modern styles such as the square arm sofa also sold well. Backs were either high, with rounded ends or took on the double curve which, in its most pronounced form, came to be known as the Sweetheart back.

The drop-end sofa was one of the most popular styles. The major factor in bringing this about was an increasing demand for upholstered furniture from the growing number of people from all walks of life who by this time lived in smaller accommodation. City populations were still growing, but the increase now was not in workers for the factories but in clerks and other office workers, many of whom lived in purpose-built blocks of flats or converted family houses.

As the average size of the modern city flat decreased, a premium was placed on the economical use of space and furniture that could be adapted to serve more than one function.

The bed-settee was ideal for studio and one-bedroomed flats and was much easier on the eye than a wall bed, and the drop-end sofa, compact and easy to convert, was for many people the ideal form of bed-settee.

Typically, the left arm of a

·PRICE GUIDE·

Sofas, Armchairs and Suites

▼ STRIKING ART DECO DESIGN WITH A U-SHAPED SEAT FRAME AND ROUNDED, STEPPED BACK. THE ARMCHAIR HAS BEEN RE-COVERED IN BLACK VELVET.

PRICE GUIDE **5**

▼ LARGE ARMCHAIR RE-COVERED IN BEIGE LEATHERETTE WITH CONTRASTING PIPING AND FABRIC COVERED CUSHION. PART OF A THREE-PIECE SUITE.

PRICE GUIDE **5**

▲ STURDY, NARROW-BACKED ARMCHAIR WITH LOW SEAT AND ORIGINAL UPHOLSTERY IN BROWN LEATHER.

PRICE GUIDE **7**

◄ PART OF A 1930s THREE-PIECE SUITE WITH ORIGINAL UPHOLSTERY IN A CUT-NAPPED PINKISH BEIGE FABRIC.

PRICE GUIDE **6**

▼ THREE-SEATER SOFA WITH ELABORATELY FLUTED, SHELL-SHAPED BACK. PART OF A SUITE.

PRICE GUIDE **6**

▼ A SOFA WITH A HINT OF ART DECO STYLING IN THE ARMS AND LEGS WHICH ARE PANELLED WITH BIRD'S EYE MAPLE.

PRICE GUIDE **7**

---

drop-end sofa was adjustable. It could be lowered to lie flush with the seat of the sofa either with a spring action or, like Sir Ambrose Heal's Knole settee, by an attached rope. Heal's design had straight sides rather than lip-over arms and was closer in style to the settees of previous centuries than to modern sofas. It was functional, with some of the angular simplicity of Tudor furniture and

represented a revolutionary break with the generally available contemporary styles.

Mass production and the influence of the machine aesthetic meant that traditionally-styled sofas had lost their elaborate baluster and cabriole legs in favour of shorter, sturdier wooden supports and castors for improved manoeuvrability. Feather-down cushions replaced stuffed-over seats and backs.

Pure Art Deco styles were the province of the wealthy and adventurous. Few people would feel that one of Jules Leleu's flauntingly asymmetrical sofas would harmonize with their other furnishings; besides, they cost the same as a small house.

The Art Deco influence was most apparent in upholstery fabrics. Even the most conventional sofas were covered in flamboyant Deco patterns.

POINTS TO WATCH

■ Check that the mechanism is in good working order and moves freely.

■ Check the upholstery; a degree of wear is acceptable and shows authenticity, but the cost of re-upholstering sofas can prove prohibitive. Re-covering may be less expensive.

■ Remove loose cushions to check that there are no loose or protruding springs.

The Wardrobe

In the Art Deco period the wardrobe, like most other furniture,
underwent a dramatic 'modernization' in style but it still owed
much to its 18th- and 19th-century beginnings

Behind large doors, the Art Deco
wardrobe had shelves, drawers and
rails which catered for almost every
item of a gentleman's dress. As well as
being useful, a wardrobe in the Art Deco
style was smart and attractive. For the
wealthy and fashionable gentleman of the
1920s and 1930s, it could also be supplied
with matching chair, small table and chest of
drawers; the ensemble created a totally
modern look in the dressing room.

Although fine clothes have always been
well cared for, the familiar wardrobe as we
know it today – with shelves, drawers and
hanging space – originated only in the 18th
century, comparatively late in the history of
furniture. It actually developed from the
linen press – a combined cupboard and
chest of drawers which was used for storing
clothes as well as household linen.

THE EVOLUTION OF THE PRESS
By the early years of the 18th century new
forms of press were beginning to be made.
The great oak types of the previous 200
years were rarely seen in important houses –
heavy oak furniture of all kinds had gone out
of fashion. Clothes cupboards continued to
be incorporated into the panelling of dressing rooms and bedrooms but they were now
made of painted deal rather than dark oak.
Free-standing presses, meanwhile, had
become noble and imposing. They followed
the arrangement of drawers below a hanging
shelved cupboard but were built in the tall,
architectural style; the most typical were
topped by a pediment supported on pilasters. Walnut and, later, mahogany, were
the most popular woods.

Fashions in furniture of the later 18th
century were many and varied, and the
clothes press kept pace with them all. An
innovation of the time was sliding shelves
that could be pulled out. The drawers in the
lower section now tended to be arranged as
a double bank of one long drawer with two
half-drawers above. The cabriole legs
raised the press – or wardrobe, as it was
now called – high off the ground.

Later in the century, neo-classical motifs
replaced rococo scrolls as typical wardrobe
decoration. Fine japanning, often in gold
and silver, or painting with neo-classical
themes, enlivened their flat surfaces. The
effect was light and delicate. Satinwood,
especially favoured by the 18th-century
furniture designer Thomas Sheraton, was
exploited for its attractive grain.

*◄ In the 1930s,
wardrobes were made
in a wide range of
woods. Walnut and
mahogany were the
most popular, though
some designers
experimented with
more exotic varieties.
This wardrobe by Heal
& Son uses a mixture
of macassar ebony
with ivory detailing.*

THE 19TH-CENTURY WARDROBE
By the early 19th century, the largest
wardrobes became monumental and imposing and were extremely spacious inside. The
Regency mahogany break-front wardrobe
for instance was wider than it was tall; a
central section consisting of drawers with
cupboard above was flanked by two tall
cupboards, either fitted with extra shelves
or with pegs.

Ordinary wardrobes, consisting of the
conventional arrangement of drawers below
a cupboard, lost none of their popularity,
however. Some of these were made with a
long mirror fixed inside one of the doors as
an additional selling feature.

Until the 19th century it was usual for
long and bulky outdoor clothes to be kept
downstairs or in passages in special built-in
cupboards. As customs changed, the
capacity of wardrobes increased accordingly, and by Victorian times, the large-

drawers for storing folded garments, complete with flush-fitting brass knobs or handles. Today the shape and design of such handles on wardrobe doors and drawers can be helpful in dating pieces.

The wardrobe with or without a mirror continued as standard bedroom furniture throughout Victorian times although space-saving built-in cupboards continued to be popular as well. In some households, where, perhaps, such luxuries could not be afforded, clothes were even kept in makeshift wardrobes consisting merely of a curtain hung across a chimney recess.

BEDROOM SUITES

By late Victorian times, when the fashion for matching sets of furniture was becoming well established, many wardrobes could be purchased as part of a suite with other bedroom furniture; although this might vary considerably, it most often consisted of a wash stand, chest of drawers, chairs, and, of course, a bed.

The desire to furnish bedrooms as tastefully as dining or living rooms produced a continuing demand for bedroom suites which factory production easily supplied.

Up until the turn of the century and into Edwardian times, revivals of classical 17th- and 18th-century furniture styles dominated the overall look of most commercially produced bedroom suites. By 1900, however, these were replaced by more modern designs, and wardrobes and bedroom suites in Art Nouveau style had become the most highly fashionable.

scale wardrobe with deep hanging space was firmly established. Victorian wardrobes reflected a number of successive furniture styles. One after the other, waves of revival styles swept across furniture design. Elizabethan, Gothic and Louis XIV were just a few of the styles resurrected before an attempt at purer forms was made by the exponents of the Anglo-Japanese or Arts and Crafts ideals in the second half of the 19th century.

All these made their mark on wardrobe design and ornamentation. However, perhaps the most typical model had a plain but bold cornice, a central door mounted with a long mirror, on either side of which lay two mock door panels. Most wardrobes still had a deep drawer above a plain lower plinth, although in some double-door wardrobes, the hanging space extended right to the floor. Some of the best-made examples still incorporated a system of shelves and

▲ *By the 1930s the idea of buying wardrobes as part of a matching set of bedroom furniture was well established, and suites of matching wardrobes, chests of drawers and beds were often deliberately incorporated into bedroom designs. This picture shows the interior design for a bedroom by French 1930s architect and designer Eric Bagge.*

◄ *Many Art Deco wardrobes were sumptuous, verging on the outrageous, in design. This example, made by Heal & Son, was covered with silver-grey spot satin edged with green braid, and had glass handles and a silver plinth.*

The Art Deco Wardrobe

THE ART DECO WARDROBE TOOK MANY FORMS, RANGING FROM REVIVALS OF CLASSICAL 17TH- AND 18TH-CENTURY STYLES TO THE MORE GEOMETRIC-LOOKING, MODERNIST PIECES GENERALLY ASSOCIATED WITH THE PERIOD.

THIS EXAMPLE, MADE OF BIRD'S-EYE MAPLE, IS A SKILFUL COMBINATION OF BOTH. THE SERPENTINE FRONT AND BRACKET FEET USUALLY ASSOCIATED WITH THE 18TH CENTURY HAVE BEEN ADAPTED TO CREATE AN ART DECO LOOK THAT IS COMPLETED BY THE CHROME AND PLASTIC HANDLES. THE DOOR OPENS TO REVEAL A FULLY FITTED INTERIOR, CONTAINING A MIRROR AND EXTRA CUPBOARDS.

① SERPENTINE-STYLE FRONT OF BIRD'S-EYE MAPLE VENEER

② CHROME AND PLASTIC HANDLES

③ MIRROR AND GLASS-FRONTED CUPBOARDS

④ CLASSICAL BRACKET FEET HAVE BEEN SLIGHTLY ADAPTED FOR A 'DECO' LOOK

⑤ DRAWERS AND INTERIOR OF MAHOGANY

Classical Revivals

THE LIGHT, ELEGANT LINES OF SHERATON FURNITURE WERE MUCH IMITATED IN THE 1930S. THIS MAHOGANY WARDROBE, WITH ITS DELICATE CARVINGS, IS A TYPICAL EXAMPLE.

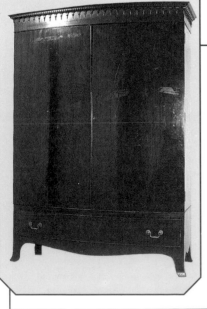

Demand for wardrobes and bedroom suites continued throughout the 1920s and 1930s. For those with traditional tastes, a whole range of furniture continued to be made in the styles of the 17th and 18th centuries.

Wardrobes and bedroom suites made in revival styles enabled people to create the complete Tudor or Georgian bedroom. More adventurous buyers chose Oriental-style lacquered or painted wardrobes, which had also been popular in the 18th century. Otherwise, there was the Queen Anne style, with wardrobes and dressing tables on cabriole legs, Chippendale examples in mahogany, and the Sheraton style, in which satinwood veneer (or, these days, cheaper maple) predominated.

SIMPLICITY AND TASTE

For some tastes, revival styles were too fancy. Priding themselves on simplicity and good taste, Heal & Sons offered a range of wardrobes and bedroom furniture of strictly simple design, in fumed or polished oak. The smallest wardrobes in the range were basic hanging cupboards with a single door; others had two or three doors, with drawers below, or consisted of a bank of drawers between two hanging sections.

Revivals of past styles on the one hand and simplicity of outline, such as that favoured by Heal & Sons, on the other, did not completely dominate furniture design in the 1920s and 1930s. Novelty was to be found

·PRICE GUIDE·

Wardrobes

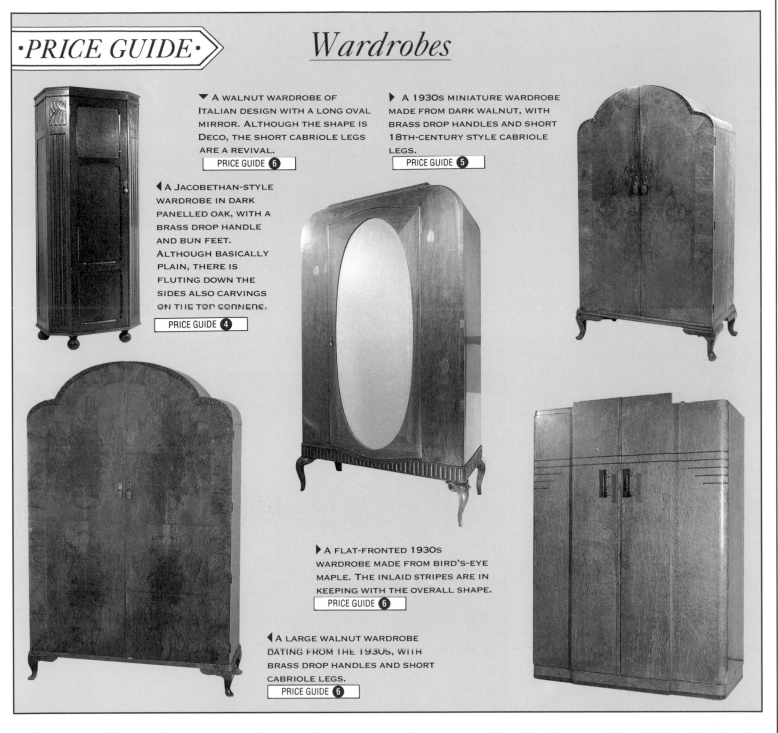

▼ A WALNUT WARDROBE OF ITALIAN DESIGN WITH A LONG OVAL MIRROR. ALTHOUGH THE SHAPE IS DECO, THE SHORT CABRIOLE LEGS ARE A REVIVAL.

PRICE GUIDE **6**

▶ A 1930S MINIATURE WARDROBE MADE FROM DARK WALNUT, WITH BRASS DROP HANDLES AND SHORT 18TH-CENTURY STYLE CABRIOLE LEGS.

PRICE GUIDE **5**

◀ A JACOBETHAN-STYLE WARDROBE IN DARK PANELLED OAK, WITH A BRASS DROP HANDLE AND BUN FEET. ALTHOUGH BASICALLY PLAIN, THERE IS FLUTING DOWN THE SIDES ALSO CARVINGS ON THE TOP CORNERS.

PRICE GUIDE **4**

▶ A FLAT-FRONTED 1930S WARDROBE MADE FROM BIRD'S-EYE MAPLE. THE INLAID STRIPES ARE IN KEEPING WITH THE OVERALL SHAPE.

PRICE GUIDE **6**

◀ A LARGE WALNUT WARDROBE DATING FROM THE 1930S, WITH BRASS DROP HANDLES AND SHORT CABRIOLE LEGS.

PRICE GUIDE **6**

in the avant-garde Art Deco style, which was launched commercially in 1925 and rapidly applied to a vast range of manufactured goods, including furniture. The hallmarks of Art Deco were clear lines and flat surfaces, with minimal decoration on angular geometric or smooth-curved shapes.

DECO WARDROBES

Following this style, the design of Art Deco wardrobes was characteristically simple. Most had full-length double doors, giving no clues as to the arrangement of shelves and compartments inside. Their only decoration was mostly in the handles, which often took eye-catching geometric shapes that might be echoed in the detail of other pieces in the suite. Wood veneers, of satinwood, walnut or maple, were exploited to the full, sometimes with a band of inlay in a contrasting wood at top or bottom of the wardrobe, or running round the outer edges of the doors. Alternatively, striking colour combinations, such as green with gold trim, brought an ultra-modern look to the bedroom.

By the 1940s, the days of the free-standing wardrobe were numbered. The built-in wardrobe became one of the standard features of post-war housing. However, after almost half a century, the wardrobe as a piece of free-standing bedroom furniture is returning to fashion.

POINTS TO WATCH

■ The Art Deco wardrobe is likely to be veneered, and also possibly inlaid. Check the veneer and inlay for damage, flaking and missing pieces.
■ The doors should close properly and sit squarely on their hinges. Are the handles firm?
■ The fittings inside should be original and preferably intact. Damage, if any, should not be beyond repair.
■ The hanging space should be of a generous depth, preferably that of the wardrobe itself.
■ Check the feet of the wardrobe; they should be stable and of overall solid construction.

The Art Deco Dressing Table

Dressing tables – from the mirrored designer-made piece to the economy
version bought at the local furniture store – were an integral part of
every Jazz Age bedroom

The dressing table had always been a favourite object in the bedroom from the days of the Victorian lady. In grander houses, men frequently had their own dressing rooms, sometimes even a separate room for bathing. The lady's bedroom therefore was her personal retreat and she frequently continued to bathe, do her hair, and all the other little acts of personal grooming that kept her busy, discreetly in her own room, rather than in the bathroom available for the general use of the household. In Victorian and Edwardian times, the dressing table offered yet another surface to cover with nick-nacks and mementos. The fashion for Art Nouveau added beautiful curved forms to mirrors, dressing table sets, and the decorative detailing of drawer handles and table legs.

In the 20th century, however, and particularly after World War I, the dressing table greatly altered in appearance, and importance. Women had independence, jobs, and formed a larger section of the consumer market. But in a reaction to the horrors of the war, they also wanted to indulge in frivolity. Nowhere is this change more evident than the styling of the dressing table during the Art Deco period. It became a veritable 'shrine to fashion', with exotic-shaped mirrors, larger than ever previously required, numerous shelves and drawers for the modern woman's range of cosmetics and accessories, and an at times fantastic use of lighting and unusual materials, to make it an eye-catching, amusing, decorative focus of a bedroom.

LIBERATED DESIGNS

The reason for this altered appearance of the dressing table was obvious – Art Deco had swept away any nostalgia for times past. Everything was to celebrate modernity, and to be decorative, eye-catching and yet at the same time, functional. These ideas perfectly sympathize with what a modern herself woman wanted to be: liberated, practical, yet attractive too. It is interesting to note that a year before the great Art Deco exhibition in Paris, the Union Centrale des Arts Décoratifs presented an exhibition which had as its sole theme, the lady's boudoir. The aim of the exhibition was to display all manner of objects, furniture, mirrors, light-fittings, carpets as well as objets d'art, which would

harmonize in the new style. It was the forerunner in style for the Art Deco exhibition of 1925, and demonstrated just how important the design of bedrooms – especially for ladies – was considered to be. Most leading designers had at least one room setting at the exhibition laid out as a modern woman's bedroom. Some of their most notable pieces were dressing tables, like that produced by the more traditionalist furniture designer, Armand-Albert Rateau for Jeanne Lanvin, from the early 1920s. It had a reversible mirror illuminated by lights inside little daisies carved and

mounted on the frame. Another important feature was its matching rosewood chair. The design combined exclusivity, expensive materials, decorative ingenuity with a high degree of practicality. Rateau's work inspired some more sober imitators. Among them was the influential French firm Süe et Mare which was noted for using deep curved shapes, carved decoration of gar-

▼ *The dressing table was the focus of a lady's bedroom where she would apply a hint of her favourite perfume or add the finishing touches to her make-up.*

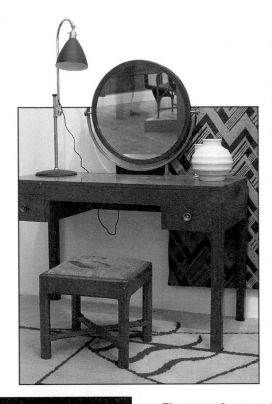

lands and flowers, contrast in woods, or gilded bronze in their pieces.

EXPENSIVE MATERIALS

The world of couture, aimed at not just wealthy wives but at the new breed of aspiring career women, had a big influence on dressing table looks, and their decoration. French Art Deco designers enjoyed using any amount of exotic materials, Jacques-Emile Ruhlmann loved to use amaranth, or overlays of sharkskin and morocco leather, and lavished all kinds of new plastics or other synthetic materials on their designs, rather in the way that couturiers liked to use exclusive fabrics and unusual accessories. In America, dressing tables often looked like left-overs from the Hollywood sets of rococo-romances, or (as in the work of Paul Frankl) like simulations of skyscrapers, executed in lacquerwork or mirrored glass.

The 1930 Studio Yearbook, London, features a design by the firm of Richter of a locust wood dressing table with inlaid bands of 'ivorine' – one of the new synthetics. Another typically up-market concept was the work of British designer Francis Bacon who showed a dressing table of black and white glass; by the mirror on the right hand side is a 'cocktail bracelet' of steel and glass – a space-saving device. The metal legs of this fantasy were coloured pink and the top surface half-frosted and half clear.

NEW LAYOUTS

The main feature of 1930s dressing tables is their great variety in shape. One innovation was the division of the dressing table into three sections, with a lower part in the centre, and drawers either on both sides or on one, with open shelving on the other. Curved fronts were popular too. Another innovation in many Art Deco dressing tables was the inclusion of a seat in the dressing table itself, by curving out one side of the table and padding the top of it. The Parisian firm of Saddier made many notable pieces like this. A matching pouffe, stool or padded chair was included in many commercial designs.

Whether the 1930s woman had an extravagant altar to beauty or a functional shelf, she would have been able to decorate it with a wide range of the new toiletries and 'tabletterie' or table sets. These now included more modern items beside hairbrush and powder bowl: cut glass lotion bottles, compact cases, possibly sets in the new plastics simulating ivory or tortoiseshell. All these new vanity items and the new-style furniture now produced for a mass market were another indication of the wide-reaching changes which had transformed people's lifestyles in the post-war years.

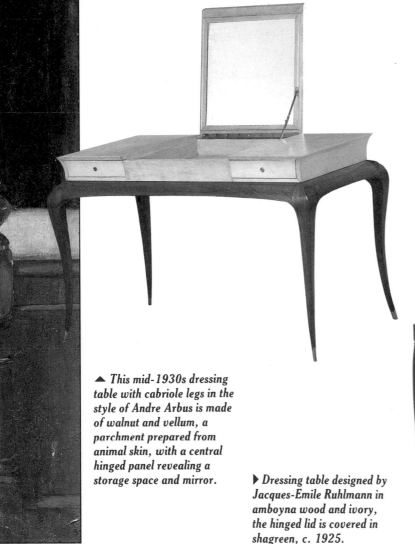

▲ This 1930s dressing table was designed along the simple, straight lines of the English furniture maker Gordon Russell and is made of solid walnut, with stool to match.

▲ This mid-1930s dressing table with cabriole legs in the style of Andre Arbus is made of walnut and vellum, a parchment prepared from animal skin, with a central hinged panel revealing a storage space and mirror.

▶ Dressing table designed by Jacques-Emile Ruhlmann in amboyna wood and ivory, the hinged lid is covered in shagreen, c. 1925.

The Art Deco Dressing Table

THE DIVISION OF THE DRESSING TABLE INTO THREE SECTIONS WAS A WELL-ESTABLISHED TRAIT BY THE 1930S. DESIGNS USUALLY INCORPORATED ANOTHER MAJOR NEW FEATURE — A VERY LARGE MIRROR. TRIPLE MIRRORS WERE OFTEN FOUND, NORMALLY WITH TWO SHORT WING MIRRORS INSTEAD OF AN ALIGNED TRIO.

THE COMMONEST MATERIAL WAS WOOD SUCH AS OAK, WALNUT OR MAPLE, PREFERABLY OF AN INTERESTING GRAIN, OR WALNUT VENEER WHICH WAS ALSO OFTEN USED. TRIMS OF UNUSUAL MATERIALS SUCH AS IVORY, PLASTIC HANDLES AND STEEL EDGINGS OFTEN FEATURED, SOMETIMES IN COMBINATION WITH SHELVING. THE DIFFERENTLY-SIZED DRAWERS CREATE A STEPPED EFFECT IN THIS CLASSIC EXAMPLE.

① 3-PIECE MIRROR
② STAGGERED DRAWERS
③ LOWER CENTRAL SECTION
④ IVORY HANDLES
⑤ INLAID GLASS
⑥ SHORT, STUBBY FEET

Designer Fancies

ART DECO WAS A PERIOD OF GREAT INNOVATIVE SPIRIT AND EXPENSIVE COMMISSIONS FOR UP-MARKET DESIGNERS, EPITOMIZED BY THIS UNUSUAL SILK PADDED AND UPHOLSTERED BUTTON DRESSING TABLE.

D uring the 1930s, focus shifted from the idea of individually made items to a real interest in mass production. This was the era of the ideal suburb, the housing estate, the 'architect-planned' house or flat. Many houses were fitted out entirely, often exactly like the one next door. This particularly applied to bedrooms, where dressing tables often disappeared as such, reduced to a large round mirror, or a wall-mounted shelf or set of shelves. Many antique pieces today may well be parts of fitted sets, removed or adapted. Alternatively, odd-shaped dressing tables could have been designed for a particular corner of a small flat or bedroom. Bedroom suites became very popular with the increasing trend towards neatness and good design in mass-market products. For a similar reason older craftsmen often split burr walnut oval loo table tops in two to make two half-oval bedheads. Burr walnut bedappled continued to be a traditional favourite often used in furniture re-creating the 'Queen Anne' style, but it too succumbed to Art Deco styling and can now be found in sets with a dressing table, chest of drawers and wardrobe.

·PRICE GUIDE· ⟩ _Art Deco Dressing Tables_

◀ ITS STYLISH BLACK LACQUER FINISH AND EXOTIC PAINTED DECORATION OFFSET THE RATHER HEAVY LOOK OF THIS 1930s PEDESTAL DRESSING TABLE.

PRICE GUIDE **7**

▶ THIS 1930s DRESSING TABLE ADOPTS A VARIETY OF DIFFERENT STYLES, YET STILL RETAINS QUITE A CLASSICAL APPEARANCE.

PRICE GUIDE **7**

◀ THE UNUSUAL LAYOUT AND SPECIAL FEATURES OF THIS LATE 1920s DRESSING TABLE IN OAK MAKE IT QUITE A RARE COLLECTOR'S PIECE.

PRICE GUIDE **6**

▲ BIRD'S EYE MAPLE WAS ONE OF THE MOST POPULAR WOODS USED IN BEDROOM FURNITURE.

PRICE GUIDE **7**

▲ MORE ECCENTRIC ASYMMETRIC DESIGNS FOUND FAVOUR WITH MORE ADVENTUROUS 1930s BUYERS.

PRICE GUIDE **7**

▲ A WALNUT DRESSING TABLE HOUSING A MULTITUDE OF DRAWERS AND COMPARTMENTS.

PRICE GUIDE **5**

BRITISH DESIGNS

A leading designer of the period was Gordon Russell, who ran a factory at Broadway, Worcestershire, turning out a wide range of reasonably priced furniture in English oak and walnut. The stretchered pedestal style was applied to dressing tables, and some of his pieces have streamlined handles, i.e. flat to the wood, with a slight handgrip with ebony or holly stringing. Another leading manufacturer was Ambrose Heal, who liked to incorporate contrasting and often striking surfaces in wood grain such as walnut veneer and the chunky

pedestal bases, often emphasized by darker mouldings and no separate feet, typical of the period. Leading designer-architect Serge Chermayeff lent his talents to a series of designs for Whiteley's store, London, for example, for 'basic furniture' offered to the public in a choice of 18 different woods. His dressing table was a very austere affair, with a plain, triple mirror, and three deep drawers on each side looking very much like modern filing cabinets, even with metal handles. Many leading manufacturers simulated the French Deco designs in cheaper materials,

using cellulose to imitate lacquer. Steel tubing, plywood, chrome, glass, even rubber, was used to extend the range of possibilities for smart designs.

JACOBETHAN STYLES

A ghastly alternative to the purer Art Deco look was the 1930s 'Jacobethan' furniture made by middle-range firms like, for example, Betty Joel Ltd (although this company also produced some beautiful dressing tables in the best Art Deco tradition). Curious circular motifs, a debased version of Art Deco themes, were often applied to the surfaces of these

otherwise chunky and not very appealing pieces.

All these efforts to bring new ideas to the furnishing factory were considered novel and exciting – though of course such a view reflects the growing economic difficulties worldwide of the period, forcing people to use cheaper materials and lower their sights about housing space, and luxury in their consumer goods. Ingenuity in fitting things into one piece applied to the dressing table too: Maples offered a design that literally opened out, with mirrored backs, in the way a modern layered sewing basket does.

The Cocktail Cabinet

Synonymous with an era of innovation, decadence and changing lifestyles, the cocktail cabinet was truly in its heyday in the Deco years when cocktails were the height of fashion

The cocktail cabinet, which was so closely integrated into life in the Jazz Age, hardly existed as a separate piece of furniture before the 1920s. Its emergence is entirely due to the change in drinking habits that had taken place after the turn of the century.

In the Victorian and Edwardian eras, it was not considered genteel to drink very much hard liquor. Gin was associated with backstreet life although whisky was considered a little better and was indulged in by the Scots and Irish, and sportsmen took nips while out shooting game. The respectable stuck to grape drinks: wines, ports and brandies, which were consumed at the dining table, in the smoking room, or at the billiard table. Drinks in decanters were kept on a sideboard or under lock and key in the butler's pantry. Perhaps a small supply of the master's favourite tipple would be kept on a tray in the library – close at hand for constant replenishment.

THE AMERICAN INFLUENCE

All this pre-supposed a regular supply of servants to bring drinks on request. After World War I, drinking and eating habits changed quite dramatically, not least because there were fewer and fewer servants. Other influences on life began to appear: the more democratic habits of the Americans were adopted, not only because they were practical, but because the burgeoning film industry made them look glamorous.

Cocktails were very much a part of this trend. Prohibition, which was introduced in 1919 and repealed in 1933, led to a huge amount of illicit alcohol being manufactured and consumed. Something had to be done to conceal its often filthy (if not blinding and poisoning) taste and mixed drinks were popularized by the Americans for this purpose, though the idea was not new. The first book on the subject, *The Bon Vivant's Guide or How to Mix Drinks*, was published as early as 1862.

▶ *For the rich elite, the cocktail rivalled champagne as a favourite drink, and was consumed both at fashionable venues and when entertaining at home.*

▼ *The simplest Art Deco cocktail cabinets resembled sideboards in shape and size. These are among the most functional and can be adapted to suit a variety of storage needs in the modern interior.*

THE COCKTAIL BAR

During Prohibition, cocktails became widely popular and socially acceptable. In 1925 the first cocktails were shown being served on stage, in 'Spring Cleaning', which was followed a year later by Noel Coward's 'The Vortex' where a cocktail drinker is seen to be the height of sophistication. In the 1930s, American barmen who had the knack of mixing the drinks, and a repertoire far superior to any other nationality, travelled to Europe to get jobs and escape the

Depression. Henry Craddock was one such American, who opened the first cocktail bar in London at the Savoy, making it a Mecca for cocktail drinkers. His work, *The Savoy Cocktail Book* appeared in 1930 with a brilliant piece of Art Deco design on the cover and has recently been reprinted.

Then drinking at home became socially acceptable – a nice way to bridge the gap between work and an evening's entertainment. The cocktail party became the smart way to entertain.

CABINET DESIGNS

All this explains why the cocktail cabinets designed in the 1920s and 1930s are more unusual, individualistic and exotic than many other pieces of Art Deco furniture. There was little or no precedent to work on, and designers had a field day coming up with new arrangements that were a loud, confident expression of the popular Art Deco ethos.

◀ The cocktail cabinets of the 1930s were amongst the most unusual and, some might say, frivolous, of the Deco period. One of the most outrageous was Christopher Mendez's cabinet built in the shape of a grandfather clock. Instead of pendulums, the case contained mirror-lined shelves with bottles and glasses.

▶ This cabinet, designed by Ruhlmann, is made from such exotic materials as macassar ebony and ivory.

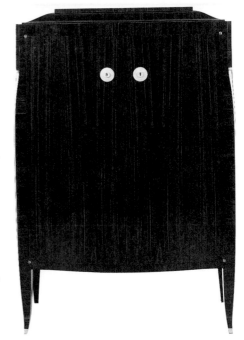

Cocktail drinking was the perfect expression of the frivolous aspirations of the Bright Young Things determined to have a good time after the horrors of the War, and outrageous cocktail cabinets were part of the fun. One famous example designed by Christopher Mendez was built like a grandfather clock: instead of the working pendulums, the case held mirror-lined shelves with bottles and glasses. The clock perfectly embodied a principal feature of early Art Deco design – the fun of concealment: bookcases were another favourite front for the drinks cabinet.

Often older Victorian or Edwardian oak, maple, walnut or mahogany display cabinets or china cupboards were also skilfully adapted to house a modern cocktail cabinet without spoiling the effect of a more period room, producing some unusual hybrid Art Deco/antique pieces.

EXOTIC MATERIALS

The Art Deco style, as its name implies, produced furniture that was always as decorative as it was functional. Cocktail cabinets, being in essence a luxury purchase rather than a necessity, were status symbols and often made of rare materials in exotic styles. Drinks cupboards that looked as if they had been imported from some far-flung colonial mansion were made in ebony and inlaid with mother of pearl or lacquered and painted with designs of swimming fish, bubbles, sunrises, moons and stars. They were also lavishly covered in sharkskin or tooled leather and trimmed with bone, bamboo or ivory.

Designers also incorporated modern features, glass being an especially popular element in many cocktail cabinets. Glass was described by a design magazine of 1934 as a substance that tends to 'make any surroundings lighter, cleaner, less stuffy, more buoyant'. The new armour plate glass did not shatter, and could support more weight, making it particularly suitable for use as shelves. A thicker glass called *vitrolite*, frequently used for floors or wall-panelling, was also a feature, often sand-blasted or etched to make decorative panels of cabinet fronts or interiors. Internal lights – often in the form of neon tubes – that came on when the door opened or the lid was lowered to provide a surface to serve drinks on were particularly popular.

INNOVATIVE FEATURES

The insides of many cabinets were lined with mirrored glass, and tubular steel or the new plastics were used for both decorative trims, and for handles or door knobs. Shuttered doors made in metal or wood often featured on round or curved cabinet fronts. Better production processes enabled designers to use thin wood veneers to dramatic effect; one particular design by the architect-designer Serge Chermayeff used coromandel, ebony and walnut veneered on to mahogany, for a rich interplay of different grains. Cheaper models used thin veneers of quality woods on plywood.

Later in the 1930s, encouraged by the government's austerity measures, cocktail cabinets followed the general trend in furniture making, and became much smaller, or were incorporated into built-in units in flats and the newer, smaller homes. Some models remained free-standing with ball castors and curved edges, rather like superior versions of ships' trolleys. Built-in varieties often consisted of wood or glass shelving, installed behind sliding glass doors, while others retained the ubiquitous trompe l'oeil effect of bookshelving that was such a popular Deco feature.

The Fluted Cocktail Cabinet

COCKTAIL CABINETS ARE ORIGINAL ART DECO OBJECTS, NOT MADE MUCH BEFORE OR SINCE. THEY USUALLY DEMONSTRATE THE BEST STYLE FEATURES OF THE PERIOD.

MANY WERE FLUTED ON THE OUTSIDE (A MACHINE FINISH), OR HAD UNUSUAL TRIMS IN GLASS, STEEL, OR EXPENSIVE WOODS LIKE EBONY. MORE SOPHISTICATED DESIGNS WERE MIRROR-GLASS LINED, AND BUILT SO THAT THE DOORS BECAME A TABLE OR A SHELF SLID OUT FOR MIXING DRINK. INTERIOR LIGHTING WAS COMMON, ALONG WITH GLASS SHELVING, AND SPECIAL STEEL FITMENTS TO HOLD BOTTLES AND GLASSES. CURVED FRONTS OR TOPS, CREATING A 'DRINKS BAR' EFFECT, WERE ALSO OFTEN FOUND.

① STRIP LIGHT

② ENGRAVED GLASS BACKING

③ INTERIOR SHELF

④ WALNUT VENEER

⑤ SEMI-CIRCULAR PLINTH

Economical Features

CABINETS MADE BY LARGE MANUFACTURERS WERE ECONOMICAL IN DESIGN AS HERE, WHERE A MAPLE VENEER HAS BEEN APPLIED TO A PLYWOOD BASE.

Extending Shelf

MANY COCKTAIL CABINETS HAD SLIDE-OUT SHELVES THAT COULD ACT AS TRAYS FOR GLASSES.

Simpler manufactured cocktail cabinets are fine pieces of design; economy simplifying some of the excesses of the luxury designer examples. True Parisian Art Deco pieces, such as those by Ruhlmann, Jules Leleu, Süe et Mare, or Dunand, are made in exclusive materials, and demonstrate a hand-crafted complexity, using fine inlays. Rare woods such as amboyna or ebony were used, richly finished with lacquerwork or mirror-glass mosaic effects, bearing heavily worked details such as carved, fluted feet, or inlaid, beaded edges.

POPULAR DESIGNS

Mass market designers took the same principles and simplified them, for factory production. Four leading Parisian department stores had studios which produced cheaper versions of top designs. England also took a strong lead from German designs, which tended to be more functional and strong. PEL was very Bauhaus influenced in its designs, and made cabinets with stainless steel. Top designers such as Serge Chermayeff and Wells Coates, made designs for the Ekco furniture company.

FURNITURE STORES

Less expensive stores, like Heal's, Maples, or Fortnum and Mason's; produced affordable cabinets and even more modestly priced was the furniture from Dunn's of Bromley, and Peter Jones in Sloane Square.

These stores helped to naturalize what was once described as 'a subdued and decent Modernism'. Designers like Gordon Russell, Betty Joel and companies such as Bowman's, PEL, and Cox & Sons, all produced quality cabinets.

Mass-produced cabinets, however, emulated various basic

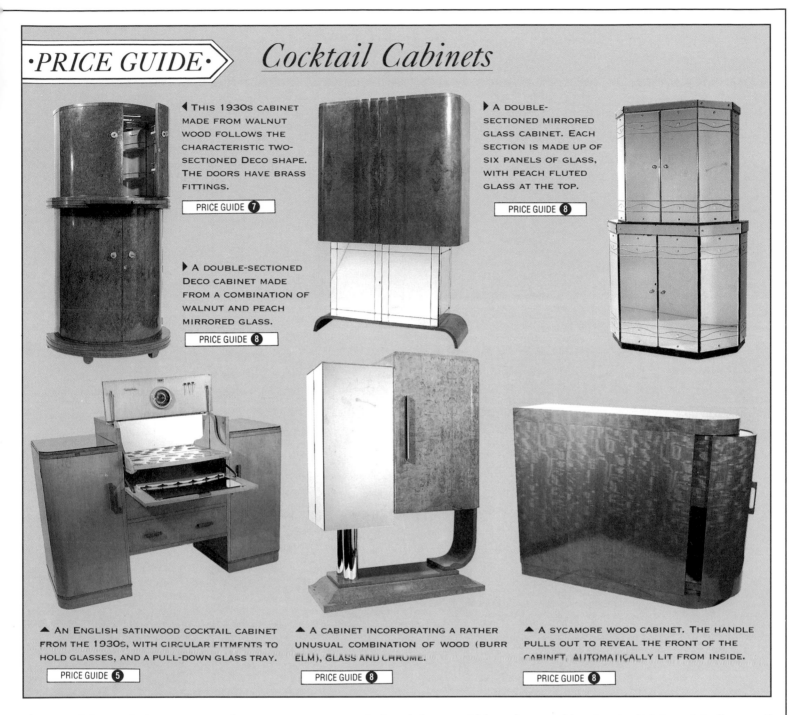

Cocktail Cabinets

◀ THIS 1930S CABINET MADE FROM WALNUT WOOD FOLLOWS THE CHARACTERISTIC TWO-SECTIONED DECO SHAPE. THE DOORS HAVE BRASS FITTINGS.

PRICE GUIDE **7**

▶ A DOUBLE-SECTIONED DECO CABINET MADE FROM A COMBINATION OF WALNUT AND PEACH MIRRORED GLASS.

PRICE GUIDE **8**

▶ A DOUBLE-SECTIONED MIRRORED GLASS CABINET. EACH SECTION IS MADE UP OF SIX PANELS OF GLASS, WITH PEACH FLUTED GLASS AT THE TOP.

PRICE GUIDE **8**

▲ AN ENGLISH SATINWOOD COCKTAIL CABINET FROM THE 1930S, WITH CIRCULAR FITMENTS TO HOLD GLASSES, AND A PULL-DOWN GLASS TRAY.

PRICE GUIDE **5**

▲ A CABINET INCORPORATING A RATHER UNUSUAL COMBINATION OF WOOD (BURR ELM), GLASS AND CHROME.

PRICE GUIDE **8**

▲ A SYCAMORE WOOD CABINET. THE HANDLE PULLS OUT TO REVEAL THE FRONT OF THE CABINET, AUTOMATICALLY LIT FROM INSIDE.

PRICE GUIDE **8**

elements of the top designs. Fluting is commonly found, but only in easily tooled areas, such as fronts, main panels or on drawers. Decorative veneers like bird's eye maple, or cherrywood take the place of rarer tropical woods.

More expensive lacquered pieces were copied by using a cellulose finish, which may now be brittle, chipped, or yellowing with age, and difficult to restore to its original colouring. Plate glass or chrome fittings, being mass-produced and were widely used, mostly in the interiors of cocktail cabinets,

and some were etched, unusually shaped, or specially cut to fit in commercially-produced cabinets.

Many cabinets were made with slide-out trays, which are long lost, or may be minus the glass shelving if it was removable for cleaning. Grooves may indicate that glass fronts to cabinets have been shattered or lost, and will need replacing. Interior lighting was a common feature of even mass-produced pieces: check that it has not been removed.

Many cocktail cabinets were built to combine with book-

shelves or sideboards: an odd-shaped piece may well be a relic from a much larger combination. Avoid pieces which are really sideboards or china cabinets, awkwardly adapted to pass as Art Deco cocktail cabinets. Look for clean, unusual, bold outlines which are often curved and unusual materials in the trims, such as good quality plastics, stainless steel, etched or coloured glass.

POINTS TO WATCH
■ Look for missing glass sections, shelving or trays.
■ Check the electrics: was

interior lighting originally part of the cocktail cabinet; can it easily be re-fitted?

■ Look carefully at veneered cabinets for signs of lifting; badly damaged veneer is hard to repair satisfactorily.

■ Look for grooves indicating that sliding glass doors are missing. The price should reflect this.

■ Many Art Deco cocktail cabinets were made as joke pieces, intentionally; do not, therefore, buy some lightweight plywood piece without regarding it as merely a novelty, and not an investment!

INDEX

INDEX

INDEX

PICTURE CREDITS